BYRON'S DON JUAN

John Murray's drawing room at 50 Albemarle Street, from a picture by C. Werner. Left to right: Isaac D'Israeli, John Murray II, Barrow, Canning, Gifford, Croker, Scott, and Byron.

BYRON'S DON JUAN
A CRITICAL STUDY

BY ELIZABETH FRENCH BOYD

THE HUMANITIES PRESS
New York 1958

Preface

During the past twenty years, since the centenary of Byron's death at Missolonghi in 1824, interest in his poetry and appreciation of his titanic role in romanticism have been steadily increasing. The pertinence and power of what Byron has to say to our generation, living through an era startlingly like his own, have given new lustre to his reputation.

Of all his vast poetic production, *Don Juan*, the last and greatest of his major works, offers the highest rewards to the modern reader. It not only stands out among his poems as the best expression of Byron, but it ranks with the great poems of the nineteenth century—Goethe's *Faust*, Shelley's *Prometheus Unbound*, Wordsworth's *Prelude*, to name only a few—as representative of the era, and of modern European civilization.

For many reasons, there has been less critical exposition of *Don Juan* than so important a poem deserves. Critics, biographers, and public interest have been so overwhelmingly fascinated with the enigmatic character of Byron himself, full of contradictions and paradox, and with the dramatic story of his life, that consideration of his poetry is often approached almost as an after-thought. *Don Juan* especially has been overlooked. It is apparently simple and lucid, it is long and leisurely, it comes at the end of Byron's career, and it is filled with irony—reasons sufficient in themselves to cause its comparative neglect. Moreover, it is a fragment and therefore less attractive for appraisal than the completed *Childe Harold*. *Don Juan* got off to a bad critical start by being published in parts and was made the object of hostile criticism from the moment of its appearance. An aura of traditional suspicion still clings to it in the popular mind.

Lord Ernle, the editor of Byron's letters and journals, in an article in *The Quarterly Review* (April 1924) occasioned by the publication of Samuel C. Chew's *Byron in England* and H. J. C. Grierson's edition of Byron's poems, sums up what is the real mystery of Byron — the hidden creative life of the poet about whom far too many of the outward details are known. For as Lord Ernle says, neither the life story, nor the observations of people like Lady Blessington, nor Byron's letters, self-revealing as they are, can explain the poet:

"Judgments founded on such external evidence fail to account for the energy, industry, concentration, and effort that are involved in the production of a vast and varied mass of poetry, none perhaps without flaw, but none, as his bitterest critic added, without value. . . . It is on such points as these that the omission of his intellectual occupations from his full and intimate correspondence becomes intensely significant. . . . One side, and that the most important side, of his existence finds no place in his letters. No one knows what proportion of his passion is devoted, for instance, to Marianna Segati and what to 'Childe Harold'; what were the dominant currents of his thoughts during the twenty-four hours of the day; which were the superficialities and which the realities of his life; which was the essential man—the dandy and the libertine or the poet."

It is necessary and right that Byron's poetry, so intensely autobiographical, should never be considered apart from the story of his life. But if we are to pluck out the heart of his mystery, we must approach him directly through his poetry, the nearest way to the essential Byron. I have tried the experiment in the following chapters of beginning a study of Byron at *Don Juan*, regarding it as an independent entity, analyzing it, and working back from it to the mind of the poet. My object has been first, to provide a guide for the modern reader to *Don Juan*, but at the same time to shed some rays of fresh light on Byron and his position in the current of nineteenth century literature.

Don Juan is the most independent product of Byron's pen, a novel in verse written in defiance of the world, in an atmosphere of increasing intellectual freedom. Freedom is not only one of *Don Juan's* powerful themes, but breathes in its scope and variety, and in the originality of its mixture of forms and styles. *Don Juan* is an epic satire based on legend, on history, and on Byron's personal experience. It mingles the best traditions of English and Italian satire and romance. Its grand subject is Byron's criticism of European civilization, but it has specific things to say about love and matrimony, travel and education, war, and contemporary English society and morality. It is the work of a humorist, comic on the surface and grave in essence.

Unique as *Don Juan* is, not only literary traditions but particular literary works played an important part in its composition. It is firmly connected on every side with great literary themes—romantic, satiric, classic and modern, Mediterranean and northern. Some of the most obvious of these I have analyzed in Chapters VII and VIII. The significance of the reappearance in Byron's work of well-worn literary motifs is twofold: it explains in part the tremendous popular appeal of his poetry, and it amplifies the conception of Byron the poet. Don Juan's trials and adventures, resolutions and bewilderments, are not only Byron's own but those of the human race. In expressing himself, Byron's utterances joined the voices of countless multitudes recorded in the permanent forms of literature. The autobiography in *Don Juan* is based squarely on universal human experience represented in the stories, poems, and reflective writings that Byron imitated.

Several studies have been made of Byron's reading to determine its ex-

tent and quality and the influence wielded by literature on his own poetry. I have followed in the wake of these studies, especially of Harold
S. L. Wiener's *Literary Background of Byron's "Turkish Tales."* Much
more work remains to be done, by a student better read in classical and
European literature than I, in investigating the literary background of
Byron's other works besides *Don Juan*. Reading was next in importance
to personal experience in the formation of Byron's ideas and images. It
is the key to the eclectic quality of his poetry. For the guidance of any
future students of this subject I have attempted to summarize the history of Byron's reading; I have enlarged the scope of Chap. VI, therefore, beyond the horizon of *Don Juan* alone. For, Lord Ernle to the contrary notwithstanding, Byron's letters and journals provide copious
evidence on one aspect of his intellectual life — his books and reading.
There may be more testimony to be gathered from unpublished Byron
archives, to which I have not had access owing to wartime conditions.

This study of *Don Juan* could not have been written without the in-
valuable assistance of the many critics, biographers, and editors of Byron. I wish especially to acknowledge the borrowing of light from the
studies of Samuel C. Chew, Claude M. Fuess, R. D. Waller, Helene Richter, W. J. Calvert, Edward Wayne Marjarum, and Ronald Bottrall. I
wish also to thank Professor Howard Mumford Jones, from whose instruction on Byron and his circle, in a seminar conducted at Columbia
University, I received great benefit and assistance.

To all my teachers and fellow students at Columbia University I extend my hearty thanks for the help and encouragement they have given
me, and especially to Professors Emery Neff, Lionel Trilling, and Su-
zanne Howe Nobbe. I am gratefully obliged to Miss Jean Macalister, of
the Columbia University Library, and to Miss Annie C. Hill, of the
Lamar Library, the University of Texas, for their assistance, and to
Professors Dino Bigongiari, Roger S. Loomis, George Nobbe, Charles
Everett, Mr. Alan Brown, Miss Julia Hysham, Miss Pauline Kramer,
and Mr. W. W. Beyer, for many helpful hints.

My thanks are especially due to Sir John Murray, of London, who
has courteously granted permission to quote from copyrighted material,
and who supplied me with a photograph of the painting which is repro-
duced as the frontispiece of this book. To the Trustees of Columbia University, who granted me a University Fellowship for the completion of
this work, I express my gratitude. And finally, I am heartily grateful to
my father, not only for much material aid, but for his sympathetic encouragement during the trials and pleasures of authorship.

E. F. B.

New Brunswick, New Jersey
    April 1944.

Contents

BYRON'S DON JUAN

CHAPTER ONE

"Against the Wind"

1

On July 15, 1819, the first two cantos of Byron's masterpiece appeared on the shelves of the London booksellers. They had been heralded by rumors circulated among the literary world for several months, hinting that the expected poem not only was novel and powerful, but was causing grave misgivings in the breasts of Byron's publisher and literary advisers. This first sample of *Don Juan*, published under such unfavorable auspices, found a very mixed reception. At first the sale was languid. Influential reviews poured torrents of abuse upon it. Journals of radical tendency pronounced in its favor. Readers who had hitherto been strong partisans of Byron recorded their disapproval and apprehension in letters to their friends. *Don Juan* administered a shock to the public, which felt that it now saw Byron for the first time in his true colors and resented the fact that the loftiness and grandeur of all his earlier poetry had cheated it into such open, passionate admiration of a truly reprehensible poet.

The public was right, not only in immediately ascribing the anonymous *Don Juan* to Byron, but in sensing its particular tone of authority. Byron, in his poetic career, had gradually liberated himself from every ulterior motive and hindering influence and was producing *Don Juan* out of the integrity of his free artistic conscience. The poem is an expression of the essential Byron, not only an exile from his homeland, but an alien to the insular English public of his times.

Thus began the disillusionment of the English public, which had been taught by its own taste and by critical enthusiasm to rhapsodize over Byron's poetry, and thus began the controversies of the critics, which helped to diminish Byron's poetic fame for nearly a century. "The Grand Napoleon of the realms of rhyme" himself declared that *Don Juan* was his Moscow. To this day it remains a poem less frequently read or understood than it deserves, though everyone willingly acknowledges its pre-eminence.

The history of the conception of *Don Juan* in Byron's mind and of its relation to his whole poetic career is of great importance in attempting to understand it. For Byron, who had been subject to many influences oppressive to his natural talents and had written from many other motives than sheer self-expression, gained his liberty gradually through experiences which had much to do in shaping and determining what his freest expression would be. Suspending for a while, therefore, the consideration of *Don Juan* itself, I shall begin with the externalities of Byron's career in relation to the making of *Don Juan*, in order that the reader may be reminded afresh of the setting or environment of this work.

Perhaps it is necessary to emphasize that Byron's career as a poet was professional. His activity in the spheres of politics and society was so spectacular as to subordinate, even for his contemporaries, his vast production as a poet. He himself cultivated the legend of his amateur Noble-Author status, careless of public opinion. He wrote very rapidly, corrected only in proof, if at all, and appeared to do everything literary in a most spontaneous fashion. He felt and expressed a contempt for the professional author — "the pen peeping from behind the ear, and the thumbs a little inky, or so." Nevertheless, his letters and journals show that his concern for poetic supremacy and fame was consistently deep and serious. Though he wrote rapidly, he relied upon the dictation of memory, for he composed his verse in his head and brooded over most of his subjects for a long time before they took shape. Independent as he was in his attitude toward public and critics, he nevertheless took care always to keep a weather-eye on the barometer of sales.[1]

Byron acknowledged his professional status, even to himself, only at last and reluctantly. Ambition for power and popularity came first and remained always the principal reason for writing. This was supplemented by the "rage, resistance, and redress," which followed the *Edinburgh Review* article on *Hours of Idleness*, and all the other snubs that life so often awarded him. Finally, after Byron had accepted his disbarment from any other career than authorship, he looked to the rewards of money. He may have been generous toward the rivalry of Moore and Scott and a few other poets, and have made disparaging remarks about those who could "bear no brother near the throne," but he was certainly not detached nor unconcerned about his own success, and wanted above everything to be First. He used Murray, the "Synod" — Murray's literary advisers — and every straw in the wind to indicate the way to success. He compromised as well as he could between his natural talents and the advice of critics and demands of the public.

2

The first critical guidance was no light touch, but a humiliating lashing that would have silenced forever any "minor" poet less pugnacious than Byron. "The poesy of this young lord," wrote the anonymous pen in the *Edinburgh Review*, January 1808, "belongs to the class which neither gods nor men are said to permit." Thus the reviewer described Byron's effusions of sentiment and humor in *Hours of Idleness*, written in imitation of Ossian, Moore, Catullus, Horace, etc. In fact, the reviewer continued, they are flat and stagnant, and not to be excused or ameliorated by the plea of youth, for look at the excellent poems of the twelve-year-old Pope. Poetry should have "a certain portion of liveliness, somewhat of fancy" — "must contain at least one thought" a little different from other writers. Imitations of what other poets have done better, for instance, of Gray's Ode on the Prospect of Eton, and of Rogers' On a Tear, are to be condemned; so also are translations, neither accurate nor concise, but only diffuse approximations. The imitation of Macpherson is so close as to be indistinguishable from borrowing, and Macpherson is "stupid and tiresome" anyway. The reviewer poured his severest sarcasm on Byron's efforts at satire on the Cambridge University curriculum and chapel choir, and concluded with ironic gratitude for what the poet had granted to the world, since it was to be the last volume from his pen.

Though Byron never forgave the writer, he learned his lesson well from that review, especially the pleas for liveliness, originality, and accuracy in poetry, and the repudiation of cloudy romanticism. He did indeed look at the poetry of Pope, and extricated himself as fast as possible from the company of insipid romantic poetasters, producing his first great success in satire, *English Bards and Scotch Reviewers*, under the aegis of Pope and Gifford. Though he was not to reap the literary benefits until later, this satire aligned him with Gifford, Frere and Canning, and the Tory Quarterly Reviewers, and, as far as literary party was concerned, alienated him from the Whigs, the romantics, and the revolutionaries.

Yet all the while he maintained his original fondness for romantic verse and fiction, for gloom and metaphysics, and eventually for Whigs, Jeffrey, Moore, Hobhouse, Hunt, Shelley, and radical and romantic principles. He took his seat in the House of Lords on the opposition benches, and then left the country for two years of travel. When he returned he found himself once more helpless and confused between the great grinding machines of literary and political parties. No wonder he was afraid to come out with the romantic *Childe Harold*, and was in an agony of alarm over Murray's submitting it to Gifford and Frere before its publication. No wonder its astonishing success and the praise from all quarters bewildered him, made him feel himself and his talent unique, and bred in him contempt for a popular and critical taste, so illogical and so unpredictable. Murray became the only guide, because he tended always strictly to business, to what would sell; and Gifford, Murray's principal literary adviser, was the oracle.

Surrounded already by a nimbus of fashion, Byron was drawn into the Murray circle, the youngest, greenest, and most unaccountable of Murray's authors. According to Dallas, Murray said he was sorry that *English Bards and Scotch Reviewers* had not been brought to him for publication. One may well believe it, since 1809, the year of its appearance, saw the first number of the *Quarterly Review*, Murray's new paper to support Tory principles and oppose the *Edinburgh's* "disgusting" revolutionary doctrines. The *Quarterly* was also to give an outlet to many people, from Scott down, who had been offended like Byron by savage attacks upon their works in the *Edinburgh*. Byron, they felt, would have belonged with them from the start, but better late than never. Yet when he did come in with them in the spring of 1812, his maiden speech in the House of Lords and his new friendship with the Hollands had committed him politically to the Whigs, and he was therefore to be kept in Murray's drawing room as a strictly literary find.

For in literary matters Murray and his friends were comparatively mild and tolerant; they even invited Hunt to write for the *Quarterly*, and Mrs. Inchbald, and others of republican persuasion. The atmosphere of Murray's drawing room above the book-shop was that of a literary club and rendezvous for authors. Every "morning" — that is, from three to five in the afternoon — Murray received whoever wanted to drop in, and here Byron met Scott for the first time, and was in daily contact with Murray's other visitors, a widely representative group: Stratford Canning, Frere, Mackintosh, Southey, Campbell, Mme. de Staël, Gifford, Croker and Barrow of the Admiralty, James Boswell the younger, Sotheby, Robert Wilmot, Richard Heber, Sir John Malcolm, who had traveled in India and Persia, W. S. Rose, whom Byron met again in Italy, Malthus, James Mill, Rogers, Moore, and Hoppner the painter. In contemporary lists of the celebrities one might encounter there, it is amusing to find Lord Byron's name usually last. He had arrived, he was a nine-days' wonder, but he was the least of the lions in these distinguished gatherings.

Gifford was the dean, the Elisha to Pope's Elijah. The great satirical successes of *The Baviad, The Maeviad*, and the *Anti-Jacobin* hung over him. Isaac D'Israeli, Frere, and Canning formed with Gifford an inner circle of satire and neo-classicism. But the circle was very broad and representative around this conservative core. Scott, with his balladry and antiquarianism, supported the new interest in history. Mme. de Staël, that enthusiastic talker, provided a high strain of romantic sentiment, with her "expert knowledge of the human heart." Her new book on Germany and her advice to "stick to the East" as the best poetical policy re-enforced with continental authority literary fashions already in vogue in England. The topics of discussion at Murray's gatherings — political economy, philosophy, theories of art and of versification, Renaissance literature, the revolution, secret histories and memoirs, English politics, and the manners of nations European and in distant lands — formed a rich and variegated nutriment for the education of any young poet. It was a school that represented the cream of both the classic and the romantic traditions.

Murray was conscious of his responsibility toward Byron's best poetic capabilities. It is amusing to see in his letters how he tries to jockey himself into position, and how quickly he learns both to dread Byron's independence and to guide it with the best tact he can muster. He begins with a fatherly attempt to discipline his new poet and, using Gifford's words as additional support, to inspire in Byron ambition to produce some really great work. As time goes on, the letters become more obsequious and enthusiastic: Murray has caught a tiger by the tail, is astonished at his luck and appalled at the daily possibilities of disaster owing to Byron's political caprice and inexperience. He relays to Byron the conservative critics' responses to each of the new poems, Gifford's, Frere's, Canning's, Dudley Ward's, and reports with growing excitement the stupendous sales achieved.

At first Byron obeyed the voice of criticism when it did not attempt to shout down his own strongest convictions. In *Childe Harold*, Canto I, for instance, he had included several satiric stanzas, as Moore says:

"full of direct personality, and some that degenerated into a style still more familiar and ludicrous than that of the description of a London Sunday, which still disfigures the poem. In thus mixing up the light with the solemn, it was the intention of the poet to imitate Ariosto. But it is far easier to rise, with grace . . . , than to interrupt thus a prolonged tone of solemnity by any descent into the ludicrous or burlesque." [2]

Gifford, Murray, and others objected to these stanzas as much on political grounds as on their violation of sentiment and literary taste, and Byron suppressed this early effusion of Don Juanism. But it remained in his mind, overflowing in satires like *The Waltz*, *The Devil's Drive*, and unacknowledged epigrams and bits of verse in the public press. Moreover, it was habitually expressed in his letters, journals, and conversation. Many of his speculations in the 1813–14 Journal were drawn out again in almost the same words in *Don Juan*, for example, those on Congreve and Vanbrugh,[3] on Jeffrey,[4] on a future life,[5] and on the visit to the Jerseys at Middleton in 1812, when he met "Longbow" and "Strongbow."

3

But the story shows Byron's increasing independence of the critics, as his success intoxicated him into thinking himself infallible. As his taste matured, the points, even of style, on which he would yield to correction became fewer. He ended by discarding most of Gifford's corrections of *The Siege of Corinth.* The rashest piece of independence from the standpoint of Murray, the Tory, was Byron's insistence on republishing, under his own name and Murray's, the pro-Whig stanzas "To a Lady Weeping," one of the many political gestures of the poet which started his persecution and exile.

By the time Byron left England after the wreck of his marriage in 1816, a *modus operandi* between him and his publisher had grown up: Byron was to have his own way whenever he wanted it, including freedom of speech on political matters (barring libel), but Murray was to furnish him with a constant stream of advice, cautions, information about the state of the market and public taste, and the applause and censures of his "Synod." Byron might heed these or not, just as he pleased. This was a satisfactory arrangement for Byron, leaving him plenty of room to grow in freedom and intransigence. But it was increasingly uncomfortable for Murray, who probably would not have put up with it if Byron had not been a best-seller. At last, the disagreements over *Don Juan* broke off their relations.

Meanwhile Byron had brought himself to a peculiar state of isolation through his voluntary exile. It is important to remember how completely he felt himself detached from almost all his former spheres of interest and opportunity. Especially he had removed himself from "the stove of society," to whose noxious heat and vapors, as he wrote Moore several years later,[6] he attributed a fatal influence on "all great and original undertakings of every kind." What pleasure there was in his new freedom had to wait, however, upon the absorption of his pain and grief. The stimuli of opposition and revenge needed to be sublimated from the merely personal to the more universal.

But he was not living in a vacuum; new experiences were pouring in upon him. To the strong influence of the places he immediately visited, Waterloo, the Rhine, and Lake Leman, were added the new influences of Shelley, of Monk Lewis, who read Goethe to him, of Mme. de Staël and her visitors, A. W. Schlegel and de Bonstetten. In this rich atmosphere of romantic literature, Byron naturally resumed *Childe Harold,* and brought it to the highest distillation of romanticism. In the shorter poems of this period, especially in *Manfred,* he poured out the wealth of passion and thought stirred in him by these influences and by the experiences he had been going through.

Childe Harold dragged on with a dying fall through 1817, grown somewhat distasteful to him. The stimulus of passion had evaporated in the unromantic atmosphere of his life in Venice, and a "deal of judgment" had taken its place. He had come to accept the hopelessness of the romantic search for ideal beauty and ideal love:

> "Of its own beauty is the mind diseased,
>   And fevers into false creation: — where,
> Where are the forms the sculptor's soul hath seized?
>   In him alone. Can Nature show so fair?
> Where are the charms and virtues which we dare
>   Conceive in boyhood and pursue as men,
> The unreached Paradise of our despair,
>   Which o'er-informs the pencil and the pen,
> And overpowers the page where it would bloom again?" [7]

Henceforth reason and the actual world would suffice for him, as they did for Pope and the Augustans. All that remained of the romantic fever would be his own pain, which it had expressed and which he would now digest in the bitters of satire, from the gayest mockery to the most deep-voiced indignation.

4

In commencing any new work, however, the practical necessity remained to be original and novel. As he was coming to these conclusions about romance and art in *Childe Harold*, he wrote to Murray the letter, so much admired by Gifford, in which he declared himself permanently on the side of Pope and the classicists. He wrote that he had recently been pondering more and reading less, and had come to the conclusion "with regard to poetry in general . . . that . . . *all* of us — Scott, Southey, Wordsworth, Moore, Campbell, I — are all in the wrong, . . . upon a wrong revolutionary poetical system, or systems." To be sure, he confesses that he has reached this conviction by a close textual comparison of their poems with Pope's. But he says that what mortified him was "the ineffable distance in point of sense, harmony, effect, and even *Imagination*, passion, and *Invention*, between the little Queen Anne's man, and us of the Lower Empire." This confession of inadequacy followed upon his acknowledgment earlier in the letter that *Childe Harold* had left him feeling depleted and without poetic prospects:

"I fear that I shall never do better; and yet, not being thirty years of age, for some moons to come, one ought to be progressive as far as Intellect goes for many a good year. But I have had a devilish deal of wear and tear of mind and body in my time, besides having published too often and too much already.

God grant me some judgement! to do what may be most fitting in that and
every thing else, for I doubt my own exceedingly."

The recurrence of emphasis in these passages on intellect, judgment, and
sense is interesting proof of the shift in Byron's attention from the emotional to the intellectual. He was ripening for a return to satire.

This letter was written on September 15, 1817, and on the twenty-
first, Hobhouse, who was still visiting Byron in Venice, records that he
"went out in gondola with Lord Kinnaird and Lord Byron to the gardens. Lord Kinnaird read to me a new poem of [John Hookham] Frere's,
excellent and quizzical — no better since the days of Swift." [8] This was
the *Prospectus and Specimen of an intended National Work* "by the
brothers Whistlecraft," in the Pulcian *ottava rima*, "intended to comprise the most interesting particulars relating to King Arthur and his
Round Table." Byron's prayers were answered, at least as far as style
was concerned; the colloquial verve and gaiety of Frere's verses set a
new tune ringing in his head, and he proceeded immediately to the composition of *Beppo*, which he shipped to Murray with Canto IV of *Childe
Harold* in Hobhouse's portmanteaux, January 1818.

The autumn of 1817 and the composition of *Beppo* marked a climax
and the beginning of a new era in Byron's career. It was not only that
his feeling of having come to the end of his rope coincided with his return
to the school of Pope and satire, nor that in Whistlecraft he found a new
style and manner; for Whistlecraft was but the last in a long series of
hints from Murray and his circle and of tentative directions from Byron's experiences, which suggested the new material he needed to match
the new style.

In May 1816, Murray had shown Byron's verses *A Sketch*, in heroic
couplet, to Rogers, Frere, and Stratford Canning, and reported to
Byron that "they agree that you have produced nothing better; that
satire is your forte. . . ." [9] In Milan, at the performance of the famous
Sgricci, Byron was introduced to the art of the *improvvisatore*, about
which he had already heard in Geneva. At Venice, the gondoliers sang
stanzas from Tasso, and Byron's attention was turned again to Berni
and Ariosto. He saw Goldoni's rational, realistic comedies. He heard the
popular *cantastorie* in the piazza of St. Mark. He read the gay colloquial verse, satirizing Venetian politics and manners, by the censored
Pietro Buratti, and he "got by heart" the *Novelle* in *ottava rima* by the
Abate Casti. Shelley wrote Byron from Bath a challenge to produce a
great work — perhaps an epic — perhaps on the theme of the French
Revolution. At the same time, January 1817, Murray began to bombard
him with requests for a work in prose and for more stories.

Murray had been delighted with Byron's letters, increasingly rich and various, and with the prose dedication of *Childe Harold*, Canto IV, to Hobhouse. He saw an opportunity for a good business venture in this new prose medium. The popular demand for works comparing the manners and customs of European countries, he thought, might be exactly satisfied by a work combining Byron's Italian experiences and story-telling abilities. He allowed Byron plenty of latitude; he would engage to keep the experiment secret and anonymous; anything would do from a "Journal of all you see" to a poem retelling "a good Venetian tale describing manners." [10]

Perhaps he knew of some of Byron's several attempts to write a novel. These probably date back to 1804 in Southwell, when Byron wrote his sister Augusta that his adventures with the neighborhood belles would furnish materials for a "pretty little Romance . . . the loves of Lord B. and the cruel and inconstant Sigismunda Cunegunda Bridgetina, etc." He tried his hand at a novel in 1807, completing two hundred and fourteen pages, of which nothing remains. Early in 1813, he commenced an epistolary novel, satirizing English society life, very like the early novels of Bulwer-Lytton, *Pelham*, for example. He soon tired of this effort and palmed off on his proposed co-author Dallas the opening letters "with these words, 'Now, do you go on.' " Dallas used the first letter to begin his novel *Sir Francis Darrell*. During November, Byron tried again, and aften ten days of experimenting, "burned his Roman, because it ran into *realities* more than ever; and some would have been recognized and others guessed at."

The fragment of horror-story Byron wrote in Switzerland, when Mary Shelley composed her *Frankenstein*, was turned over to Dr. Polidori, completed by him, and published with many misunderstandings and apologies as *The Vampire*, 1819.[11] But Moore reports that Byron began at the same time as the *Vampire* "another romance in prose, founded upon the story of the Marriage of Belphegor, and intended to shadow out his own matrimonial fate." This he burned when he heard from England that Lady Byron was ill.[12]

The need for confession under the guise of fiction cropped out again in Venice in the form of an unfinished novel relating the adventures of a young Andalusian nobleman, Don Julian. Hobhouse says he read the beginning of this novel in January 1818, and noticed its resemblance to the *Mémoires d'un Jeune Espagnol*, the fictional autobiography of J. P. C. de Florian, published in 1807 and again in 1812.[13] Byron's attempt ran this time to one hundred "paper-book" pages, which he sent to Moore with the rest of his Memoirs in September 1821. Moore appends a passage from this fragment disclosing its Don Juanesque qualities; [14] it relates the break-up of the marriage between Byron and Annabella.

The Memoirs, — those famous memoirs that were composed by Byron 1818–21, given to Moore, and burned directly after Byron's death, appear to have had a novel-like quality. "The amusing account given of some of the company [at Lady Jersey's farewell assembly for Byron in London, April 1816] . . . of the various and characteristic ways in which the temperature of their manner towards him was affected by the cloud under which he now appeared — was one of the passages of that Memoir it would have been most desirable, perhaps, to have preserved." [15] Peter Quennell conjectures that the composition of the Memoirs at the same time as *Don Juan* may have fortified Byron's opinions and clarified his experiences, and that *Don Juan* is therefore, "so to speak, only an essential residue" of the material of the Memoirs.[16]

But to return to the winter of 1817–1818 and *Beppo,* which was the response to Murray's appeal for a Venetian tale exhibiting Italian manners in contrast with British. Murray continued his demands for a work in prose, and between the urgings of both Murray and the Venetian circle of friends that Byron should become an interpreter of Italy to England and of England to Italy, the idea was dinned relentlessly into Byron's head. Hobhouse joined the campaign, writing to Murray after *Beppo* was finished that he should foster the idea of a work describing Italy, not in guidebook style, but "by subjects — literature, antiquities, manners, politics, &c." For a while Byron and Hobhouse planned to compose a joint work, based on the suggestions in Hobhouse's notes to *Childe Harold,* Canto IV.

Byron, however, was not to be bogged down in any remorselessly prosaic work. The all-important question was whether *Beppo* would succeed with the public. He had found in it a style as near prose as poetry can be, a style that suited him exactly, in which he could speak in his natural voice, as if he were writing a letter, witty, gay, satiric. It furnished him as a storyteller with room for both dramatic characterization and action, and also subjective confessions and comments. Nevertheless, *Beppo* was to be published anonymously, as a trial balloon; "that kind of writing . . . suits our language, too, very well," but "we shall see by the experiment. If it does, I'll send you a volume in a year or two, for I know the Italian way of life well, and in time may know it yet better. . . ." [17]

The reception of *Beppo* in Murray's circle was instantly favorable. Frere, who had to be persuaded that it was not by W. S. Rose, was generously delighted and compared Byron's "protean talent," with fulsome yet subtle flattery, to that of Shakespeare. Scott, who was to review *Beppo* along with Whistlecraft and Rose's *Court of Beasts,* was equally diverted. But Byron was right in mistrusting the public's ability to see through fun and absurdity in this new style. Frere had had difficulties on this point with Whistlecraft, aggravated by Murray's timid method of publishing it without advertising or acknowledgment. He compared Whistlecraft's title page to a man who comes into a room "with a strange, uncouth foreign uniform. If he looks shy and diffident, he is immediately the last man in the company, and nobody troubles themselves about him. If he puts himself confidently forward, he becomes an object of general notice and curiosity." *Beppo*, however, was modern, and more transparent and intelligible than Whistlecraft. Murray reported the favorable verdict to Byron, June 16, 1818, that everyone "continues in the same very high opinion of its great beauties," and, most important, that he has sold six times as many volumes of *Beppo* as he has of Whistlecraft, of which the public "cannot see the drift." [18]

Murray left Byron no chance to cool off. His next letter, July 7, took up the question of a work to open the autumn season. "Have you not another lively tale like 'Beppo'? or will you not give me some prose in three volumes? — all the adventures that you have undergone, seen, heard of, or imagined, with your reflections on life and manners." The answer to that was two-fold: the prose Memoirs, and *Don Juan* written in *ottava rima*. Satire, confession, invective, and burlesque were all united in the freedom of the novel and the large picture of society.

In the exchange of letters about these and other projects, Byron sought information on "the state of the reception of our late publications"; if Murray would tell him exactly, he would know how to proceed:

"I once wrote from the fullness of my mind and the love of fame, (not as an *end*, but a *means*, to obtain that influence over men's minds which is power in itself and in its consequences,) and now from habit and from avarice; so that the effect may probably be as different as the inspiration."

This calm, businesslike exchange between publisher and poet is a remarkable contrast to the hectic account given by Moore of the inception in the febrile Byronic mind of *Don Juan*, Byron's manifesto and challenge to society. [19]

5

By November 12, 1818, Canto I and the Dedication to Southey [20] were completed and shipped off to Murray. Julia's letter to Juan, and three more stanzas of the Dedication were added a few weeks later, and Canto II reached Murray some time in April 1819. But the two cantos were not issued until July 15, and then not only anonymously like *Beppo*, but without even Murray's name on the title page.

The fears of Murray and the adverse criticisms of Byron's friends, who constituted themselves a "cursed puritanical committee," as Byron called them, to pass upon the manuscript, were the cause of all this de-

lay and doubt. Byron had to reason, cajole, and persuade — all at long
distance by means of letters — in order to bring Murray to the publishing point. He was pinning his whole poetic future at this time on
Don Juan, and there was enough praise in Murray's and the others'
comments to second his own conviction that the poem was as well worth
publishing as anything he had ever done. *Don Juan* was not only a new
major bid for literary glory; it represented Byron's effort to reform
the literary taste of the times in favor of Pope, to strike a blow against
cant and bores, and to uphold the glorious causes of political freedom
and freedom of thought. He anticipated and wanted controversy and opposition.

He found it immediately, before publication, in the opening skirmishes with his friends. Their specific objections to Canto I, made without even waiting to see how the poem was to progress, were three-fold.
Hobhouse recalls that he and S. B. Davies read Canto I together over
breakfast. "I have my doubts. . . . The blasphemy and bawdry and
the domestic facts overpower even the great genius it displays." [21] The
blasphemy consisted in the parody of the ten commandments, Stanzas
205–206, "Thou shalt believe in Milton, Dryden, Pope," etc. The
bawdry, of course, was the whole fabliau of Don Juan, Donna Julia,
and Don Alfonso; and the domestic facts were embodied in the description of Donna Inez and her husband, Don Juan's parents. Moore con-
curred with Hobhouse; *Don Juan*, Canto I, was unpublishable because
"Don Juan's mother is Lady Byron." When, however, he read the proof
sheets of Canto II at Murray's, he felt more enthusiastic about the
poem. "Young Haidée is the very concentrated essence of voluptuous-
ness," but the allusions to Lady Byron are still objectionable. Hookham
Frere, in conversation with Hobhouse and Moore, developed in more
general form the objection to the combination of easy morals and vio-
lently anti-Tory satire: since Byron belonged to the opposition party
to a profligate court, he should if anything be Puritan, certainly not
more profligate than the ruling party. [22] "A friend of freedom should
be a friend to morality." Finally, Frere continued in Hobhouse's report
of this conversation, "there was preparing a convulsion between the
religionists and the free-thinkers. The first would triumph and the latter be extirpated with their works. He instanced Hall Stevenson, a fashionable rake writer once in vogue, who was put down by common consent
of the moral readers of George II's time, and is now forgotten, though
excellent in its way. . . . I felt that I was talking in some sort to a rival
of 'Don Juan's' style; but then, as what he said was sensible, I did not
care for the coincidence." [23]

Whether Byron was as much mystified and confounded by these objections as he appeared to be, it is difficult to say. He had grown rather

far away from England by this time, and was not in touch with the temper and sentiment of London. The extraordinary seriousness of his friends towards a poem that was intended, in these early stages, "to make giggle" must have surprised him. For a while he agreed not to publish, but requested fifty copies to be printed and distributed to a list of gentlemen whose names he would send later. But it irked him that all the criticisms were directed at the "morality" of the poem, while nothing but high praise was expressed for its poetry. "If they had told me the poetry was bad, I would have acquiesced; but they say the contrary, and then talk to me about morality. . . . I maintain that it is the most moral of poems; but if people won't discover the moral, that is their fault, not mine." This was all the "cant of the day":

"I despise it, as I have ever done all its other finical fashions, which become you as paint became the Antient Britons. If you admit this prudery, you must omit half Ariosto, La Fontaine, Shakespeare, Beaumont, Fletcher, Massinger, Ford, all the Charles Second writers; in short, *something* of most who have written before Pope and are worth reading, and much of Pope himself. *Read him* — most of you *don't* — but *do* — and I will forgive you; though the inevitable consequence would be that you would burn all I have ever written, and all your other wretched Claudians of the day (except Scott and Crabbe) into the bargain." [24]

Perhaps Murray was swayed by this reasoning; or perhaps he gave up in despair that Byron ever would write "a great work — an Epic Poem, I suppose," as Foscolo, Gifford, everybody wanted him to do, or a sober piece of prose on the manners of the Italians. At any rate, he began to feel more kindly toward *Don Juan*, and kept the question of publication open. At last Byron risked a peremptory order that the cantos should not be privately printed but actually published:

"Methinks I see you [Byron wrote] with a long face . . . anticipating the outcry and the scalping reviews that will ensue; *all that* is my affair; do you think I do not foresee all this as well as you? Why, Man, it will be nuts to all of them: they never had such an opportunity of being terrible; but don't *you* be out of sorts."

Everything depended now on how the public would receive *Don Juan*, for even Hobhouse was becoming reconciled, and Kinnaird was appeased by a direct assertion from Byron that Donna Inez was not intended for his "Clytemnestra." There was a threatening rumble or two in the press, even before the publication, but when the storm broke in the reviews it was terrific. As might have been expected, the parties took their stand along political lines, although the object of their defense or attack was the morality of the poem. The reviews ranged from a complete defense

in Hunt's radical *Examiner* [25] to the opposite extreme of attack in the
Tory *Blackwood's Magazine*.[26]

Love, honor, patriotism, religion, — thus the reviewer in *Blackwood's*
wrote — are mentioned in *Don Juan* only to be scoffed at, though the
genius and power of the poem are unimpeachable. This is the best poem
for a "mixture of ease, strength, gayety, and seriousness extant in the
whole body of English poetry." What a pity that it is pitched in such
a "low moral key"! Byron is resolved to show us that he is "a cool unconcerned fiend." Worse, this "filthy and impious" poem contains an
attack on Lady Byron, and the description of the shipwreck is disfig-
ured by a deplorably inhuman sense of humor.

Byron read the reviews while waiting impatiently for weeks after the
publication to learn about the all-important matter of sales. The result
was dispiriting. In October, he wrote to Hoppner:

"The poem has *not sold well,* [only 1200 out of 1500 copies]. . . . The third
Canto is in advance about 100 stanzas; but the failure of the two first has
weakened my *estro,* and it will neither be so good as the two former, nor completed unless I get a little more *riscaldato* in it's behalf. I understand the
outcry was beyond every thing — pretty Cant for people who read *Tom Jones,*
and *Roderick Random.* . . . There hath been asterisks and . . . 'domned
cutting and slashing.' " [27]

6

Thus the poem, begun with certain motives of opposition and self-
expression, but primarily as a good literary and business venture intended to repeat the success of *Beppo* and enlarge it, turned gradually
into a battle standard of revolt.

At first the opposition of the critics acted like a progressive stimulant
on Byron. His combativeness rose and strengthened his resolution to
vindicate not only Pope but now himself against the false poetics of the
day. Comforting Murray's chicken-heartedness, he seized upon the lucky
mistake of the editor of "my grandmother's Review — the British" to
"defend himself gaily" in a letter which he sent Murray with *carte-
blanche* to publish in any way he pleased.[28] He gave Murray and the
Quarterly Reviewers permission to cut him up root and branch, make
him a spectacle to men and angels, provided only that they would let
him publish *Don Juan* unaltered.[29]

But the indifference of the public, the poor sale of the first cantos, and
the activity of the pirates were a wet blanket to Byron's spirits. Continuing the composition of Cantos III and IV, he was perplexed by the
difficulties of remaining true to his own convictions and tastes in this
poem that he knew to be his best work, and at the same time of modifying
it sufficiently to suit the popular taste and make it sell. Meanwhile the

great question mark hung over it, whether Murray could secure legal support for the copyright, or whether all their labor would be lost to the pirating booksellers. Murray encouraged him to continue, while he solicited preliminary legal opinions on the first two cantos before pressing suit publicly to restrain the piracies. Mr. Shadwell and other lawyers of the Chancery Bar fortunately decided in Murray's and Byron's favor, adding an interesting critical note, "that one great tendency of the book was not an unfair one. It was to show in Don Juan's ultimate character the ill effect of that injudicious maternal education which Don Juan is represented as having received, and which had operated injuriously upon his mind." [30]

Murray reported these favorable opinions to Byron, who had come to rest in Ravenna after a year of wandering and unsettled life. They revived his spirits somewhat, and with the threat of piracy removed, he set to work to finish Cantos III and IV, which were mailed to London by the middle of February 1820. He had some doubt, however, he wrote to Murray, "whether they ought to be published, for they have not the Spirit of the first: the outcry has not frightened [it had, according to a letter he wrote to Kinnaird in October] but it has *hurt* me, and I have not written *con amore* this time. It is very decent, however, and as dull 'as the last new Comedy.' "

Byron now began a campaign to prepare the way for these new cantos when they should be issued. He commenced a translation of Pulci's *Morgante Maggiore*, which he thought would make Murray "stare":

". . . it must be put by the original, stanza for stanza, and verse for verse; and you will see what was permitted in a Catholic country and a bigotted age to a Churchman, on the score of religion; — and so tell those buffoons who accuse me of attacking the liturgy." [31]

This piece of literal translation was literal for a purpose. Hitherto the English public had had translations of only excerpts from Pulci. Byron's translation was to be printed side by side with the original, so that anyone with only a smattering of Italian could see that nothing had been falsified by the translator. It would be a most important piece of artillery in his campaign against the canters of religion and morality, who prided themselves on the free speech and liberality of Britain, and denied Byron the right to exercise them. Byron took the utmost pains with every word to make sure that his translation was accurate. Pulci represented not only an historical precedent for free speech, but a poetical authority, consecrated by antiquity and by the contemporary enthusiasm in England for the Italian chivalric romances. Evidently even the literati of London did not know their Italian epics so well as they should have done, since they made such ridiculous mistakes about Ariosto's verse

and style, when Byron was nominating Scott the "Ariosto of the North."
Maybe some of the harsh criticism against the "inhumanity" and "im-
piety" of *Don Juan* could be dispelled by educating the public better in
its originals, just as the outcry of the moralists might be laid not so much
to "refinement" as to humorless stupidity.

On the Pope side of the campaign, Byron composed the answer to the
critical article in *Blackwood's* of August 1819. The reply is dated
Ravenna, March 15, 1820, and was sent to Murray two weeks later,
but the ideas for it had lain in Byron's mind for several months before.
I should not be surprised if much of the autobiographical and apologetic
parts of it echoed his prose Memoirs, the first part of which had been
handed to Moore in October. Byron was given to repeating himself. The
letter, dedicated to D'Israeli, is humorously denominated an additional
quarrel and calamity of an author, but its tone is mainly serious and in
the personal parts bitterly sad. From personal apology, he diverges to
make his first critical defense of the beauties of Pope and Dryden and
his first reasoned and public attack on modern poetical taste, which can
permit such aberrations as the Lakists, Scott, Byron himself, and all
their imitators.

As a further stroke in the good cause, he wrote to Murray, on March
28, that he would now like to publish *Hints from Horace*. When Moore
came to this letter in writing Byron's biography, he was completely non-
plussed by "the revival of this strange predilection. . . . Such a delu-
sion is hardly conceivable, and can only, perhaps, be accounted for by
that tenaciousness of early opinions and impressions by which his mind,
in other respects so versatile, was characterized." [32] But Byron's desire
to publish *Hints from Horace* at this time was completely logical as part
of his literary campaign.

At this point, however, the relations between Byron and Murray began
to grow strained. Murray probably had no particular sympathy for
Byron's resolve to wage poetical warfare. If Byron was going to turn
doctrinaire, and that on the unpopular and old-fashioned side of the
fence, besides sending him poetry that either brought hornets' nests
around their ears or promised to have no sale whatsoever and nothing
but ridicule, Murray was not going to make one of the party. He was
probably, as Smiles suggests, further discouraged by the advice of
Croker, who wrote him one rainy Sunday afternoon, March 26, 1820,
his opinion of the new cantos, *Don Juan* III and IV. After commenting
on their "tediousness" and yet their "merit of all kinds," Croker dis-
cusses their "Principles," warmly defending Byron against the great
injustice done him on this score by Murray first of all, and by all the
world. He brushes aside all the moral objections as wholly unworthy,
and says it is no wonder if Byron has been goaded by "indiscreet, con-

tradictory, and urgent *criticisms*, which, in some cases, were dark
enough to be called calumnies," into expressing political and personal
opinions which he probably never felt. The moral objections will blow
over, but here is the crux of the matter: "such passages as those about
Southey and Waterloo and the British Government and the head of that
government" are "cruelty to individuals," "injury to national character," and "an offence to public taste." What in the world can Byron
mean by turning Radical? It must be the influence of Messrs. Hobhouse
and Leigh Hunt. A man of Byron's birth, taste, talents, and habits, "can
have nothing in common with such miserable creatures as we now call
Radicals." Yet Croker has just heard a disturbing rumor that Byron
had actually promised to come over to England and lead the revolution.
Let Lord Byron revise these two cantos, and not "make another step in
the odious path which Hobhouse beckons him to pursue." [33]

It is amusing to note that though Croker knew that Hobhouse was
languishing at that moment in Newgate for Radicalism, he did not know
that Hobhouse and Byron were temporarily bitterly estranged, or the
reasons for their estrangement. Radical Hobhouse had piqued Byron by
his Puritanical criticisms of *Don Juan* I and II. In return, immoral
Byron had circulated a rough ballad poking fun at Hobhouse's radicalism and his alleged defection from the Whig Party. Croker, in fact,
knew nothing of Byron's present temper, of his new inflexibility to criticism, of his contentiousness, and especially of his implication, as a leading member of the *Carbonari*, in Italian plots for revolution.

7

Murray, however, knew all these facts and read Croker's letter in their
light. He must have decided to wear Byron out by disapproving silence
and neglect, or at least to salvage only the poet while turning a cold
shoulder on the controversialist. He kept the *Juan* cantos on the shelf,
did not publish the Pulci, or the "Danticles," or the *Blackwood's* answer, or the *Hints from Horace*. Byron was beside himself with impatience at seeing Murray let the time slip by. He tried to accommodate
himself to Murray's interests and wishes, at which he was guessing because Murray wrote not at all, not even to acknowledge receipt of manuscripts. The *Observations* upon the article in *Blackwood's* he allowed
should not be printed at this time. Perhaps he was himself worried that
printing anything which might be twisted into a confession of his authorship of *Don Juan*, when he was considering going to England in the
autumn, might cut him off from seeing Augusta or his little daughter
Ada. The copyright suit had not yet been publicly settled.

Meanwhile, since the door appeared to be closing on his *Don Juan*, he took up a new line of writing — the tragedies modeled on classic principles. These too belonged to his new role of defender of the faith, "the Christianity of English poetry, the poetry of Pope." They occupied his attention through most of 1820 and 1821. It is not my purpose here to enter into the question whether Byron intended these for the stage, though I agree with David V. Erdman's reasoning that Byron was making a new bid for great popularity and applause in a career as a dramatist. If epic failed, tragedy might win the day. If Byron had succeeded in that line, possibly we should have had no more of *Don Juan*, in spite of Shelley's high approval of it and encouragement to continue this truly original and great work — "something wholly new and relative to the age, and yet surpassingly beautiful."

Byron dangled *Marino Faliero* before Murray's eyes to restore him to a publishing humor, and agreed to no separate publication of Cantos III and IV of *Don Juan*; they could be slipped in with the first two in a future edition. "I shall be glad to hear from you," Byron wrote, "and you'll write now, because you will want to keep me in a good humour till you can see what the tragedy is fit for. I know your ways, my Admiral."

There is no need to go on with the melancholy story of neglect, misunderstandings, and cross purposes, of delays in publishing, suppression of dedications, omissions, and errors. Canto V of *Don Juan*, finished in December 1820, was at last published with Cantos III and IV in August 1821. Contrary to Byron's expectations, the sale this time was tremendous, like the old days and the *Corsair:* "the booksellers' messengers filled the street in front of the house in Albemarle Street, and the parcels of books were given out of the window in answer to their obstreperous demands." [34] But apparently popularity had come too late. Byron had signed in a letter to Teresa Guiccioli, on July 4, a promise not to continue *Don Juan*. The martyr "*to* and *by*" the women was martyred once more.

However, Byron's spirit was not broken by all the discouragements of the two past years. He continued the defense of Pope in the letters to Murray against Bowles's *Invariable Principles of Poetry*, dated February and March 1821. He urged Murray to republish his friend Hodgson's two poems directed against *Childe Harold*, but "all for Pope," and to have Gifford undertake a new life and edition of the master.

At the end of June, "John Bull's" encouraging letter reached the Right Hon. Lord Byron; it begged him to "stick to *Don Juan*, . . . it is the only sincere thing you have ever written; and it will live many years after all your humbug Harolds have ceased to be. . . ." In August, Shelley came to visit Byron at Ravenna. In almost every letter for months past, he had been spurring Byron on to undertake a great poem. He sympathized with the depression of spirits under which Byron was laboring. "You say," he wrote, "that you feel indifferent to the stimuli of life. But this is a good rather than an evil augury. Long after the *man* is dead, the immortal spirit may survive, and speak like one belonging to a higher world." [35] Now he continued in conversations that lasted till dawn the encouragement and inspiration that had meant so much to Byron in Switzerland five years before. Trelawney says that Shelley told him he had urged Byron at Ravenna to "come out of the dismal 'wood of error' [*Cain?*] into the sun, to write something new and cheerful. Don Juan is the result."

Shelley's words lingered in Byron's mind as he packed his books and papers to move to Pisa in September. "I have read over the Juans, which are excellent," he wrote to Murray. "Your synod are quite wrong; and so you will find by and by. I regret that I do not go on with it, for I had all the plan for several cantos, and different countries and climes." The sight of the "new Juans" so carelessly printed, the news of their popularity, the failure of everybody to comprehend his dramas and their intentions (Gifford's dislike was particularly mortifying), and Murray's neglect of his affairs, all united to stimulate him again to new enthusiasm for great works. As a result, he sent Murray a set of "articles" for a new arrangement between them — only certain books to be sent to Byron, no reviews, etc. — all to the end that his Genius may "take its natural direction, while my feelings are like the dead, who know nothing and feel nothing of all or aught that is said or done in their regard." [36]

All that remained to be done was to be released from his promise to Teresa. This was successfully accomplished a few months later, and *Don Juan* proceeded with only minor interruptions, and in spite of Murray's declining to publish it any further, until the expedition to Greece put a halt to it forever.

The story of the making of *Don Juan* is the story of Byron's declaration of independence — independence of Murray and the critics, of "petticoat influence," of popular British fashions in sentimentality and Philistine hypocrisy, and of the ruling Tory politics. It marks his gradual emergence into freedom from the trammels of his own former self. Struggling through a thicket of difficulties and discouragements, Byron wrote and published his greatest poem in spite of the world. Whatever one may think of the fragmentary and unpolished quality of *Don Juan*, its very existence is an extraordinary proof of Byron's creative power and artistic integrity.

CHAPTER TWO

"A Versified Aurora Borealis"

Before we attempt a critical appraisal of *Don Juan,* it may be well to refresh our recollection of its actual contents. Any reader already well acquainted with it may, of course, omit this chapter. But the vast arabesque of narrative and digression, too leisurely and complex for modern taste, is hard to retain. For the sake of convenience, I shall produce here a simplified and literal synopsis of *Don Juan,* with no attempt to elaborate its ironic or aesthetic values. Every serious reader of the poem should make his own analysis, canto by canto.

In the modern editions, *Don Juan* begins with the dedication to Southey, which was not at first published, although it was circulated in pirated broadsides.[1] Southey is accused of having turned his political coat to secure the Laureateship; he is an "Epic Renegade." Coleridge, "explaining Metaphysics to the nation," [2] and Wordsworth, guilty of the *Excursion,* are included in the attack; they have all been rendered narrow, fusty, and unintelligible by battening on each other's brains at Keswick. Let Posterity decide whether they are worth more than Scott, Rogers, Campbell, Moore, and Crabbe. The field of poetry is wide, and far be it from Byron to try to change or subdue these three, or to begrudge them their due meed of poetic fame. The example of Milton, however, whom Time has vindicated, staunchly loyal tyrant hater to the end, accuses them; Milton would never have bowed, as they have bowed, to Castlereagh. Italy and Ireland testify to the scandalous character of that tinkering slave maker.

Canto I. The poet (for Byron pretends to be an anonymous Spanish writer) mockingly imitates Tasso's catalogue of possible historical heroes. Rejecting them all for some falling off of their heroic reputations, he chooses Don Juan, a familiar figure whom we have all seen in the pantomime. Unlike the epic poets, he will not begin *"in medias res,"* but at the beginning:

> "The regularity of my design
> Forbids all wandering as the worst of sinning."

Don Juan was born at Seville on the Guadalquivir, the son of Don José, a true Hidalgo, and Donna Inez, a learned lady. The matrimonial

22

quarrels of José and Inez, which affected Juan to the neglect of his education and manners, were reaching the point of divorce proceedings, when José died of a tertian fever. Juan, left heir under his mother's guardianship, was given a private education by tutors who used carefully expurgated texts of the classics. The poet himself would not have educated him in seclusion, but would have sent him to college, where he would have learned a great deal about everything except books.

At sixteen, Juan meets Donna Julia, the young wife of Don Alfonso, who had been a former suitor of Donna Inez. The propinquity of this romantic young pair, strangely encouraged by Donna Inez, inevitably results in their falling in love. On the sixth of June, at half-past six in the evening, Juan at last realizes that he is in love with Julia, as they sit together in the summerhouse; and Julia abandons her Platonic resolutions and capitulates. The poet apostrophizes Pleasure, and lists the sweet things of life, the sweetest of all being First Love. Then he enumerates the marvellous discoveries and inventions of this new age, in medicine and war and every art affecting the body of man, but none so marvellous as Man himself, whose destiny is obscured beyond the gates of death.

The poet, meanwhile, has taken a poetical license to skip six months and proceeds to the rapid narrative of the November night farce in Donna Julia's room. Don Alfonso, whose suspicions, on his first inspection for a hidden stranger, are lulled by Julia's harangue, returns again to apologize, discovers Juan's shoes, and the game is up. Juan escapes, but Alfonso sues for a divorce. Inez, vowing to the Virgin several pounds of candles to remove this stain from Juan's reputation, sends her son off to travel. Donna Julia is consigned to a convent, and writes her famous farewell letter to Juan.

To conclude the Canto, the poet returns to questions of literary and moral criticism, giving his own set of poetical rules. He declares that this poem is an epic based on truth and Aristotle's rules, and that it is extremely moral. Whoever says it is not, lies (if he is a clergyman) or is mistaken (if a critic). At any rate, the poet has taken the precaution of bribing the reviewers (the *British Review*, only; he has been told it is no good trying to corrupt the *Edinburgh* or the *Quarterly*). Lifting the gossamer of anonymity for a moment, Byron professes that he has lost his combativeness and self-assurance, and laments his own lost youth.

Canto II Juan's errors at sixteen are hardly surprising considering the faults of his education and stupidity of his tutors. Well, so the world wags, and meanwhile the poet cannot resist apostrophizing the beautiful girls of Cadiz. While Inez at home takes up Sunday School teaching for naughty children, undefeated by her failure with her son, Juan sets sail from Cadiz on the "Trinidada" bound for Leghorn. He takes an exile's farewell of Spain, mourns over Julia's letter, but in the very throes of love is overcome by seasickness. Love may withstand "noble maladies," but "vulgar illnesses" are usually too much for it.

Then follow the storm, the shipwreck, and the horrible tortures of the survivors in the long-boat. Juan loses all his companions and everything he possessed, and alone reaches land more dead than alive. Haidée, the daughter of the Greek pirate and slave-trader on whose island Juan has been washed up, rescues him and tends him back to health, concealing him in a cave by the sea. Inevitably they fall in love with each other, and the progress of their amour occupies the rest of the canto. The humorous, tender narrative is accented by brief digressions, at first salty and gay — on Pasiphaë's attachment to the Cretan bull, on Ceres, Venus, and Bacchus, and on the pleasure of learning a foreign language from a pretty young girl. As the romance progresses, the poet's choruses rise, from the praise of hock and soda water, the true joy of watching a sleeping loved one, the love of women, their sad fate, and the revenge they take for inevitable betrayal, to an apostrophe to love, the "God of evil." At last returning to a calmer, lighter mood, the poet apologizes for Juan's inconstancy, tries to explain it philosophically and anatomically, and takes farewell of the reader.

Cantos III and IV, originally written as a unit, contain the rising action, the climax, and catastrophe of Haidée's story. Her father Lambro, mistakenly reported dead, returns home to surprise Juan and his daughter and the whole island in the midst of a great celebration. Juan is seized and transported to Constantinople, where he is left in the slave-market, weak with wounds and grief.

The digressions, occupying fully a quarter of the stanzas and more segregated and connected than in the former cantos, are personal, apologetic, and combative. Byron defends his bad habit of digressing by saying that "*longueurs*" are to be preferred to the inanities of the Lake poets. He comments on his state of mind. Intellectual pride, he says, especially in youth, leads us to conceptions too vast for our powers. But Time, the leveler of all things, together with Adversity, tames youth, cures pride, and teaches us to reflect with wonder on our past emotions. Byron, however, still has feelings, not having been dipped in Lethe, and "if I laugh . . . 'Tis that I may not weep." He intends nothing subversive in this poem, as his critics have accused him, but only to be merry. His manner is exotic to the English language, being Pulci's, but he has chosen a modern subject, since Pulci's knights and dames are now obsolete. Let the critics carp, if they wish to read into his poem what positively is not there; speech and thought are free in this liberal age.

The favorite Byronic theme of the power of poetry and the transiency of Love, Glory, and Fame is the deepest tone in these reflections. The description of the court poet, a trimmer and laureate like Southey, who sings nevertheless the patriotic "Isles of Greece," leads directly to reflections on the power of the written word, "which makes thousands, perhaps millions, think," which outlasts even the name of its author. A hundred stanzas later, Byron returns to the theme. He says, in answer to his critics, that he used to love a literary fight, but is too old for that now, and will leave his own reputation to the decision of posterity. Fame is transient, and the love of glory futile; everything will eventually crumble into anonymous dust. Nevertheless, poets will continue to write, for it is their inescapable urge to express passion in words and to mirror the images of life. Censorship spoils many a pretty poem. How curious for Byron that he was once a "literary lion" and has now been exiled by the "blue-coat misses of a coterie." He has heard of Humboldt's cyanometer for measuring the intensity of blue in the sky, and would like to use it on "Lady Daphne." Thus the oratory and melodrama of these cantos melt away into satiric scherzo.

Canto V, introduced by a criticism of amatory writing, a description of Constantinople and environs, and the poet's attachment to the name of Mary, settles down to Juan in the slave-market, shivering in the bleak autumn day and the misery of his reduced circumstances. Juan, and his new acquaintance the English captive Johnson, are sold to an old black eunuch, who rows them off up the Bosphorus. Disembarking at a little creek below the back gate of the palace gardens, they thread their way in the dark toward the great lighted building. Juan proposes killing the eunuch and escaping, but the Englishman dissuades him in favor of going on and getting their dinner. Inside the palace, the eunuch dresses his captives, Johnson in Turkish finery, and Juan as an odalisque for the seraglio. This comic scene gives place quickly to the grand drama of the interview between the Sultana Gulbeyaz and Juan, interrupted at the close of the canto by the arrival of the Sultan himself and all his train.

The longest digression occurs early in the canto, when, considering whether the slave-trader's conscience troubled him at dinner after selling his fellow men, Byron wanders on, musing on mortality and his experience with the sudden death of the Ravenna Chief of Police. The crux of the matter is the mind's apparent dependence on the body and bodily functions:

> "And is this blood, then, formed but to be shed?
> Can every element our elements mar?
>   And Air — Earth — Water — Fire live — and we dead?
> *We*, whose minds comprehend all things? . . ."

It is an unsolvable mystery.

A later digression satirizes the detailed description of the travel books, but though Byron spares an itemized account of the palace, he does meditate on the gloominess of deserted halls and galleries, big houses, churches, and the tower of Babel, and recalls Horace's blast against Architectural Folly, when we should be thinking of our tombs. In the seraglio scene, the digressions are mere asides of the poet, on the rapidity necessary in courtships in hot climates, on the inability of the royal to understand the feelings of their inferiors, and on other examples of women scorned — Potiphar's wife, Lady Booby, and Phedra. The satiric description of the Sultan delivers sideswipes at George IV and the diplomats who make wars.

More than two years passed before Byron took up his poem again. The volume containing Cantos VI–VIII has a prose preface acknowledging the source of the Siege of Ismail scenes, defending the attacks on Castlereagh, now dead by his own hand, and repudiating any concern about the charges of blasphemy and indecency leveled at Byron by the present generation of Englishmen, notorious hypocrites.

Returning to his story in *Canto VI*, Byron marvels at the impulsiveness of Gulbeyaz, a typical woman who thinks with her heart. Though her behavior was admittedly wrong, her position as fourth wife and sharer of her lord with fifteen hundred concubines furnishes her some excuse. Don Juan in his feminine disguise finds himself in a favored position, dismissed to spend the night in the harem with the bevy of lovely odalisques — "Oh, enviable Briareus!" The "Mother of the Maids" surely has a sinecure, merely to keep in order fifteen hundred girls with only the Sultan to cause strife among them. From tender descriptions of Lolah, Katinka, and Dudù, and their innocent questioning of "Juanna," and from digressions on the Age of Gold, on pins in women's dresses and the joys and griefs of playing lady's maid, Byron takes an astonishing leap back to his ontological theme: "What are we? and whence came we?"

In this lulled and timeless mood, we see the sleeping beauties of the Oda suddenly awakened by Dudù's scream and hear with them, in all innocence, the naughtily disappointing recital of her symbolic nightmare. But dawn is breaking, and Gulbeyaz, all amort with jealousy, interviews Baba the eunuch, and orders the death of Juan and Dudù.

Canto VII. From love, jealousy, and danger in the seraglio, and leaving Juan's fate in suspense, Byron turns to war and glory at the Siege of Ismail on the Danube in the Russian-Turkish war. Love and Glory are both fleeting flames like the Aurora Borealis, and his poem is also an Aurora, flashing "O'er a waste and icy clime." He deprecates the criticism that accuses him of scoffing. He laughs at all things, for all things are a *show*. When many a great poet and philosopher and every modern preacher lift their voices on the nothingness of life, Byron will not be silenced.

Empty military glory and futile conquest constitute the nothingness of the siege and battle of Ismail, and they are contrasted with the lavish expenditure of effort, gallantry, pain, blood, and life itself. The lightness of touch in the mock epic catalogue of heroes with tongue-twisting Russian names, or monotonous English Thomsons and Smiths, or nameless Frenchmen (for it is treasonable nowadays to admit any gallantry in the abhorred foes of England), and the flat, matter-of-fact narration of the action are jolted only by the description of Potemkin, the arch villain, who from mere lust of power ordered all this slaughter:

> " 'Let there be Light!' said God, and there was Light!
> 'Let there be Blood!' says man, and there's a sea!"

For the rest, from Juan and Johnson, who turn up on the eve of the assault with the eunuch and two harem ladies, to General Suvaroff, the Hero-Buffoon, the actors are mere fallible fools, obeying orders or chasing glory. The peroration on the eve of battle, complaining that modern war is not Poetic, invokes eternal Homer, Bonaparte's bulletins, the Shade of Leonidas, and Caesar's Commentaries, to assist in the description of the work of Glory. The last stanza dwells oratorically on the awful pause before the charge, "dividing Life from Death."

In a true epic, *Canto VIII*, the Taking of Ismail, would have been straight dashing narration. Nowhere does the special manner of Byron's satiric epic show its colors more obviously than in this passage. The narrative is embedded in editorial digressions and is shot through with ironic caustic comments. Byron turns the spotlight over the broad scene of charge and counter-attack, picking out individual actions of valor and self-sacrifice. Thus he points up the contrast between the senseless bloody conquest and sacking of Ismail and the generosity of the human beings defending and attacking. At last the Christian Cross "red with no *redeeming* gore" glares where the Crescent has been, and Suvaroff writes the dispatch to the Empress Catherine: "Glory to God and to the Empress! Ismail's ours," which shocked Byron to the core. They are the most tremendous words since "Mene, Mene." No one will ever forget them:

> "For I will teach, if possible, the stones
> To rise against Earth's tyrants."

Byron's generation will never see a free earth, but Posterity will; and let them read this story of Ismail as if, though worse, it were comparable to the tales of savagery of ancient Britons, or to meaningless hieroglyphics and the riddle of the Pyramids.

Juan, who has distinguished himself for gallantry in the battle and has acquired the little Moslem orphan Leila, rescued from the Cossacks, is sent to Catherine in St. Petersburg with Suvaroff's dispatch.

Cantos IX and X, beginning with the dedication to Wellington (or "Villainton") and a reprise of the metaphysical speculation on death, span Juan's experiences at the Court of St. Petersburg. Looking like Cupid in the disguise of a Lieutenant of Artillery, he presents the dispatch to Catherine and is instantly rewarded by that susceptible monarch with elevation to the "high official station" of favorite. His Spanish relatives, to whom he writes of his adventures and his new position, begin to think of tripping to St. Petersburg to secure places through his favor. His mother writes him, congratulating him on reducing his expenses, warning him against the Greek Orthodox Church, and exclaiming over the Empress's surely maternal love for him; she also informs him that he has a little brother, born in second wedlock.

But Juan, whether from pining in that cold climate, or boredom in the huge arms of royalty, or the cankerworm of some obscure care, falls into a fever. The court physicians probably would have killed him, had his constitution not been so strong. At a loss, they pronounce the climate too hard for him and recommend travel. Catherine sends him on a secret mission to Great Britain, which is in negotiation with Russia over many matters. Departing in great style, Juan and Leila traverse Europe, cross the Channel, pay the customs bill at Dover, and enjoy a rapid journey by English post through Canterbury toward London.

Canto IX continues the old themes for digression — women, love, time and eternity, tyrants and revolution, death and the bondage of the body. But immediately after the recital of Donna Inez's letter, an apostrophe to Hypocrisy introduces a new emphasis on the theme of sin in high places, especially in England. The first sight of the cliffs of Dover and the view of London from Shooter's Hill raise the poet's lament for England, hardened in imperial sin.

Juan, however, rapt in admiration, is rudely and speedily introduced to crime in "Freedom's chosen station." A gang of highway robbers holds him up, and he is profoundly disturbed and saddened to think that he has been "obliged to slay a free-born native in self-defence." Has he, perhaps, mistaken a welcoming custom of the country?

In *Canto XI*, we follow him, through the suburbs and streets of London, to the hotel patronized by foreign envoys; then up the social ladder, through ministers and underlings (even the clerks were so much impressed with him that they "were hardly rude enough to earn their pay") to presentation at Court and in West End society.

Byron, intimately acquainted with all these scenes and people, makes the most of the double view, his own and Juan's. To heighten the ironic relativity of these diverse viewpoints, Byron calls in a favorite theme, the destruction wrought by passing time. In a famous *"ubi sunt"* passage, he recounts the astonishing changes since 1815, enough to "suffice a moderate century," in society, in politics, in the distribution of wealth, even in the change from beer to gin. He advises Juan to enjoy the day, for

"Tomorrow sees another race as gay
        And transient . . .
                and above all keep a sharp eye
        Much less on what you do than what you say.
        Be hypocritical, be cautious, be
        Not what you *seem,* but always what you *see.*"

The hypocritical postwar society of England is to be the theme of the English adventures.

Canto XII is taken up with the omnipotence of money and the specific evil of the "marriage mart." The satire is ultimately aimed at Malthus, who has condemned the human instinct of philoprogenitiveness and has reduced marriage, even in theory, to arithmetic.

Canto XIII, turning "serious," treats the superficies of high society and introduces Lady Adeline Amundeville, Lord Henry, and their house party guests at Norman Abbey:

"Society is now one polished horde,
        Formed of two mighty tribes, the *Bores* and *Bored.*"

Canto XIV, the beginning of Lady Adeline's matchmaking on Juan's behalf at the house party, is set in a frame of metaphysical speculation on appearance and reality. Byron defends this speculation against the charge of irrelevance; he is writing truth, not fiction, and as he tackles that most unnatural, artificial subject, Society — somewhat neglected of late by poets — he needs to keep a truthful perspective and a firm grip on facts.

Juan makes a great success with the hunters in the field and the ladies in the drawing room, and especially captivates the passionate, amoral Duchess of Fitz-Fulke. Lady Adeline, from an infinity of motives and circumstances, has her attention fixed upon Juan by this threat to his social safety, and herself falls in danger of thinking too much about him. The exposition of her character, her motives, and her relations with her husband, the good nobleman Lord Henry, who is abstracted by his political business, carries Byron's serious indictment of English high society. It appears most forcibly in an extraordinary geyser of digression, following the discovery that Lady Adeline suffers from vacancy of heart and meddlesomeness because her husband will not or cannot satisfy her craving for affection. Happy, says Byron, are they who have an occupation. Idleness is fertile for evil, and from the ennui of High Life

> "arise the woes of Sentiment,
> Blue-devils — and Blue-stockings — and Romances
> Reduced to practice, and performed like dances."

Oh, Wilberforce! he cries, now that you have freed the heavy-laden
blacks, try shutting up the idle whites, the bullies and the tyrants, and
teach them that what's sauce for the goose is sauce for the gander. Or
shut up the world at large, let Bedlam out, and you will not find much
difference, for there is not a jot of sense among Mankind.

In *Canto XV*, Adeline attempts her match-making, and we are introduced to Aurora Raby, the English gem in contrast to Haidée, the Greek
flower. The surface of the story is eked out by the fashionable dinner,
with satire on French cookery and gourmets. But Byron still feels difficulty in dealing with his prosaic and artificial subject. Fiction must be
founded on reality, and only philosophy, or, more likely, religion can tell
what that is. He flounders for firm ground under the wishy-washiness and
unreality of society ; he must introduce "Politics, Policy, and Piety" to
"dress" and "stuff with sage" that "very verdant goose." At last he
resorts to the Supernatural, and ends his flippancy in a sudden elevation
to the sublime: "Between two worlds Life hovers like a star," a stanza
that sounds like a compressed paraphrase of the ninetieth psalm.

But the ghostly visitations described in *Canto XVI* turn out to be as
indeterminate and confusing and disillusioning as any other of Juan's
experiences. The poem is broken off unresolved. Seeming and being,
hypocritical cant and reality, are the keys to the last part of *Don Juan*.
The subtle modulations of thought repay close study, as Byron's verse
hovers, sometimes humorously, sometimes venomously, over the subject.
He should not be believed when he writes :

> "My Muse, the butterfly, hath but her wings,
>   Not stings, and flits through ether without aim,
> Alighting rarely ; — were she but a hornet,
> Perhaps there might be vices which would mourn it."

No brief summary can do justice to *Don Juan*. It is a whole archipelago of narrative islands, some marshy and some firm and solid, float-
ing in a vast sea of Byronic speculation. The reader must explore it for
himself. Byron's varying moods illuminate it with a play of shifting
lights, now tender and rosy, or dark and gloomy, and then with a
crackling display of wit, or lightning stabs of passionate or prophetic
insight. It is a panorama of the world as Byron saw it.

CHAPTER THREE

"Epic Satire"

1

Considering the doubts, delays, and obstructions attending the composition of *Don Juan*, we may well be surprised that it turned out as coherent as it is. But the changes Byron made in his plans and purposes, though partly due to his difficulties, were also inherent in his subject matter and manner and in his growing conception of the poem. While maintaining, through all the choices of unfolding plot, the steady development of his hero's character, the orderly progress of his story, and the style and method of the cantos, Byron enlarged the purpose. *Don Juan* begins in fun, but it ends in bitterness and sadness. The crescendo of tone, the broadening and deepening of scope are well supported through the first twelve cantos. Then the poem takes a dip again into frivolity, though there are indications that much greater seriousness is to come. All the entangling lines for the English episode, when Don Juan is to become the "cause for a divorce," are left in the air, but they point towards a savage exposé of British hypocrisy. The theme of political freedom also is to be worked out not only in comments and episodes, but in the eventual entanglement of the hero in revolution — the French revolution, Byron promises, in his forecasts to Murray and others.

Professor Chew has summarized lucidly the evidence in Byron's letters and recorded conversations concerning his plans for *Don Juan*.[1] Beginning possibly as a burlesque of the Spanish legend of Don Juan, "the poem grew under his hand into the great satiric picture of modern society that it is." "You ask me," Byron wrote to Murray, August 12, 1819, "for the plan of Donny Johnny. I have no plan. . . . Do you suppose that I could have any intention but to giggle and make giggle?"

But by February 16, 1821, he was able to write to Murray:

"The fifth canto is so far from being the last of *Don Juan* that it is hardly the beginning. I meant to take him a tour of Europe, with a proper mixture of siege, battle and adventure, and to make him finish like Anacharsis Cloots in the French Revolution. . . . I meant to have made him a *Cavalier Servente* in Italy, and a cause for a divorce in England, and a sentimental 'Wertherfaced man' [Moore had just used this phrase in his *Fudge Family in Paris*] in Germany. . . . But I had not quite fixed whether to make him end in Hell,

or in an unhappy marriage, not knowing which would be the severest. The
Spanish tradition says Hell; but it is probably only an Allegory of the other
state."

Byron shows inconsistency, characteristically satiric even in this more
explicit forecast. An ending in Hell would be compatible with a guil-
lotining, like Anacharsis Cloots' finale, in the French Revolution, but the
unhappy marriage would not be. Byron added still another possible
ending in conversation with Hunt in 1822, that Don Juan should turn
Methodist. But these inconsistencies are merely half-serious persiflage,
for the revolutionary goal appears to have predominated. "Byron,"
Chew continues, "told Medwin that he thought of introducing a scene
of the plague, and that he planned that Leila was to be in love with Juan
and he not with her. 'He shall get into all sorts of scrapes, and at length
end his career in France. Poor Juan shall be guillotined in the French
Revolution.' "

Later, Greece may have been drawn into Juan's itinerary. Chew notes
that on the way to Greece in 1823, Byron "remarked that if the coming adventures were of a serious cast they should be material for a fifth
canto of *Childe Harold;* if comic, they should go into *Don Juan.*" The
accusation (if true) made by Countess Guiccioli many years later in her
Recollections, that Moore and others in London had burned five genuine
cantos of *Don Juan* composed at Missolonghi, supports the inclusion of
Greek adventures:

"The scene of the cantos that followed," Teresa wrote, "was laid first in
England and then in Greece. The places chosen for the action naturally
rendered these last cantos the most interesting, and, besides, they explained
a host of things quite justifying them. They were taken to England with Lord
Byron's other papers; but there they were probably considered not sufficiently
respectful toward England, on which they formed a sort of satire too out-
spoken with regard to living personages, and doubtless it was deemed an act
of patriotism to destroy them." [2]

This fascinating bit of news, however, as Chew notes, must be put beside Byron's statement to Moore, in a letter dated March 4, 1824, that
in the press of Greek business he was not, as the newspapers reported him
to be, living a quiet life on an island continuing *Don Juan* or any other
poem. The few stanzas of Canto XVII discovered among his papers and
first published in 1905 apparently represent all that he accomplished
on the poem during the last year of his life.

The extension of the number of cantos projected, from twelve, to
twenty-four, to fifty, and finally to one hundred, is only a sample of the
Pulcian freedom Byron permitted himself. But the multiplicity of plans
and intentions also illustrates essential Don Juanism, that is, Byron's

interpretation of the Pulcian manner. On the one hand, Byron thought of his coming adventures in Greece as material for *Don Juan* provided they were comic; on the other, he seriously declared that *"Don Juan* will be known by and bye, for what it is intended — a *Satire* on abuses of the present state of Society, and not an eulogy of vice. . . ." [3] Now he calls his poem epic, however irreverently, bows to Horace, Aristotle, Milton, Dryden, Pope, or invokes eternal Homer to help him paint a siege more bloody than the siege of Troy. Now Ariosto and Pulci are his masters, as with "capering spirits" he sails his "still sea-worthy skiff" of Poesy, or promises

> "to prattle
> Like Roland's horn at Roncesvalles' battle."

Frequently, then, he complains that he has lost the thread of his story, indulging his vice of digression; that he has forgotten what he meant to say:

> "But let it go: — it will one day be found
> With other relics of 'a former World' ";

or that he has deviated into matters rather dry.

> "I ne'er decide what I shall say, and this I call
> Much too poetical: men should know why
> They write, and for what end; but, note or text,
> I never know the word which will come next."

Thus he underlines ironically the moral "stuffing" of his story.

This is the tone of the humorist, of a master who, though imitating a model, is perfectly willing and able to subordinate imitation to his own whim or free invention. Byron's Don Juanism belongs to no school; it does not set itself up adherent to any System. It is heir of all the ages, can use or toss aside any literary reference or philosophical idea, any fact or mood that comes to hand. It is rich and free. As Byron himself said, "The soul of such poetry is its license." He expected his audience to recognize and relish not only his free imitation of the Italians but every least allusion to the world of letters or of European society.

To write a great poem was, we can be sure, Byron's unswerving intention. With Murray's, Gifford's, and Shelley's exhortations ringing in his ears, with the admired example of Scott, "the Ariosto of the North," to emulate, and the despised *longueurs* of Southey with his *Madoc* as a mark to shoot beyond, he must aim high, and epic was still the topmost branch of poetry. Thinking over all the modern epics he had to compete with — *Télémaque, l'Henriade, Oberon,* Lucien Bonaparte's *Charlemagne,* to mention only a few — he resolved that his should be an epic with a difference, namely, that it would be true, and that it would have an ordinary, modern, faulty human being for hero. The ancient heroes, all except tyrants like Alexander, have been forgotten; they mean nothing to the modern world, or worse than nothing:

> "But oh! ye modern Heroes with your cartridges,
>   When will your names lend lustre e'en to partridges?"

Wellingtons and Bonapartes turn into venal politicians or bloody tyrants. Imaginary heroes, on the other hand, will not serve. A *preux chevalier* like Huon, the hero of *Oberon*, exists only in fairyland, with the king of the fairies to watch over him and help him out of scrapes that belong to sentimental romance, with all sorts of miraculous, incredible devices.[4] His like is not to be found in real life.

Solemnity and sustained heroics, Byron thought, are not true to life, and besides they were not for an author who shied at the possibility of failure and ridicule. *Don Juan* should combine the congenial manner of the Italian jocose epics with the advantages of the best in satiric prose romance: Lucian, Rabelais, *Don Quixote, Gil Blas, Gulliver's Travels, Candide, Tom Jones, Peregrine Pickle, Tristram Shandy.* Byron would adopt the easiest form of fiction, the story told by the omniscient author in his own person, who comes out to the front of the stage like Fielding, whenever he feels called upon to address his audience directly. He will disguise the author at first a little, since the poem is to be published anonymously, and he will begin small and very jocose with Don Juan's earliest scrape:

> "but whether
> I shall proceed with his adventures is
> Dependent on the public altogether."

"My poem's epic," Byron declared toward the end of the first canto, and meant it as sincerely as Fielding meant his declaration of epic pretensions in *Joseph Andrews.*[5] The question whether *Don Juan* should be classed as an epic is a moot point, for its epical qualities are subordinate architectural ornaments. Ariosto-like introductions and conclusions to cantos, "new mythological machinery and supernatural scenery," catalogues of heroes, invocations to the Muses, are decorative flourishes or mere sarcasm and irony. Love, wreck, and war are classic epic themes, but they belong also to the realistic novel. Wordsworth's Preface of 1815 lists among the types of Narrative Poetry, "that dear production of our days, the metrical Novel. Of this class, the distinguishing mark, is, that the narrator, however liberally his speaking agents be introduced, is himself the source from which every thing primarily flows." The real model of *Don Juan* is the picaresque novel, the great catchall of narrative and reflection, subject to no law but the author's desires. A spontaneous proof that the reading public saw *Don Juan* immediately in this light is the fact that some of the earliest spurious cantos that came from the piratical presses were picaresque romances.[6] Would-be continuators of the anonymous and unprotected poem took up their pens to write under the inspiration of the same Muse, and turned out stories of adventure in distant climes or at home in the underworld of London.

2

Though Byron, a passionate devourer of fiction and a naive story-teller, paid lip service to the supremacy of epic, his natural poetic tendency was moral, Virgilian rather than Homeric. It was not lightly that Byron declared, in words that shocked the *Blackwood's Magazine* editor because they came from Byron, "In my mind, the highest of all poetry is ethical poetry, as the highest of all earthly objects must be moral truth." [7] For Byron, therefore, as for Shaw in *Man and Superman*, the legend of Don Juan was merely a framework on which to hang his view of human life and his moralistic philosophizing.

Until Byron used it, the Don Juan legend had followed a well-established conventional pattern in all its appearances in the theater. Byron probably knew a number of these. He had frequently seen the pantomime based on Thomas Shadwell's *Libertine*, first produced by Garrick and revised by Delpini, with music by Gluck. Thus Byron announces his choice of hero as

> "our ancient friend Don Juan —
> We all have seen him, in the pantomime,
> Sent to the Devil somewhat ere his time."

He may have seen a presentation of Tirso de Molina's play *El Burlador de Sevilla*, still popular in Spain in 1809. This play, the first great dramatic success based on the widespread legend of Don Juan, dates from the early seventeenth century. There is no evidence that Byron was acquainted with Molière's *Le Festin de Pierre*, but he certainly must have seen at Venice not only the *Don Giovanni* of Mozart and Da Ponte, but also Goldoni's comedy, based on Molière, *Don Giovanni Tenorio, o sia Il Dissoluto*. In the latter, Goldoni revenged himself on a faithless actress by incorporating the story of her treachery in the plot and making her play her own role of the traitor. Even if Byron never saw this play, he knew, from an amusing and notorious passage in Goldoni's memoirs, about this autobiographical use of the Don Juan legend.[8]

In 1816–1817, as E. H. Coleridge and Miss Helene Richter point out,[9] Byron had his attention twice directed to the legend. In the novels

of Casti, he met a flippantly satirical handling of the theme in the story
of *La Diavolessa*. But especially in the *Biographia Literaria*, Chapter
XXIII, he read S. T. Coleridge's original critique of Shadwell's *Libertine*.[10] Coleridge brought up the questions of the true nature of Don
Juan and the morality of his story in order to condemn, by contrast, the
hero and the morals of Maturin's *Bertram*. As *Bertram*, with its exag-
geratedly Byronic hero, was one of the last plays Byron had sponsored
through thick and thin in his Drury Lane committee work, he naturally
read with care Coleridge's famous criticism of the play and of all "Ger-
manic" romantic drama.

Coleridge first notes that the *Atheista Fulminato*, as he calls Shadwell's play, is a wholly imaginative production — "nothing of it belongs
to the real world." The characters are "creatures of the brain; as little
amenable to the rules of ordinary probability, as the Satan of *Paradise
Lost*, or the Caliban of *The Tempest*, and therefore to be understood
and judged of as impersonated abstractions." Don Juan, Coleridge goes
on, has every endowment of birth, talents, and material fortune, but is
ruled entirely by self-will. "Obedience to nature is the only virtue: the
gratification of the passions and appetites her only dictate." The abstraction of Don Juan's character consists in the union of superior gifts
and entire wickedness in one and the same person, an unnatural mixture,
similar to Milton's Satan, which the audience can enjoy only as an
artistic ideal figure by their willing suspension of disbelief. Our disbelief
in the existence in real life of such a character is made up for by our
admiration of his superior qualities. We want especially to be able like
him to attract heroic devoted love for ourselves alone, in spite of our
bad qualities. The sheer power of Don Juan — to awaken devotion to
himself, and to wield intellectual overlordship, even over his own guilt and
the avenging power of the supernatural world — is his supreme attraction. In this he resembles Shakespeare's villain heroes. Coleridge's analysis all leads to his appreciation of the fine moral effect of the supernatural in the *Atheista Fulminato*, and his condemnation of the confused
morality and meaningless use of the supernatural in such plays as
Bertram.

The question is whether Byron's characterization of Don Juan and
narrative of his adventures owe anything to the legendary figure, represented in all these plays. Miss Richter agrees with Byron's editor
(E. H. Coleridge) that Byron must have derived his new conception of
Don Juan from S. T. Coleridge's description of him as the natural man,
to whom the only sin is to act contrary to his own nature. Indeed, Coleridge's acute analysis might pass muster as a character sketch of Byron
himself in the light in which the English public of 1816 saw him. Coleridge's critique probably set the egocentric Byron thinking about the

usefulness of the legend for his own purposes, and he proceeded to adapt it with perfectly fresh and unconventional freedom to his own view of human life. But far from being affected positively by the legendary hero and his career, Byron seems to me to have reacted strongly against the supernaturalism of the drama and the abstraction of the hero's character remarked upon by Coleridge.

Byron's Don Juan is no more like the legendary Don Juan than he is like the earlier Byronic heroes. For the traditional Don Juan is a libertine, a man of endless and heartless seductions, a monster fitly consigned to the Devil in a blast of thunder. He belongs to a kind of licentious romanticism, which, in serious or ribald plots, linked Satanism and the phenomena of human love and marriage. To be sure, Byron had dabbled in this sort of literature. He read Le Sage's *Le Diable Boiteux*, which, by the way, he suggested as a more fitting sobriquet for himself than Lamartine's *"chantre d'enfers."* He imitated Machiavelli's *Marriage of Belphegor*. He told Moore he thought of trying a poem somewhat on the order of Cazotte's *Le Diable Amoureux*, but doubted that he had tenderness enough to succeed in it. But above all, he knew Goethe's *Faust*, and recognized Goethe's universal humanizing of the theme of love and evil. In *Manfred*, written just before *Don Juan*, and in *Cain*, composed during a pause in *Don Juan*, Byron himself dealt with the Faust legend. Now, as Miss Richter boldly asserts, taking up the other great European legend of the insatiable Renaissance hero, Byron treated symbolically the Juan-saga as the companion piece of the Faust-saga.[11]

But Byron's Juan is neither a diabolical monster, nor a Faustian superman, nor even a blithe rascal like the conventional *picaro*. He is an ordinary human boy, whose adventures, though spectacular and bloody, are thoroughly mundane. He resembles Tom Jones or Candide more than the orthodox picaresque heroes. For Tom Jones and Candide eventually learn from their experiences, and Don Juan gives promise of doing so; he is at least a sadder if not a wiser youth when the poem is broken off. Whereas the true *picaro*, whether mischievous or good, maintains a static character. For example, Roderick Random, no matter how often the human race has risen up and smitten him, is the same naive, sentimental, heroic rawbones at the end that he was at the beginning.

Critics have remarked upon the passivity of Juan's character, as of Tom Jones's, objecting that it is a serious flaw in any hero. Juan is whirled along on the stream of chance and change, scarcely developing the adroitness of the opportunist. Things happen to him before he can think even once, and he seems to have to be prodded into accepting the gifts the gods send, without having will enough of his own to accept or reject. Only in moments of extreme danger does he rise to act of his own volition: when he fights his way out of Donna Julia's room, when he takes charge during the wreck of the "Trinidada," when he defies Lambro, when he goes gaily and resolutely to meet an unknown fate in the seraglio, and when he acts the chivalric hero at the battle of Ismail. But these, Byron explains, are the instinctive behavior of noble blood and hardly to be credited as conscious acts. Miss Richter notes Juan's inarticulateness. The author has given him scarcely any lines to say, yet we believe implicitly in his charm and grace.

As far as truth to nature goes, this characterization of the late-adolescent boy, especially of one who had been brought up in the cloistered manner Juan had, seems highly credible. The formal education of Tom Jones was neutralized by the intellectual quarrels of his tutors, and he was cast into life to act instinctively according to his innate goodness. Juan, likewise, released from the rigid and meaningless governance of his mother, may be expected to show a combination of numb bewilderment and instinctive animal courage. His innate good disposition carries him through every trial. (Byron professed to believe in innate feelings, but not in innate ideas.) He learns discretion and worldly wisdom, and he shows fortitude in enduring hardships and sorrow, though he cannot altogether avoid the physical and psychic reaction natural after all his brutal, crowded experiences. He is not completely cured of folly and hot-blooded impulses, but he certainly shows at the end of the poem that he is ready to consider more seriously his own behavior and the deeds and professions of others. We suspect that he is entering the typical youthful phase of the adolescent moral censor, which Byron himself exhibited when he wrote *English Bards* and *The Waltz*. Juan, in fact, is as much the young Byron as Tom Jones is the young Fielding. The author looks back from middle-aged wisdom with a wry smile on the follies and idealisms of youth:

"In both *Tom Jones* and *Don Juan*," writes Ronald Bottrall, "the natural man who acts according to impulse is contrasted with the hypocrite, or the hypocritical society, which acts according to convention. The antithesis is between conduct and inclination or intention. In both, evil in the hero is mainly sexual; or at worst, anything vaguely against the social usage; but the evil of society is seen as a fundamental and rooted inability to be honest and truthful, or to care for the individual human life." [12]

On the score of the form Byron adopted for *Don Juan* and the adventures he included in his narrative, Miss Richter points out that he made very scant use of the legend and its examples. Juan's shipwreck and his rescue by a child of nature, who falls in love with him, is perhaps the single motif of the legend which he uses:

"How little Byron thought about following the real Juan-saga, is best shown in the circumstance that he neglected to perfect the invariable companion of Juan in the form of his servant. Thereby he cut away from its former likeness half of the myth, in which the emphasis is less on the hero than on the complementary pair. . . . Would not one suppose that the servant especially would have a particular charm for Byron, through the possibilities of allowing him to utter, ironically, mother wit, coarse humor, naive cleverness, and of making him a sort of fool or chorus to the hero? But what does Byron do? He held back all these possibilities for his own person. He himself undertakes the roles of Gracioso, Sganarelle, Leporello, of Mentor and of Chorus." [13]

Other differences between the legend and Byron's *Don Juan*, noted by Miss Richter, like the change in the hero's role from heartless seducer to helpless prey of the women, or the enlargement of the scope from mere amatory intrigue to include war, politics, and society, or the half-serious, half-mocking use of the supernatural, may be left to later chapters.

3

Fiction was valuable for Byron, if not only, at least especially when it was founded upon fact. He wanted *Don Juan* above all to be a story of real life. Returning to his statement of plans, we find that he mentions not only the Spanish legend but also Anacharsis Cloots. Among Byron's books on contemporary French history were two small volumes edited by John Adolphus, entitled *Biographical Anecdotes of the Founders of the French Republic*, London, 1797. They contain about two hundred brief articles, based on the accounts of French émigrés in London, and presented from a mildly sympathetic and moderate viewpoint toward the Revolution. The article on Cloots reads as follows:

"*Anacharsis Cloots* (His baptismal name was Jean Baptiste: he adopted that of Anacharsis) was born in Cleves. Although a Prussian, a Baron, and a man of fortune, he seems to have imbibed, while yet a boy, a taste for liberty; and, indeed, notwithstanding his singularities and extravagancies, he never appears to have belied his original opinions. At an early period of life, he travelled into all the different countries of Europe; and being rich, noble, and sprightly, he was every where received with attention.

"While in England, he frequently visited Mr. Burke, to whom he was introduced by means of letters from some very learned and respectable men on the Continent.

"The interview between the Philosopher of Beaconsfield, and the 'Orator of the human race,' will be deemed less whimsical, perhaps, than may be at first imagined; when it is known, that Mr. Burke, at the period alluded to, was neither the pensioner nor the pander of royalty, but upheld a lofty character for independence, and possessed some of those very singularities so conspicuous in his friend Anacharsis.

"M. Cloots was not only the nephew of a man of letters (Cornelius

Pauw . . .), but actually a man of letters himself. In 1792, he published a small octavo volume, entitled *'La République Universelle, ou Addresse aux Tyrannicides;'* which was printed at Paris, in 'the fourth year of the Redemption,' and had *'Veritas atque Libertas,'* by way of motto. Voltaire having styled himself the Representative of Philosophers, the author pretends to be 'the Representative of the Oppressed;' and claims an 'universal apostleship for the gratuitous defence of the millions of slaves, who groan from one pole to the other.' In this tract he asserts, that nations are not to be delivered by the blade of a poniard, but by the rays of truth — 'Steel can kill only the tyrant, but tyranny itself may be destroyed by knowledge.'

"The following is a speech delivered by Anacharsis, at the bar of the Legislative Assembly, to which he had conducted a deputation of Dutch, Spaniards, Italians, Germans, Americans, and Asiatics, a little before the grand confederation —

" 'Legislators!

" 'The awe-inspiring standards of the French empire are about to be displayed on the 14th of July, in the Field of Mars, the same place where *Julian trampled all prejudices under foot!* This civic solemnity will not only be the festival of the French, but that of the whole human race. The trumpet, which indicates the resurrection of a great nation, has resounded to the four corners of the world; and the joyful songs of a chorus of twenty-five millions of freemen have awakened the nations buried in a long slavery. . . .' "

The speech continues on the theme of world-wide liberation from tyrants and despots through the example of the French Republic. After an examination of Cloots's atheism, the article concludes:

"Anacharsis, Prussian by birth, a Frenchman by adoption, and a citizen of the world by choice, at last found means to become a member of the National Convention. On the grand question respecting the death of the King, he voted in the affirmative; and with the same breath passed sentence on the head of the house of Brandenbourg, and Louis XVI — 'Et je condamne pareillement à mort l'infame Frédéric Guillaume!'

"Soon after this he was implicated in the affair of Père Duchesne, arrested, sent to prison, and (as Robespierre *never forgave*) he was put to death on the 24th of March, 1794. It is but justice to state, that he continued faithful to his principles, and that he appears to have died innocent. It is not a little singular, that he insisted on being the last person executed that day, in order to have an opportunity of instilling certain principles into the mind of each, by means of a short harangue, which he pronounced as the fatal guillotine was about to descend on his neck."

Byron could not fail to be struck by this eccentric and picturesque figure, with its mixture of cosmopolitanism, rugged independence, fiery love of liberty, freedom of thought, stoical endurance, and prophetic oratory.

The name Anacharsis alone would catch his eye, the name of the philosophical traveler in ancient Greece as Childe Harold was in modern Greece. Jean Baptiste, we learn, rejected his Christian names in recognition of his anti-Christianity, and adopted Anacharsis shortly after the appearance in 1789 of Barthélemy's celebrated novel, *Le Voyage en Grèce du jeune Anacharsis*. This historical, philosophical novel of the ancient world of Greece and the Eastern Mediterranean in the fourth century B.C. was the talk of Paris, and Cloots saw his prototype in the Scythian foreigner, the younger Anacharsis, who traveled as an intelligent observer of customs and governments, comparing civilizations.[14] The phil-Hellenism of this novel could scarcely have failed to attract Byron's notice.[15]

The Voyage of Anacharsis, like another of Byron's favorites, Wieland's *Agathon*, looks back to Fénelon's *Télémaque*, and the origin of the Bildungsroman. The idea of these novels is that a young man not only will develop his character but will learn cosmopolitanism and philosophical relativism from comparing different civilizations at first hand and from undergoing a variety of experiences in his adventures. The three here mentioned are historical novels about the remote past; *Don Juan* deals with the recent past; but all aim alike at the manners and ideas of the present.

With his prejudice for a foundation of fact beneath all fiction, Byron would be drawn to the story of Anacharsis Cloots, and all its filaments of association in contemporary politics and thought; and with his inveterate egoism, he would be caught by those points in Cloots's opinions and circumstances which so much resembled his own. If Anacharsis Cloots is, at least in part, the original of Byron's Don Juan, we recognize immediately that Byron divided the suggestions inherent in him between Juan and himself. The outward facts and circumstances he left to his hero, and the opinions he retained for his own expression. This process resembles what Miss Richter has noticed in Byron's usurpation of Leporello's role in the legend.

4

With the career of Anacharsis Cloots as a general pattern, the time scheme of *Don Juan* naturally suggests itself. The hero's birth and boyhood are rapidly summarized, and the action opens when he is sixteen. Counting backward from the one fixed date, the siege of Ismail in 1790, we can date the Donna Julia episode from June to November 1789. Juan is shipwrecked, say, in January 1790, lives with Haidée on the Greek island through the early Mediterranean spring and summer, and is shipped off to Constantinople in the autumn. There he is sold at auction, passes one night in the seraglio, and escapes with Johnson, Baba, and "two Turkish ladies," arriving at Ismail on the Danube in mid-December

1790. In January 1791 he is dispatched to St. Petersburg, and spends the next few months as favorite of the Empress. His health failing in that cold climate, he is sent as special ambassador to England, arriving at the height of the London season, probably May or June. "Grey was not arrived," and Chatham was dead, the newspapers were carrying paragraphs about Horne Tooke, and George IV was still "the Prince of Princes." After a few hectic weeks in high society, Juan follows the "fatal fair," Lady Adeline Amundeville, and his friend Lord Henry, down to Norman Abbey for the September house party. So much for the historical accuracy of the fact-loving Byron, but the reader need not be reminded that the ideas and manners all belong to a period twenty or thirty years later. "The world he writes" is the Napoleonic world. Nevertheless, in a poem championing Freedom, both personal and political, it is altogether fitting that the era outwardly intended should be that of the French Revolution; the contrast between the high hopes and idealism of that period and the cynicism and disillusionment of 1818–1819 merely underlines Byron's satire.

Byron, of course, probably did not have this time scheme completely in mind before he started composing the poem. It is doubtful, for instance, whether he foresaw Juan's involvement in the Russo-Turkish war and had already selected the Siege of Ismail before he dispatched Juan eastward through the Mediterranean, or whether that siege came to hand opportunely and was selected partly because its date fitted the part of the story already published. It is even more doubtful that he would have destined Juan from the beginning to take part in the historic negotiations between Russia and England in 1790–1791. And there are discrepancies. Juan, for example, is accurately stated to be eighteen when he reaches London, but a canto or so later, Byron absent-mindedly makes him twenty-one, since he is said to be only forty days younger than Lady Adeline who had just reached that ripe age. However, this discrepancy in reckoning makes no difference in the appearance and manner of Don Juan, who is still described as a beardless charming youth, a grown-up Cupid.

It is, of course, foolish to hold poets and novelists too rigidly to a matter-of-fact calendar. But observing Byron's care in adhering to a time scheme in a story apparently so carelessly and episodically narrated is instructive as well as amusing. It temporarily folds back the layers of wrappings around the story and reveals its hard factual skeleton, justifying Byron's claim to realism and truth. Moreover, if Byron intended to pursue the Anacharsis Cloots pattern and finish Juan off in the Reign of Terror, we can foresee perhaps a little less dimly how the second half of the story would have gone. There would have been ample time for adventures in Germany, Italy, Greece, and Paris at the rate

Juan had been already traveling. Troubles with women and increasing involvement in politics and revolution would have shared the action.

The settings of the action were dictated to some extent by the localities and manners Byron himself knew. But from the moment in Canto V when Juan enters the Bosphorus gate of the seraglio, to the point in Canto X when he reaches the castellated Rhine, Byron was altogether dependent for settings on those "materials" that he told Murray he had. Even when he knew a locality or scene at first hand, he seems to have borne in mind the literary descriptions he had accumulated in the years of reading memoirs and travels. For example, he confessed to using Tully's *Tripoli* as well as his own memory in the description of Lambro's house and Haidée's costume. If one may trust Medwin's statement, Byron revealed to him the way in which his mind subconsciously relied on book "materials." Speaking of the future of Don Juan after Canto V, he said:

"Well, they make good their escape to Russia; where, if Juan's passion cools, and I don't know what to do with the lady, I shall make her die of the plague. There are accounts enough of the plague to be met with, from Boccaccio to De Foe; — but I have seen it myself and that is worth all their descriptions." [16]

What of the characters in this Epic Satire? They must be as varied as possible, in order that the contrasts between East and West, between War and Peace, between Nature and Civilization, and between Man and Woman, may be as sharp and as comprehensive as Byron's experience could make them. What a gallery of figures he has produced! Bourgeois, hypocritical Donna Inez; the unspoiled child of nature Haidée; pirate-patriot Lambro; Gulbeyaz, the seraglio queen; Johnson, the soldier of fortune; bloody proletarian Suvaroff; Catherine II; brilliant woman of the world Lady Adeline, and her parliamentarian husband Lord Henry, who surely are the prototypes of Trollope's Plantagenet Palliser and Lady Glencora. These are only high spots in a galaxy more varied than in any of Scott's greatest novels. The list may be extended almost endlessly, from poor Pedrillo, who was eaten in the longboat, to the duenna Lady Pinchbeck. Among them all young Juan moves, growing in two, short, crowded years from the dreamy adolescent to the experienced, serious, and saddened young diplomat. He does double duty in the story, as protagonist, whose character development is all-important and carries the moral of the tale, and as observer, whose reactions to the various situations in which he is placed reveal, even more forcibly than the profuse authorial comment, the meaning of the scenes.

In *Don Juan*, Byron fused double purposes and double models to produce a peculiarly Byronic medley. Jest and earnest, epic and satire, are almost indissolubly mixed together. Starting with the career of a legendary hero, he superimposed the historic pattern of a real figure in the

French Revolution. To classic epic, he added not only the Italian jocose epic, but the picaresque novel, named by Fielding "comic epic in prose." Responding to Murray's demand for an autobiographical work relating "all the adventures that you have undergone, seen, heard of, or imagined, with your reflections on life and manners," he produced not only a novel in verse but a satire on modern Europe.

CHAPTER FOUR

Don Juanism

The one point on which all critics of Byron's poetry agree is the unique success of his style in *Don Juan*. Even Swinburne, in the midst of his depreciation of Byron, grants that in "the Bernesque style," *i.e.* the burlesque, in the manner of Berni, continuator of Boiardo's *Orlando Inamorato*, "Byron was supreme . . . a king by truly divine right"; indeed, Swinburne has left us the most often quoted description of the verse of *Don Juan*.

"The style of *Don Juan*" is a somewhat inexact phrase, for the most obvious quality of the poem is its variety, its multiplicity of styles, or, more accurately, of tones. Byron uses the full orchestra, everything from the piccolo to the double bass, though the prevailing tone is somewhere in the middle register, humorous and ironical. The pathetic voice-breaking, the sudden rise to oratorical grandeur or sublimity, the deadly seriousness of invective or prophecy, all characteristic of Byron's grand romantic manner, are used sparingly in this poem, and are all the more effective by their infrequency.

But even when the tone is light and laughing, the subject matter and Byron's intention are fundamentally grave. While most of the fun of reading *Don Juan* is in hearing the suppressed laughter in Byron's voice as he recites, — that tone that so many of his friends and observers remembered with pleasure, — one must not fail to hear the earnestness ironically concealed. Take, for example, the introductory stanzas of Canto V, the seraglio adventure:

> "When amatory poets sing their loves
>   In liquid lines mellifluously bland,
> And pair their rhymes as Venus yokes her doves,
>   They little think what mischief is in hand;
> The greater their success the worse it proves,
>   As Ovid's verse may give to understand;
> Even Petrarch's self, if judged with due severity,
> Is the Platonic pimp of all posterity.

> "I therefore do denounce all amorous writing,
>   Except in such a way as not to attract;
> Plain — simple — short, and by no means inviting,
>   And with a moral to each error tacked,

45

Formed rather for instructing than delighting,
    And with all passions in their turn attacked;
Now, if my Pegasus should not be shod ill,
    This poem will become a moral model."

To jest in earnest is the object of Don Juanism, and it is impossible to separate the humorous tone from the moral sincerity.

Byron uses all the humorous writer's tricks. One may point out parody, puns, epigrams, modern allusions with a humorous or satiric import, double meanings, surprise endings, anti-climax, and ridiculously clever rhymes. Most of these one may find in every canto in great profusion. They are virtuosities, high lights, spangles in the style. But the pervasive humor may not be separated from the subject matter, from Byron's management of the story, and from the impression of his personality on every page. We soon come to notice it most only when we miss it, on those occasions when Byron lays it aside for dark and gloomy, sentimental, or blazingly rhetorical passages.

If the prevailing tone is ironically humorous, it is also conversational, not to say confidential and even chatty. The audience, sometimes posterity as with Fielding, sometimes Byron's friends or his enemies or Europe's millions, but usually his British public, is as important to the existence of the poem as Byron himself and his bag of tricks and subjects. *Don Juan* should always be read as if Byron were reciting it, impromptu, in an after-dinner company. The spice of danger implied in sitting opposite a poet spouting unpredictable verses, who may cease merely to entertain and turn and rend his auditors at any moment, is the desirable seasoning for this pleasant intimacy. *Don Juan* is a skillful dramatic monologue, based on the art of the *improvvisatore*, but excelling it as much as Pulci surpassed the ballad entertainments of the market-place *cantastòrie*.

We have already mentioned the approximation of Byron's letters, journals, memoranda, and incidental verse [1] to *Don Juan*. His conversation also contributed to its style. Though Medwin's book is untrustworthy on points of fact — Medwin was naive and limited in his comprehension of Byron, who took pleasure in fooling the impressible captain — it is unsurpassed for preserving the quality of Byron's talk when he was at ease in a small masculine circle. Actually, Medwin's gullibility assisted his faithful reporting, though sometimes one suspects that his literalness is intentional and that he perfectly well saw through his subject. It is difficult to find a short representative passage entirely free from Byron's posing and Medwin's naïveté, but take this one as a sample:

" 'I have received,' said he, 'from my sister, a lock of Napoleon's hair, which is of a beautiful black. If Hunt were here, we should have half-a-dozen sonnets

on it. It is a valuable present; but, according to my Lord Carlisle, I ought
not to accept it. I observe, in the newspapers of the day, some lines of his
Lordship's, advising Lady Holland not to have anything to do with the snuff-
box left her by Napoleon, for fear that horror and murder should jump out
of the lid every time it is opened! It is a most ingenious idea — I give him
great credit for it.'

"He then read me the first stanza, laughing in his usual suppressed way. —
     'Lady, reject the gift,' &c.
and produced in a few minutes the following parody on it:
     'Lady, accept the box a hero wore,
       In spite of all this elegiac stuff:
     Let not seven stanzas written by a bore,
     Prevent your Ladyship from taking snuff!' " [2]

Medwin's pages taken all together have the ring of authenticity.
Byron's style of talk, like his style of letter writing, was vivacious,
full of anecdote and literary reference, stuffed with his political, religious, and literary prejudices, and always returning to himself and his
own concerns. Apparently, if one liked the man and showed it, he re-
sponded with complete ease and liberality. In a strange company, a
large group, or with uncongenial people, Byron was stiff and silent,
partly from shyness and partly from old-fashioned notions of patrician
etiquette. Worry and grief also had the natural effect of silencing him.
Hunt remarked that Byron was hesitant and awkward in expressing
himself, but after revolving an idea in his mind for some time could
deposit it neatly in a written stanza. But Hunt never knew the mature
Byron under favorable circumstances. The shock of the death of Al-
legra and then of Shelley, and the worry and disappointment over his
very connection with Hunt on the *Liberal* would be more than enough
to eclipse Byron's conversational ease.

It is a pity that Moore and others besides Medwin did not play the
Boswell to Byron more often. But they have left innumerable testi-
monials to the charm of his conversation. Countess Guiccioli, whose witness, of course, is not unprejudiced, speaks of him when he was excited
by a peculiar degree of penetration and insight:

"Then his conversation really became quite dazzling. In his glowing language
all objects assumed unforeseen and picturesque aspects. New and striking
thoughts followed from him in rapid succession, and the flame of his genius
lighted up as if winged with wildfire. Those who have not known him at these
moments can form no idea of what it was from his works. For, in the silence
of his study, when, pen in hand, he was working out his grand conceptions, the
lightning strokes lost much of their brilliant intensity; and although we find,
especially in 'Don Juan' and 'Beppo,' delightful pages of rich comic humor,
only those who knew him can judge how superior still his conversation was." [3]

She quotes Millingen's description of the interest, the merriness, the mercurial variety, and the frankness of Byron's talk,[4] and what Colonel Stanhope said about the "volcanic" mind of Byron:

"As a companion [Colonel Stanhope continued] . . . no one could be more amusing than Lord Byron; he had neither pedantry nor affectation about him, but was natural and playful as a boy. His conversation resembled a stream; sometimes smooth, sometimes rapid, and sometimes rushing down in cataracts. It was a mixture of philosophy and slang, of everything, — like his 'Don Juan.' "[5]

Byron could write a terse epigram, but his usual style is expansive rather than concise. Though there are not many stanzas in *Don Juan* that we would positively wish away, the poem flows along with conversational ease, taking up far more space than would be necessary to achieve even the variety of effects that he intended. One may compare, for example, the stanzas in Canto IV, 8–28, on the ideal perfection of Juan's and Haidée's love, with Keats's Odes on a Grecian Urn and to a Nightingale.[6] The subject and the effect that both poets wished to produce are substantially the same; yet Byron requires five times as much space as Keats. The comparison shows clearly the difference between Keats's distilled, sustained style and the headlong volubility of Byron. Not being himself one to "smooth, inlay, and clip, and fit" fine verses, Byron preferred to write a rough draft and then to add his second thoughts. First thoughts for him were best thoughts. He remarked that Hogg had warned him he should never succeed in writing for the stage because he could not "condense his powers of writing sufficiently." It is this large, unwary liberality of style that made Swinburne liken *Don Juan* to the ocean and its stanzas to the broad backs of the waves.

Byron was more at home in the Spenserian stanza and the *ottava rima* than in the heroic couplet; they gave him more room to turn around.[7] A comparison of *Julian, a Fragment*,[8] the first attempt that Byron made to describe a lone, exhausted survivor of a wreck, with similar passages in *Don Juan*[9] and *The Island*[10] may show the importance of prosodic form to Byron's success in poetry. *Julian* was cast, like the *Corsair* which Byron had just completed, in the new flowing style of couplet made fashionable by Crabbe. The couplets are blocked off in stanzaic paragraphs, as if Byron were groping again toward the larger freedom of the Spenserian stanza. Four years later, however, in treating this same scene in *Don Juan*, he had the room in the *ottava rima* stanza that his voluminous Muse needed and was consequently much more successful. But when he tried again, in *The Island*, five years later still, to repeat something of the same subject in the tenaciously admired heroic couplet, his Muse faltered and failed. It was the choice of prosodic form that made the difference between success and failure.

Byron's art in *Don Juan* has been compared, even by himself, to the art of the *improvvisatore*, but his acquaintance with this style of impromptu versifying provided him with little more than a suggestion for the style of *Beppo* and *Don Juan*. Hobhouse has left an entertaining though derogatory account of the performance of Sgricci that he and Byron witnessed in the Scala theater at Milan.[11] The poet was contending for the "crown of Corinna" and the Lombardy audience was critical. A preliminary orchestral overture accompanied the preparation by the audience of slips of paper containing suggested subjects, which were handed up to the stage, judged by a committee, folded up, and shaken in a vase. The first subject drawn for the *"versi sciolti"* event was the taking of Algiers. "At last Sgricci appeared, and was received with shouts of applause. He was fantastically dressed: his long black hair flowed wildly over his face and shoulders, and his neck was bare. He wore yellow Turkish slippers. He began at once to pour forth his unpremeditated verse." The subject for the *"terze rime"* proved to be "Artemesia at the tomb of Mausolus"; and after some discussion and rejections by Sgricci, the tragedy selected was "Eteocles and Polynices." Hobhouse felt that Sgricci's poetry was very mediocre, and the performance boring; the audience agreed with him as far as the tragedy was concerned, and no doubt Byron shared his views. The Italian language and the art of verse, he and Hobhouse felt, were deplorably degraded by the rage for these mediocre follies.

Though the conversational and spectacular aspects of this kind of poetry were naturally agreeable to Byron, he profited far more from literary models both Italian and English. Above all he owed a debt to Pulci, the inventor of the manner and method of *Don Juan*,[12] which he finally acknowledged (*Don Juan*, IV, 6) after assigning it erroneously to Berni and Whistlecraft.

Byron had long shared the fashionable English interest in the great Italian renaissance poets. His library in London was plentifully stocked with Ariosto and Tasso, and in his early letters he made several admiring references to their power. From the commencement of his study of Italian in Greece in 1810, a long list of evidences might be assembled to show his early and continued enthusiasm for the Italians. From his acquaintances in London, he must also have absorbed a good deal of information about Italian poetry, and some about Pulci in particular. John Herman Merivale, for instance, published pioneer articles in the *Monthly Magazine* between May 1806 and June 1807, introducing the British public to the *Morgante Maggiore*, and imitated Pulci in his

Orlando in Roncesvalles, published by Murray in 1814. Byron admired this poem and said that its meter was "uncommonly well chosen and wielded." [13]

In March 1813, Byron met Leigh Hunt, who was making the fifty-six volumes of the *Parnaso Italiano* "his favorite reading" during his political imprisonment. Hunt loved Pulci "for spirits, and a fine free way" and was pleasurably impressed by his combining a belief in a "religion of charity" with satire of Christian dogma. Tolerance and tenderness of heart, Hunt found, were an appealing mixture in Pulci, and his gaiety and levity redeemed him from the type of "melancholy absurdities" into which Dante's seriousness led.[14] Hunt never failed to recommend the reading he enjoyed. He and Byron undoubtedly discussed Italian literature as well as liberal politics during the prison visits. When Byron was called upon to correct Hunt's *Story of Rimini* and accept its dedication, he praised and defended it, not only out of loyalty to Hunt, but from the honest conviction that it had "two excellent points . . . — originality and Italianism." [15] His sole objection to *Rimini* was that the style smacked of Wordsworth's "vulgar System"; but Hunt pointed in self-defense to the example of the Italians, particularly Ariosto.[16] It is impossible to suppose that the qualities of Pulci's verse did not also at some time enter into these discussions, for Pulci first introduced discursive style and colloquial speech in connection with high subjects.

Perhaps Byron first learned from P. L. Ginguené's *Histoire Littéraire d'Italie* that Pulci was the true originator of the Italian literary chivalric epic style. Frere confessed [17] that his attempt to imitate Pulci in Whistlecraft, begun in 1813, "originated in reading Ginguené's account of Pulci in which some extracts are inserted as characteristic of his style." The knowledge that Frere was composing these jocose verses, and possibly also that Ginguené was the source of his inspiration, was common property among his friends. No copy, however, of Ginguené appears in the catalogue of Byron's books sold in 1816, and no reference to it in his letters until 1820, but an edition of it published in Paris in 1811, the year of its first appearance, is listed in the 1827 sale catalogue. Byron must have acquired it in Venice, though perhaps not until he was ready to translate Pulci, when, remembering Frere's experience, he turned to Ginguené for guidance. Byron thought him perhaps superficial in scholarship, but superior to Sismondi and Tiraboschi, his former guides, and even more entertaining than his favorite Baron Grimm. Ginguené devotes hundreds of pages of detailed description and criticism to the Italian chivalric epics, and Byron, who very well knew how to avail himself of short cuts to knowledge, profited from his fertile suggestions.

In April 1819, Ugo Foscolo's brilliant article on the "Narrative and Romantic Poems of the Italians" appeared in the *Quarterly Review,*[18] in response to public interest in the subject, following the publication of Whistlecraft and Rose's *Court of Beasts*. From a consideration of Casti, Tassoni, and Forteguerri, Foscolo branches out into authoritative exposition of the origins and development of Italian epic; he corrects and elucidates the account given in Ginguené, supplying facts not known to that French critic. He gives full credit to the differences of customs, manners, tastes of the Italian public in the fifteenth and sixteenth centuries, which Ginguené's more classic, national criticism had not fully understood. He hopes that Frere will continue his "Specimen," and

"perhaps create a style which, retaining the blithesomeness and ease of his models, will become completely English, and be truly naturalized by English wit and English feeling. But he must do his best to gain the suffrages of the ladies, who, in every country, and particularly in England, are after all, the supreme arbiters of the destiny and reputation of the new poetry. This he may easily effect by exciting the softer passions. Since the irrevocable decree of Sancho Panza, such warlike beauties as Bradamante and Marfisa are no longer in fashion; and a damsel, who hath once cut off the head of a giant, ceases thenceforward to be killing, nor do we sympathize with her, whatever misfortunes may afterwards befal her. But if the author will only condescend to introduce a heroine, crowned with poetical laurels, driving out of the Campidoglio in her triumphal car, chanting an altisonant ode in prose, and making love by algebra, many fair readers will be dissolved in tears and rapt in ecstasy." [19]

Foscolo's challenge to Frere was renewed to Byron, when Murray wrote that he, Foscolo, Gifford, everyone, hoped Byron would produce an Epic. Byron's answering roar in his letter of April 6, laid down the law on *Don Juan*, and defied Foscolo, the critics, the ladies, and the public, to do better, or to disturb his peace of mind if they did not like it.

However rich or scanty Byron's firsthand knowledge of the Italian epics may have been before 1820, he fully grasped their characteristics and learned to use them in English. R. D. Waller has given an admirable description of Italian mock-heroic romance, the lack of unity in construction, the length determined arbitrarily by the poet, the variety of characters and incidents, the breadth of scene, and the digressions, relevant and irrelevant, grave and comic:

"The style which varies naturally with the poet, abounds in pointed wit, epigrams, and sudden bathos (here assisted by the structure of the octave with its home-striking final couplet), and is often conversationally intimate in tone. Again, in the case of Pulci and some minor writers the vocabulary and phraseology are at times comically vulgar and plebeian. In manner and in metre it is the freest of all verse forms." [20]

Byron, however, took a good many hints from his predecessors Rose and Frere in acclimating the Italian manner to English. William Stewart

Rose's free translation of Casti's *Animali Parlanti* [21] is in six-line rather than eight-line stanzas. Its extremely clever satire tells the story of contemporary English politics under the veil of animal fable. Though the scene of the action is in India, nothing hinders the poet from dragging in contemporary matters in England by way of comparison — for example, Bell's schools, and Cambridge University reform. Likewise, Byron, writing a supposedly Spanish story in *Don Juan*, Canto I, hits at English education, and in Canto III, describing a Greek court poet, lashes Southey and the Lakists. Rose's description of the lion whelp's education under the tutelage of the Ass reminds one of Byron's sarcastic comments on the ignorance of the Sultan and his sons and daughters, *Don Juan*, V, 148–153. One of Rose's digressions in Canto III deals with a favorite subject of Byron's, the mysteries of the feminine mind.[22] When Byron begins to tackle the subject of Great Britain in Canto XII, and staggers at its difficulty compared to any other society, he reverts to Rose's fable:

> "All countries have their 'Lions,' but in thee
> There is but one superb menagerie."

Rose even interpolates Byronesque comments on his own style, for example, in Canto III:

> "Let Scottish loons lay on, and thresh and thump,
>   And for our flights as brain-sick fancies brand 'em;
> I like such thoughts as come, hop, step, and a jump,
>   And pass so quick you scarce can understand 'em.
> They please me as a misty landscape pleases,
> Provided that it neither rains nor freezes.

> "Besides, I like to let my pinnace drive,
>   Sure she can wear, although she may not tack;
> In the bold hope that if I'm left alive,
>   Some friendly wind or wave may waft me back.
> Where was I, though, before this burst irrelevant?
> — I recollect: I left off at the Elephant."

No wonder Frere thought Rose must surely have written *Beppo*.

While Rose adapted to English Casti's eighteenth century refinement of the Pulcian style, Frere in his *Prospectus . . . by the brothers Whistlecraft, The Monks and the Giants*,[23] directly imitated Pulci's *Morgante Maggiore* itself. Perhaps the greatest service Whistlecraft rendered Byron was to show him how to pass beyond the halfway mark of success achieved by Frere in importing the Pulcian manner into English. Frere transplants the story of the monks and the giants from the Continent to Britain; instead of Charlemagne and Orlando, he gives us King Arthur and his knights. But though there are modern allusions and digressions, the subject matter still remains in the past and the realm of legend. What Pulci might conventionally have treated as historical reality for his audience, had no appeal beyond fantasy, no seriousness, no real grip on the imagination of nineteenth century Englishmen. Warned by Frere's example, Byron adopted Pulci's modernity of spirit and left his outworn subject matter alone.

Nevertheless, without too great a stretch of possibility, one might point out hints great and small from Whistlecraft, that Byron enlarged on in *Don Juan:* the transparently disguised narrator of the poem, for example, and the defiance of Aristotle's rules:

> "Bold Britons take a Tankard, or a Bottle . . .
> And so proceed in spite of Aristotle —
> Those Rules of his are dry-dogmatic stuff. . . ."

Frere, like Byron, leans ironically upon an authority — in Frere's case "Morgan's Chronicle" — and makes a Chaucerian appeal to the strict necessity of adhering to fact in his narration:

> "Historians are extremely to be pitied. . . .
> The following scenes I wish'd to have omitted,
> But Truth is an imperious obligation." [24]

Byron rivals Frere's three stanzas of pig-Latin, describing the attack of the Giants upon the Monks, in his pharmaceutical recipe for Juan's medicine prescribed at St. Petersburg. Perhaps Frere's satire of high society manners at King Arthur's court, with its catalogue of dishes at the feast and comments on good old English fare — not "truffles and ragouts, and various crimes" — and with its character sketches, obviously with topical reference, suggested to Byron the possibilities developed in the dinner parties at Norman Abbey. The Siege of the Giants' Castle also parallels, however remotely, Byron's Siege of Ismail. On the whole, Byron seems to have taken hints from Frere only to improve upon them, and to have been encouraged to use his natural voice by the successful examples of Frere's and Rose's colloquial, conversational English.

Ronald Bottrall, in his "Byron and the Colloquial Tradition in English Poetry," declares that Byron took only the externals of the *ottava rima* from Frere, Casti, and Pulci. The real voice he uses is like Pope's, like the style of his own letters and journals, which was indeed the colloquial style of the English aristocracy "from the Restoration down to Chesterfield and Sheridan." With *Childe Harold* and *Manfred,* he got over the influence of Shelley toward rushing, confused, sublime metaphors, and returned to his own voice. Chaucer, Donne, Dryden, Pope,

and Byron, says Bottrall, are the colloquial tradition, using the vigor of
colloquial English, its word order and rhythms, as the basis of their
verse, and maintaining it as literary English during eras of non-drama-
tic poetry. From Dryden, Byron learned how to paint a satiric "character," and from Pope he learned the trick of poetic anticlimax, the use
of metaphors and images arranged in a satiric order. Where Pope concludes a couplet with a satiric descent to the absurd, Byron completes a
thundering octave with a crashing vulgarism:

> "Don Juan saw that Microcosm on stilts,
>   Yclept the Great World; for it is the least,
> Although the highest: but as swords have hilts
>   By which their power of mischief is increased,
> When Man in battle or in quarrel tilts,
>   Thus the low world, north, south, or west, or east,
> Must still obey the high — which is their handle,
> Their Moon, their Sun, their gas, their farthing candle."

Or this stanza, which seems almost an echo from *The Rape of the Lock:*

> "Then dress, then dinner, then awakes the world!
>   Then glare the lamps, then whirl the wheels, then roar
> Through street and square fast flushing chariots hurled
>   Like harnessed meteors; then along the floor
> Chalk mimics painting; then festoons are twirled;
>   Then roll the brazen thunders of the door,
> Which opens to the thousand happy few
> An earthly paradise of *Or Molu.*"

Bottrall points out the affinity of Byron's new method of story-telling
in *Beppo* and *Don Juan* to Chaucer's, his Chaucerian skill in using digressions to set the stage and the mood, to create suspense and build to
a climax, and the Chaucerian trick of using realistic dialogue at the very
narrative crisis of the story, as in *Don Juan*, I, 142–163. Whether Byron
looked directly to Chaucer for these devices, or more likely to Sterne on
the one hand, and to Congreve and Sheridan on the other, Bottrall's conclusion is suggestive and valid:

"Byron was working out a technique to do much the same work as Chaucer had
done before him — to sum up a society and an era. Byron is much narrower in
his range and in his sympathy than Chaucer, but he is far wider than Shelley
or even Wordsworth."

We might extend Bottrall's list of English colloquial stylists, from
the poets alone, to include Burton, Swift, Fielding, and Sterne, writers
more to Byron's taste than Chaucer, whom he did not understand, and
Donne, whom he appears never to have read. Fielding particularly fur-

nished Byron with models for *Don Juan*, not only in the character of his hero, in the suggestion of the managerial author, and in many a mock-heroic flourish and comic-epic legislation, but in the gentlemanly and scholarly style. How to treat realistic subject matter without unintentional vulgarity was the problem. Byron has testified to his admiration of Fielding on this point in one of his anti-Bowles letters. The Cockney poets, he wrote:

"remind me of Mr. Smith and the Miss Branghtons at the Hampstead Assembly in 'Evelina.' . . . Far be it from me to presume that there are now, or can be such a thing as an *aristocracy* of *poets;* but there is a nobility of thought and of style, open to all stations, and derived partly from talent, and partly from education, — which is to be found in Shakespeare, and Pope, and Burns, no less than in Dante and Alfieri. . . . *Vulgarity* is far worse than downright *blackguardism;* for the latter comprehends wit, humour, and strong sense at times; while the former is a sad abortive attempt at all things, 'signifying nothing.' It does not depend upon low themes, or even low language, for Fielding revels in both; — but is he ever *vulgar?* No. You see the man of education, the gentleman, and the scholar, sporting with his subject — its master, not its slave. Your vulgar writer is always most vulgar the higher his subject; as the man who showed the menagerie at Pidcock's was wont to say, 'This, gentlemen, is the *Eagle* of the Sun, from Archangel in Russia; the otterer it is, the igherer he flies.' "

Knowledge, wisdom, and mastery form the center of poise from which the author derives the nobility and the strength to tackle any subject.

As for Sterne, we observe that he was not only a master of the purposeful digression, but that he has even more than Pulci the power of flitting whimsically from grave to gay and back again. His Shandean mobility of temperament resembles Byron's though it exceeds Byron's in high-strung nervousness, sensitiveness, and sentimentality. Like Byron, Sterne could float a shred of story in an ocean of rambling reflection and metaphysical speculation. While Byron was re-reading Fielding in Italy, he did not neglect Sterne. He quotes occasionally from *A Sentimental Journey* in his letters, and the remnants of his library sold in 1827 contained a copy of *Tristram Shandy.* How well he learned to employ the Shandean manner may be judged from these stanzas of *Don Juan*, Canto II, which might have been written by the sentimental traveler himself. Byron begins his Platonic apology for Juan's fickleness in so soon forgetting Julia for Haidée:

"I hate inconstancy — I loathe, detest,
    Abhor, condemn, abjure the mortal made
Of such quicksilver clay that in his breast
    No permanent foundation can be laid;
Love, constant love, has been my constant guest,

And yet last night, being at a masquerade,
I saw the prettiest creature, fresh from Milan,
Which gave me some sensations like a villain.

"But soon Philosophy came to my aid,
    And whispered, 'Think of every sacred tie!'
'I will, my dear Philosophy!' I said,
    'But then her teeth, and then, oh, Heaven! her eye!
I'll just inquire if she be wife or maid,
    Or neither — out of curiosity.'
'Stop!' cried Philosophy, with air so Grecian,
(Though she was masqued then as a fair Venetian;)

" 'Stop!' so I stopped. — "

There is more than mere imitation of tone, vocabulary, and sentence
structure here. Byron has put on, at least for the moment, the very garment of Sterne's humor — gallantry, sentiment, naughtiness, philosophy, and high comedy blended together.

It is worth noting, also, that Burton's *Anatomy of Melancholy* was
a favorite book not only of Sterne but also of Byron. The classical play
with erudition, the mixture of metaphysics and high comedy in both
Sterne and Byron have a Democritus Jr. air about them. If Byron, in
the pursuit of his Muse, could follow Sterne's example by writing the
first sentence and trusting to Providence for the next, he could likewise
say with Democritus and Burton:

"And if I laugh at any mortal thing,
    'T is that I may not weep. . . ."

For the atrabilious humor of Burton, assuming the Democritan garb,
and laughing with a catch of pity at himself and the whole human race —
Vanitas vanitatum! Hypocrites, fools, and knaves, we are all mad together — underlies the skepticism and ridicule of *Don Juan.* Byron,
like Dr. Johnson, and many another eighteenth century wit and poet,
read his Burton faithfully.

The Shandean influence rendered *Don Juan* more planless than the
Italians themselves, encouraged the digressions to bulk larger and more
important, and the humor, cynicism, and satire to be broken in upon
almost unawares by beauty and sentiment.[25] But with Byron's debt to
Sterne, we acknowledge his place in the Lucianic tradition in English
and French literature, where he belongs from his earliest youth, long
antedating his sojourn in Italy. Byron is of the company of Burton,
Butler, Anthony Hamilton, Swift, Fielding, Sterne, and Voltaire.

The style of *Don Juan,* we have found, was the product both of Byron's natural proclivities and of his imitation of Italian and English
models. We are left with the question, what of it? What is it good for?

Is Don Juanism merely a clever mingling of Italian medley poetry and the best traditions in English satire, as *Don Juan* itself, we have said, represents a marriage between the epic and the picaresque novel? *Don Juan* is a virtuoso performance, to be sure, in which Byron has the fullest opportunity to exhibit his wonderful powers of imitation. But it is rendered sincere and original by the force of Byron's own assimilating power and his individuality. *Don Juan* is a literary cosmos, not a chaos, for the modulations of subject matter and style are so contrived that the whole is as solid and brilliant as a faceted diamond. The unifying force of Byron's consciousness is the fire at the center of it.

The value of Don Juanism, or of what has been called the medley style of poetry, depends upon the brilliance and power of the mind that creates it. Beyond the mere desire for light entertainment, the reason for constructing this kind of poem is to emphasize a view of life that Byron holds to be centrally true. Like Wordsworth, he thought of poetry as the dream of sleeping passions,

"A shadow which the onward Soul behind throws."

In his search for reality, Byron had long decided that his immortal soul was his immortal mind, that indissoluble fiery particle which sees and comprehends all things, recognizes the garment of the world as a passing show, and transcends all material aspects in its immaterial eternal consciousness. The Whole is greater than the sum of its parts; the only valid and central reality is the creative mind. Thus Byron claims the right to play objectively with temporality. The poem at bottom will be subjective, ideal, and eternal, for its unifying element is his own personality.

CHAPTER FIVE

"Love — Tempest — Travel — War"

Although the style of *Don Juan* is personal and subjective, the themes are universal and are handled objectively — playfully, on the surface, as Byron freely confesses, but with an underlying seriousness. The grand theme, implicit in the story and the satire, is Nature vs. Civilization, or as Byron might have defined it, if anyone had pinned him down with a question, Truth and Feigning, or Reality and Appearance. In Byron's mind, it runs through everything, from natural and political history to metaphysics. Byron's preoccupation with it is typically romantic.

To clothe the major argument, he uses a multitude of themes, departments of human experience and thought, some of which he takes the trouble to name from time to time in the course of the poem. The lists differ in details, but the best summary appears at the end of Canto VIII — "Love — Tempest — Travel — War." In Canto XIV, after many preliminary hints in Cantos X–XIII, he adds:

> "A bird's eye view, too, of that wild, Society;
> A slight glance thrown on men of every station."

He remarked to Medwin that *Don Juan* is about Love, War, and Religion, the classic subjects of the epic. We might append to the list, also, the topics for digression — what Byron calls his "lucubrations" — on metaphysics, freedom, education, literary criticism, his personal confessions, and a host of lesser subjects.

But omitting all these, tempting as they are, for the purpose of brief but comprehensive discussion I propose to analyze only what Byron has to say on Love, Tempest and Travel, War, and Society. In chapters VII and VIII, I shall sketch something of the literary background of these subjects in Byron's reading, which contributed to his exposition of them.

At the outset, we must note that the principal substance of Byron's thought is conveyed in his story. It is easy in reading *Don Juan* to be too much diverted by the digressions and to regard the story as comparatively trivial, a thread of interest barely strong enough to hold the poem together and keep the reader's curiosity alive from canto to canto. Byron writes as if he were himself very little concerned with it and was being forced only by convention to return to it and keep it spinning.

58

We might easily be deceived by this negligent attitude and assign it to feebleness and inertia in storytelling, forgetting that a large part of Byron's poetic apprenticeship consisted of concentrated galloping narratives. But there is an important difference in the *Don Juan* narrative from the short tales like the *Corsair* or *Mazeppa*. In the tales, the emphasis is upon action and passion, but in *Don Juan* Byron was attempting to *add* to a straight story of adventure the novelistic virtues of elaborate psychological realism and intellectual theme. Instead of the romantic world of oriental or Gothic coloring, *Don Juan* treats of the real world, and all its values are true to life. This made a different and a much greater tax on Byron's powers of invention, imagination, and expression. We must remember the unsuccessful attempts he had persistently made to write novels, and his recent experience in composing dramas.

Whether *Don Juan* is a successful novel or not, it must be judged as a novel, on its merits as a story, if we care to understand what Byron has to say through it. To be sure, the first person digressions re-enforce and explain the story, but even without the digressions the story would stand firm. Byron's ideas are implicit in the characters and the action.

This is a new departure in Byron's practice in writing narrative poetry. His definitions of poetry — that it is a mirror of life, the passions in action — were made in refutation of the practice of psychological novelists, especially Madame de Staël, who "reason upon the emotions." Now he is borrowing their technical weapons to refute their prevailing views. We are reminded of Goethe's judgment, that Byron "as soon as he thinks, is a child." But Goethe put this judgment in so forcible a metaphor merely to stress the greatest power of Byron — the power to give expression in words to the electric thrill of passionate emotion. Goethe meant that Byron was not a clear and original thinker; he did not mean to call him brainless and unreflecting. Granted that Byron is muddled, inconclusive, and derivative in his ideas, nevertheless it is important to recognize the intellectual content of *Don Juan*, if only to understand and feel more intensely its passion.

1

As Byron turned over "all the adventures that he had undergone, seen, heard of, or imagined, with his reflections on life and manners," the epic theme of love naturally occupied a very large position in his thoughts. For all his too well known amours, strange to say, Byron has been accused of exhibiting very little knowledge of the female heart because he made the women in his verse tales stereotyped romantic dolls. As a matter of fact, he was a very accurate reader of feminine character, aided, perhaps, as Moore suggests, by the feminine traits of his own mind. He had made a prolonged and deep study of women and the passion between the sexes, not only in his own experience but from books. He had much to say upon love — first love, pure natural love, impure selfish love, the hypocrisies of fashionable love, love in marriage, and marriage without love — and upon the effect of love in the lives of women and the careers of men.

In his reading on this subject, Byron had acquired a wide knowledge of quasi-philosophical and psychological thought about love and the nature of man. On the one hand, he had read practically everything in self-observation and analysis from Montaigne to Rousseau, and the criticisms and endorsements of these philosophers in the comments of people like Grimm and Diderot. On the other hand, he knew the mass of fiction portraying and analyzing the progress of love, especially books like Marmontel's *Contes Moraux*, which tend to reduce romantic imaginations and substitute worldly wisdom on matters of love and marriage. He knew and condemned Mme. de Staël's highly elaborate psychologizing on the tender passions. He was among the first to admire Constant's *Adolphe* as profoundly true and realistic in characterization, though he thought it highly improbable in plot. Wieland's *Agathon*, we know from Moore, was supplying him with its realistic information on the progress of passion as he embarked on Canto III of *Don Juan*.

Byron could not fail to agree with Grimm, who said, in justifying Montaigne and Bayle for what has been called "the licentiousness of their bold reasonings on human nature":

"They thought they might permit themselves to enter into rather minute details upon the subject of a passion which has so much influence on the whole economy of our existence; which formed, and which constantly modifies society, and is in fact, the most active and the most powerful principle by which it is moved." [1]

Byron was for pushing the inquiry further, to find out new truths about this mainspring of human life. Commenting at the end of Canto XIV on the growing relationship between Adeline and Juan, he writes:

> ". . . for Truth is always strange —
> Stranger than fiction; if it could be told,
> How much would novels gain by the exchange!
> How differently the World would men behold!
> How oft would Vice and Virtue places change!
> The new world would be nothing to the old,
> If some Columbus of the moral seas
> Would show mankind their Souls' antipodes."

Not less truth is needed, but more; and Byron believed that faithful adherence to clearly observed facts is the way to acquire it. With this conviction of the importance of love and of faithfulness to reality in describing it, Byron chose the famous legend of Don Juan and set about retelling it in the light of truth. Love is the most important theme in the poem, viewed from the standpoint of the general theme, Nature vs. Civilization.

To begin with Byron's conclusions, we may gather from some one hundred stanzas scattered through *Don Juan* the essence of his thought on love. It is complete and satisfactory, artistically coherent with the actions and characters of the poem, but it is not theoretically consistent, and it is filled with romantic paradox and wonder and awe at the unplumbed mystery, Man. To the first mention of love in Canto I, the digression on the sweetness of first love, Byron instantly appends the corollary of wonder at Man, the inscrutable creation.

In the story of Don Juan, Byron rejects the simple diabolism of the Spanish legend. Fundamentally, he says, the nature of man is good, and love is one of his most beautiful and sublime instincts. If Don Juan becomes a libertine monster, a man worthy of Hell, the fault lies in society, which has wrecked his primal nobility and twisted his good impulses to evil ends. This is Byron's Rousseauism.

But almost in the same breath, he repudiates this view as too narrow and incomplete. Love is now the God of Evil (II, 205–207); not Evil in itself, but the gateway of all evil. Part of the evil occasioned by love is to be laid to society, it is true; but the individual cannot be exempted, for the transient purity of love gives place only too soon to selfish passions, extravagances and errors which bring upon the individual his own proper punishment:

> "The Heart is like the sky, a part of Heaven,
>   But changes night and day, too, like the sky;
> Now o'er it clouds and thunder must be driven,
>   And Darkness and Destruction as on high:
> But when it hath been scorched, and pierced, and riven,
>   Its storms expire in water-drops; the eye
> Pours forth at last the Heart's blood turned to tears,
> Which makes the English climate of our years.
>
> "The liver is the lazaret of bile,
>   But very rarely executes its function,
> For the first passion stays there such a while,
>   That all the rest creep in and form a junction,
> Like knots of vipers on a dunghill's soil —
>   Rage, fear, hate, jealousy, revenge, compunction —

> So that all mischiefs spring up from this entrail,
> Like Earthquakes from the hidden fire called 'central.' "
>
> (II, 214–215)

With this rather unsatisfactory piece of poetical anatomy (Hobhouse objected to it as grotesque), Byron tries to express his understanding of the dual nature of man, wherein the physical and spiritual, the evil and the good are inextricably mixed. From the perversion of a pure instinct to an unbounded passion come all the woes we bring on our own heads:

> "The Nightingale that sings with the deep thorn,
> 　　Which fable places in her breast of wail,
> Is lighter far of heart and voice than those
> Whose headlong passions form their proper woes.
>
> "And that's the moral of this composition,
> 　　If people would but see its real drift. . . ."
>
> (VI, 87–88)

Evil is inherent in the nature of man; he does not have to learn it from society, though society frequently succeeds in first evoking it. The heart and the liver are both parts of man's nature, and evil and pure instincts spring side by side. Thus Byron attempts to reconcile Rousseauism with the older views of human nature in the philosophies of Aristotle and Calvin.

Closely allied with Byron's wonder at human nature in general, but on a lower and slightly patronizing plane, is his philosophizing on the nature of women. He recommends to "young beginners" in the science of psychology a "quiet cruising o'er the ocean, Woman." [2] Here he also makes a distinction between women in a state of nature, like Haidée, and women whose bondage to society damages more or less their natural goodness and calls out in them their worse natures.

It has been suggested that Byron shared Pope's rather cynical view in his *Moral Essay on the Characters of Women*, that women are mere pretty animals who possess but two ruling passions: the love of pleasure and the love of sway. But though Byron did not like to see a woman eat, he was not so contemptuous as that. In *Don Juan*, he assigns as woman's ruling passion the need to love and to be loved:

> "Man's love is of man's life a thing apart,
> 　　'T is a woman's whole existence; Man may range
> The Court, Camp, Church, the Vessel, and the Mart;
> 　　Sword, Gown, Gain, Glory offer, in exchange
> Pride, Fame, Ambition, to fill up his heart,
> 　　And few there are whom these cannot estrange;
> Men have all these resources, We but one —
> To love again, and be again undone."
>
> (I, 194)

So Julia, from the convent where she has been shut up, writes her fare-well letter to Juan as he is setting forth on his adventures. This truism, by the way, first met Byron's attention in Mme. de Staël's *Corinne*. It stands as a text for the fates of all the heroines of *Don Juan*, from gentle Julia and innocent Haidée, to the great whore Catherine II, who was at least "three parts woman."

Pity for the sad lot of women is a keynote in many passages. Women, Byron thinks, can really love but once, and that love is invariably be-trayed:

> ". . . for Man, to man so oft unjust,
>> Is always so to Women: one sole bond
> Awaits them — treachery is all their trust;
>> Taught to conceal, their bursting hearts despond
> Over their idol, till some wealthier lust
>> Buys them in marriage — and what rests beyond?
> A thankless husband — next, a faithless lover —
> Then dressing, nursing, praying — and all's over."
>> (II, 200)

> "Poor Thing of Usages! coerced, compelled,
>> Victim when wrong, and martyr oft when right,
> Condemned to child-bed, as men for their sins
> Have shaving, too, entailed upon their chins, — [3]

> "A daily plague, which in the aggregate
>> May average on the whole with parturition, —
> But as to women — who can penetrate
>> The real sufferings of their she condition?
> Man's very sympathy with their estate
>> Has much of selfishness, and more suspicion,
> Their love, their virtue, beauty, education,
> But form good housekeepers — to breed a nation."
>> (XIV, 23–24)

This, and much more, from Byron, who called himself the "martyr to and by women," is sympathy indeed. Thus he enlarged on the Elvira theme of the legend. His sympathy for women leads him to condone, while wondering at, their conscious arts and wiles, handed down traditionally from maid to maid, to fit them first for the marriage market and then for the managing of a husband. It excuses their casuistry in love, their reck-less impulsiveness, and their tigress-like fury when they are betrayed.

The simplicity of this Byronic view of women, however true to nature and to the condition of women in Byron's day, belies somewhat the sub-tlety and the effect of infinite variety in the portraits of individual women in *Don Juan*. Byron's observation and dramatic characterization in this particular are more comprehensive than his philosophizing. These women, fundamentally mere lovers and objects of love, like the earlier Byronic heroines, are now endowed with complete personalities, and exhibited at every age and at every stage of their careers. In the earlier tales, the predominant importance of the Byronic hero relegated the heroines to the background, where they show only in silhouette. In *Don Juan* they are set forth "in the round." Byron recognized their loyalty and capacity for friendship. He understood the spiritual craving in love experienced by the good and sensitive woman. Lady Adeline, for example, found something lacking in her noble husband, Lord Henry:

> "A something all-sufficient for the *heart*
>   Is that for which the sex are always seeking:
> But how to fill up that same vacant part?
>   There lies the rub — and this they are but weak in.
> Frail mariners afloat without a chart,
>   They run before the wind through high seas breaking;
> And when they have made the shore through every shock,
> 'T is odd — or odds — it may turn out a rock."
>
>   (XIV, 74)

On the whole, he admitted the potential humanity of women, but thought it criminally stifled by the prevailing conditions of society.

Byron's view of marriage is uncompromisingly unfavorable; some of the bitterest verses of *Don Juan* are reserved to condemn this, to him, uncomfortable and artificial state of being. Love is an institution of nature, but marriage of society, and the two are rarely compatible. This romantic view, hallowed by the ages, was no conventional pose with Byron. His own experience of unhappy marriage and of cicisbeism in Italy confirmed what he read from Pope's *Eloisa* to Rousseau's *Nouvelle Héloise*. Especially in England, he says, where marriages depend upon money, no matter what hypocritical society may declare to the contrary, matrimony is the opposite of love. He takes up Scott's phrase and proves that Love is not the ruler of Camp, Court, and Grove, but that Money is. (XII, 13–16.) In a bitter syllogism, he shows that heaven cannot be love, because heaven sanctions only matrimony, and everybody knows that, first, matrimony and love are incompatible, and second, all unmarried love is sin and therefore unheavenly.

Especially he condemns the hypocrisy of society and individuals toward love. He begins in Canto I attacking the hypocrisy of parents and husbands toward love and marriage, and in the last cantos he is still spurring to the charge. All hypocrisy in love is wicked and one of the prime evil effects occasioned by love, especially the hypocrisy of "Platonics" and other forms of self-deception. As a literary critic, he condemned the hypocrisy of romantic amatory writing. He thought the duty of the poet is to speak out plainly and with full responsibility, and he tried in the various and successive love episodes of *Don Juan* to exemplify his conception of the truth about love.

Byron's purpose in the first canto, the Julia episode, is to present a picture of first love, callow, dreamy, and naïvely sweet, against a background of gross hypocrisy. The effect is to be bittersweet, and is to be accomplished by a lightness of touch typifying adolescent calf love seen in retrospect. The style and attitude must be comic, brushing with laughter even the humiliation of Juan escaping naked through the dark streets, and the tragic fate of Julia buried alive in the convent. First love, as far as man is concerned, Byron seems to say, is light love, thoughtless and unreal, in both its animal and its sentimental aspects, and therefore good material for farce comedy. Illusions fade, and romantic notions are soon forgotten, leaving nothing behind, or at most only a slightly bitter taste. Vanity of vanities!

> "Alas!
> All things that have been born were born to die,
>   And flesh (which Death mows down to hay) is grass;
> You've passed your youth not so unpleasantly,
>   And if you had it o'er again —'t would pass —
> So thank your stars that matters are no worse,
> And read your Bible, sir, and mind your purse."
>   (I, 220)

This is first love in civilized Seville, and it is touched and debased, for all except Juan, by hypocrisy. Byron more than hints that the reason Donna Inez was not prompt to separate Juan and Julia, when the fact that they were falling in love became obvious, was that Inez, now a widow, had once been courted by Julia's husband, Don Alfonso, and that she was consequently jealous of Julia and wanted to destroy her reputation and even her marriage. Using Juan as an unwitting tool, she succeeded in separating Julia from Don Alfonso by divorce and getting her locked up in a convent. In Canto X we learn from Inez's letter to Juan at St. Petersburg, that Inez has married again and Juan already has a little brother. The inference is that she married Don Alfonso.[4] At any rate, the jealous hypocrisy of Inez and Alfonso is clearly sketched. Even Julia's hard fate does not violate poetic justice, since she too was a self-deceiver in love, though from weakness and her unfortunate position, rather than from malice. The strongly wicked flourish as the green bay tree; while the weakly sinful are cut off in their prime.

As for Juan, Byron's ridicule of his adolescent romance is tenderly severe. Like Wieland's Don Silvio de Rosalva, Juan has been brought up in ignorance of reality under the tutelage of a strict and unsympathetic female relative. The effect of this mortmain education and strict protection is to re-enforce the adolescent state of insulated solitude. Wandering like Don Silvio through the woods dreaming unutterable dreams, Juan indulges in reveries that remind us of the inquiries meditated by D'Israeli's romantic bluestockings in *Flim-Flams*:

> "He thought about himself, and the whole earth,
>   Of man the wonderful, and of the stars,
> And how the deuce they ever could have birth;
>   And then he thought of earthquakes, and of wars,
> How many miles the moon might have in girth,
>   Of air-balloons, and of the many bars
> To perfect knowledge of the boundless skies; —
> And then he thought of Donna Julia's eyes."
>   (I, 92)

Romance for Juan burgeoned in the wilderness "where Transport and Security entwine," [5] whether he was physically present in the woods or in Donna Julia's bedroom; in his romantic insulation, Juan never considered that he should "beg 'Security' will bolt the door," and he is rudely awakened to the prosaic ignominy of concealment, discovery, scuffling, and stripping, being lucky to escape with his life and reach his home "in an unseemly plight." The episode is forever closed for him on shipboard, when, reading Julia's farewell letter and vowing never to forget her, he is overtaken by seasickness. Romantic love can survive violent ills, fever and wounds, but a cold in the head or an attack of seasickness is invariably too much for it.

The curtain is dropped upon the farce comedy, and after an interval, we are introduced to the second love episode, a passionate, naturalistic pastoral. The contrast to the stuffy civilization of Seville is intense; in the sea-washed island under "all the stars that crowded the blue space," Juan and Haidée

> "form a group that's quite antique,
> Half naked, loving, natural, and Greek."

Shocked awake by his severance from all familiar surroundings and by the terrible experience of suffering and death at sea, Juan finds real romance for the first and the last time. He and Haidée love not *like* the children of nature, as in the feigning of the pretty romances Byron deplored. They *are* children of nature, and their love is the real, natural passion. But it is attended by youthful inexperience and recklessness which are bound to prove its undoing. Headlong passion in a natural state of innocence collides with the cruel passion of Lambro, who typifies the barbaric civilization of the Orient. The fatal ending of the Haidée episode, brought about by the extravagant passions of all three actors — Juan, Haidée, and Lambro — is Byron's comment on the fragility of natural love in an unnatural world. Byron says that they were lucky to have their happiness interrupted by violence, and not slowly diminished by age and care and indifference.

Juan is now truly bereaved, but his dim and superficial understanding of what has happened to him is complicated through new adventures by new shocks and disillusionments. The variation of physical and spiritual trials to which he is subjected is intricately life-like. Wounds and fatigue, physical hardship and danger, desperate uncertainty and change of scene keep his inward self under a kind of anaesthesia and postpone grief and maturity. His reactions to each new situation are physical reflexes. Gulbeyaz's fatuous love-making causes him to burst into tears with the memory of Haidée and with pride injured by his fall into slavery. Then at Gulbeyaz's humiliated weeping, he automatically unbends and begins to yield. Under the soldier Johnson's influence, he forgets love-making and sorrow for the glories of military action. But in the heat of the carnage of Ismail, he is swept by a wave of self-gratifying pity and devotion for the orphan Leila. From glitter to blood and back again to glitter, Juan is hurried along to the overripe civilization of the Empress Catherine's court. The pace of events and sensations is so swift — though unfortunately not Byron's pace in relating them — that Juan has no time to pause and take stock. The result is an illness that affects both his body and his spirits. He is hopelessly entangled in the contradictions that the world and his own behavior have presented to him.

The relationship between Juan and Leila, though left in an unfinished state, is clearly meant to illustrate yet another type of love. We can only speculate on what role Leila would have played in the English episode; perhaps she was to remind Juan of Haidée, and to disturb him with the recollection of oriental love when he is deeply embroiled with the English "gem" Aurora, and the ladies of Amundeville and of Fitz-Fulke. Byron is at some pains to explain the curious affection between Juan and his ward; [6] it was neither parental nor fraternal and still less a sensual love. He loved her because he had saved her from death and slavery and ignorance; she was his peculiar property. Yet the egotism of this love did not make it possessive; it remained altruistic and generous, and it is an ironic comment that the best that Juan could do for his ward was to take her to London and confide her to the duennaship of Lady Pinchbeck.

In contrast to Juan's unselfish affection for Leila, his love for Catherine was purely selfish and sensual. Byron is careful to explain how a youth hitherto described as naturally generous and pure-hearted could be suddenly perverted by temptation. The weakness was his vanity — that "imperious passion, Self-love." Catherine's favor flattered his van-

ity both in his male physical prowess and in his sudden elevation thereby
to be "a sort of King." In yielding to this impulse, Juan fell still further
into the inevitable consequences of dissipation. His fever and ennui were
not only the reaction from all his past experiences but a speedy repay-
ment for his errors.

This dazzling period in Juan's life, it is worth noting, Byron presents
in pantomime. Not a word is spoken by any actor on the scene, though
the written words are quoted of Suvaroff's infamous billet and of the
physicians' probably equally infamous receipt for Juan's medicine. Byron dwells on the brilliance and luxury of the St. Petersburg court, but
he glides over the surface of the love episode with "Russia's royal har-
lot," giving only "the bloom of favouritism," and not its "blush":

> ". . . far be it from my Muses to presume
>   (For I have more than one Muse at a push)
> To follow Juan beyond the drawing-room. . . ."

This is a confession that the whole story of Juan in his "high official situation" is not only so offensive to an English reading public that it can
be glanced at only lightly and from a distance, but that it is equally distasteful to Byron's serious Muse. To treat with the same frankness and
freedom this period of dissipation in Juan's life as he had treated the
former more natural love affairs would be to violate the moral and artistic tone of his poem:

> "He lived (not Death, but Juan) in a hurry
>   Of waste, and haste, and glare, and gloss, and glitter,
> In this gay clime of bear-skins black and furry —
>   Which (though I hate to say a thing that's bitter)
> Peep out sometimes, when things are in a flurry,
>   Through all the 'purple and fine linen,' fitter
> For Babylon's than Russia's royal harlot —
> And neutralise her outward show of scarlet.

> "And this same state we won't describe; we would
>   Perhaps from hearsay, or from recollection;
> But getting nigh grim Dante's 'obscure wood,' . . .

> "I won't describe, — that is, if I can help
>   Description; and I won't reflect, — that is,
> If I can stave off thought. . . .
> I *won't* philosophise, and *will* be read."

By means of innuendo and downright epithet, by digressions now suggestive of what is left unsaid, and now frankly irrelevant, like the one to
Jeffrey and "Auld lang syne," as if to relieve the odiousness of the sub-

ject, Byron worries his way through the Catherine episode. The reader feels that he is relieved to get Juan well out of St. Petersburg, having given him, by a view of the seamiest side of love, that worldly wisdom which will prepare him for English scenes of high life in which he is to move as a young diplomat.

Still convalescent Juan arrives in England and enjoys a period of indifference to womankind resulting from his physical and psychic reactions. However, a short time is sufficient for youth to recover at least outwardly most of its elasticity. Inwardly his experiences have left corroding deposits which produce in him a comparative soberness, a more worldly circumspection, and a tendency to brood in melancholy fashion when he is alone. He feels "restless, and perplexed, and compromised" by Lady Adeline's machinations and advice; he "feels somewhat pensive, and disposed for contemplation rather than his pillow"; he "muses on Mutability, or on his Mistress — terms synonymous." In this mood, he sees a ghost. The poem leaves him surrounded by more or less consciously predatory women, his mind perplexed by a mingling of sorrow-tinged nostalgia, disenchantment, longings, and metaphysical speculation. He has reached the last stage of adolescence and begins to contemplate life with the tear-dazzled doubt and wonder proper to romantic youth:

> "Between two worlds Life hovers like a star,
> 'Twixt Night and Morn, upon the horizon's verge."

Juan, within the limits of his fictional character and situation, has reached the state of mind Byron was in when he returned to England in 1811.

The love affair foreshadowed between Lady Adeline and Juan, flanked on the one side by the fleshly Duchess of Fitz-Fulke, and on the other by the spiritual Aurora Raby, obviously intended for matrimony, was probably meant to epitomize Byron's experiences with the fashionable ladies of England between 1812 and 1816. This section of *Don Juan* is as autobiographical as a story so completely fictionalized can be. It extracts the essence of Byron's reflections and adventures in English high society. None of the ladies so carefully described is a portrait, but each is a distillation. Lady Pinchbeck has something of Lady Melbourne's characteristics, but she is a composite of duennas and dowagers, an eternal type. Lady Adeline reminds us sometimes of Lady Caro Lamb,[7] and sometimes of Lady Frances Webster; but there are qualities in her of Lady Oxford, Lady Jersey, and who knows what other ladies besides. She is an ideal type — good, restless, brilliant, worldly, misunderstood, "champagne in ice." She is reincarnated later in dozens of fashionable novels, in Trollope's Lady Glencora Palliser, for instance, and in Meredith's Diana. All we know is that for Juan she is to be "the fatal fair."

Without condemning any individual in this story as utterly black,
Byron is going to show the rottenness of the social system to which they
belong. They will wreck Juan with their scheming, contriving, and cross
interests, and then, herding together hypocritically, they will expel him
with all the blame concentrated upon him. It is too bad that Byron could
not have completed this section of his poem; it would have been a more
satisfactory revenge and apologia than any burned memoirs with their
irrelevant and inconvenient personal details.

None of Juan's love episodes is for Byron strictly autobiographical,
but the whole story contains his explanation of the havoc wrought in
his life by love affairs and the ruin of his reputation. This, Byron says,
is how the human being is evolved whom the world ignorantly dubs a Don
Juan. Hypocrisy, violence, and vicious self-indulgence in individuals
combine with an unnatural civilization to ruin the pristine beauty and
purity of the human heart.

2

The general theme of *Don Juan*, Nature vs. Civilization, is illustrated
not only in the love episodes and their effect upon the hero, but in Juan's
travels. As we have already noted, Byron deliberately enlarged the scope
of the legend and broadened his hero's career by taking him on a tour of
Europe and giving him the conventional picaresque novel adventures.
Don Juan is a story of travel as well as a story of love, and travel ranks
in importance only second to love as the source of change in Juan's character. Just as Byron enlarged upon the Elvira theme of persecuted innocent womankind, so, in the inclusion of shipwreck and travel, he expanded
according to his own gifts and interests the hints in the original Don
Juan legend. What exactly had Byron to say in his use of the themes of
tempest and travel?

The story of Don Juan in Tirso de Molina's *El Burlador de Sevilla*
begins with a seduction in Italy from which Don Juan escapes to Spain.
His ship is wrecked on a rock off Tarragona, and only he and his valet
escape by swimming. A poor fishergirl succours Don Juan, and he repays
her hospitality by seducing her. The convention of shipwreck and near-
drowning persisted in all the subsequent versions of the story, except
Da Ponte's and Goldoni's, as if to illustrate the proverb that the villain
cannot drown but is reserved for a more appropriate death.

But the tempest and the sea journey mean more for Byron than a mere
following of the Don Juan legend, or indeed of epic and picaresque novel
conventions. It is appropriate to the general theme that a violent convulsion of physical nature should follow, in this series of romantic-real-
istic contrasts, the tempest in the teapot of civilized Seville.

Byron had almost as strong a prepossession for the sea as Shelley had.

Galt recorded in that memorable passage describing him as a "mystery wrapped in a winding-sheet and crowned with a halo," that the young Byron spent hours on their voyage from Gibraltar sitting alone in the rigging contemplating the ocean. Hobhouse remembers a passage in Byron's memoirs that described the long hours of swimming and daydreaming on the rocky coast of Greece. To swim, off the Lido, in the bay of Leghorn, even to the excess of making himself ill with sunburn and exhaustion, was as much a necessity of Byron's spiritual being as of his physical.

The ocean stood for escape and liberation to Byron. Those who remember the wonderful effect of climax and release produced by the famous lines to the ocean at the end of *Childe Harold* will recall that it is achieved by a sudden shift of viewpoint. The Pilgrim of Eternity does not stand on the seashore of ruined empires and look at the unchanging ocean; instead, he contemplates the shores of Africa and Europe from the middle of the Mediterranean. It is a view landward from the sea, and at once the ocean becomes the impassive, unchanging floor of the world, while the solid lands around turn into "the graves of Empires" that "heave but like some passing waves," as Byron restated it at the end of Canto XV in *Don Juan*.

The untamed sea, symbol for Byron of escape, oblivion, and eternal nature, provided in his own experience the sheer space and loneliness that were enough to sponge out old life and refresh him for the new. But for Don Juan, who experiences the sea at its most impersonally cruel and tedious, the wreck and the sufferings in the longboat and the final exhausting efforts of swimming were meant to intensify the naturally purifying effect of a sea voyage. As we have already suggested, they make credible his Garden-of-Eden innocence and his integrity in the Haidée episode. Natural love and passionate violence are appropriately introduced by a rude commotion in physical nature and a stark tale of human struggle for survival against natural forces.

Sticking to reality, however, Byron could not give his hero a sea voyage, much less a wreck, every time he wanted to ring down the curtain on one of his shattering experiences and prepare him and the reader for the next. True, Don Juan has another short voyage from Lambro's island in the Cyclades to Constantinople. But the mere sight of Ilion in the distance, though it affords Byron and the reader a breathing space to muse on mutability, could not refresh the wounded forlorn Juan.

Byron here introduces other conventions of picaresque fiction; first, the troupe of wandering actors. Byron claims that the story of the Italian opera company sold into slavery by their impresario is a fact, the truth of which he learned in Venice in 1817. The topics, however, of "Raucocanti's eloquent recital" he may have derived from Goldoni's

amusing comedy *L'Impresario della Smyrna*, — the whims of the prima
donna, the bellowing basso, the dancers, the cracked voices, the catarrhs,
and the jealousies. But this dim diversion and object lesson in optimism,
and even the passing of time and healing of his wounds were hardly sufficient to restore Juan to a semblance of hope and health. What syncope,
time, travel, and new scenes were not wholly able to accomplish, philosophy completed, in the shape of the sturdy Englishman, Johnson. Candide also found solace in a philosophical fellow traveler, when his spirits
were at their lowest ebb. Johnson, taking up where Raucocanti's cheerful
optimism left off, flatters and shames Juan by precept and example into
a courageous frame of mind:

> "By setting things in their right point of view,
>   Knowledge, at least, is gained; for instance, now,
> We know what slavery is, and our disasters
>   May teach us better to behave when masters."

Travel serves not only to pass the time and change the scene, so that
the hero may grow up and the whole view of European society be un-
rolled before his eyes; but travel and the firsthand experience it brings
are meant to be as powerful educators of Juan as any of his affairs of the
heart.

Steeped in the English aristocratic tradition of the grand tour, Byron wrote to his mother in 1808:

". . . when I return [from the tour of the East] I may possibly become a
politician. A few years' knowledge of other countries than our own will not
incapacitate me for that part. If we see no nation but our own, we do not give
mankind a fair chance; — it is from *experience,* not books, we ought to judge
of them. There is nothing like inspection, and trusting to our own senses." [8]

This humanistic conviction remained with him all his life. He learned to
hold a cosmic view not only from Cuvier but from a glimpse of the stars
through Herschell's telescope, and he acquired a continental outlook not
only from books but from experience. Though he read travel books
eagerly, he knew how and why to distrust them.[9] He plumed himself, if
not on the extent, at least on the duration and the thoroughness of his
travels. It might be shown that travel was the source, or at least the re-
enforcement, of his political views and activities. In literature, he scorned
the stay-at-homes like Hunt and Keats and Wordsworth and Southey —
what could they know of the world? Making the most poetic capital of
his travels, he dealt with the best-known publisher of travel literature.

If one contrasts the travelogue qualities of *Childe Harold* and *Don
Juan,* the different uses made of travel in each poem strikingly illustrate
the growth of this conviction in Byron's mind and his intention con-

cerning travel in *Don Juan*. *Childe Harold* is a sight-seeing tour, a nega-
tive forth-faring to seek escape. The monuments of the past, whether
the handiwork of man or of nature, are its objects, as the ruin of empires is its embracing theme. Modern civilization and contemporary life
enter the picture only as foils, or to point the moral lessons of antiquity.
In *Don Juan*, however, we travel in the world of 1789–91. Sight-seeing
occupies a minimum of either Juan's or the reader's attention. If Juan
does not feel like looking at Cape Sigeum, usually the reader is not allowed to look at it either. If Juan stops at Canterbury to inspect the
Cathedral and its relics, it is to point up a contrast between his dreams
of old English heroism and the actuality of the highway robbery about
to occur to him; or to give a chance for sarcasm on un-Christian Christians, through the irony of Leila's remarks on the Cathedral. These are
the only bits of sight-seeing *per se* recorded at any length in *Don Juan;*
for the rest, Juan is hurried in a "kibitka," or the Empress's imperial
coach, or the English stage-coach, through scenes suggested with only
enough detail to provide that sense of elapsing time and space necessary for the story.

The important objects of travel in *Don Juan* are modern societies and
modern people and their effect on the unfolding consciousness of the
hero. *Don Juan* is not a travelogue, but a *Wanderjahr*. The reader sees
the world, now through the eyes of Byron, and now through those of
Juan, but the different angles of vision are trained on the present, on the
modern, actual world. *Childe Harold* is a passive contemplative travelogue; *Don Juan* is the travels of a man of action.

To the educative influences of contact with rude nature and personal
experience of distance and physical hardship, Byron adds firsthand
acquaintance with a wide variety of peoples, places, and manners. But
he makes another use of travel, as the technical device for conveying
satire. He uses the technique of travel and the eyes of a voyager from
another civilization to give the utmost point to the satire on his own.
Juan, assisted by Byron's asides, is the favorite eighteenth century traveling philosopher from China all over again, only in the dress of a modern Spaniard-cosmopolite. The natural man, whether he is a Spaniard,
or a Chinese, or a Scythian (as in the *Voyage of Anacharsis*), views society through unaccustomed eyes and thus sees it truly. Travel in *Don
Juan* serves a double purpose. It fosters and chastizes the hero, educating him as no mother or book learning in Seville could do; and it educates
the reader, by juxtaposing view after view of the modern real world.

Juan's itinerary is dictated partly by the legend and by Byron's own
experience, but also by the purposes of satire and the use of the travel
theme to illustrate Nature vs. Civilization. The story necessarily starts
in Spain, in keeping with the legend, and the Spanish civilization is even

more pointedly ripe for satire than the English. It goes to England inevitably, since English society and English responsibility in continental politics are principal butts of the satire. But what is the significance of Greece and of Russia? Greece, enslaved under Turkey, and Russia, tyrannical and treacherous, the remote corners of Europe, provide contrasts to the homelands of both Juan and Byron, and give unparalleled opportunities for reflection on the themes of nature and civilization, war, tyranny, and freedom.

It would be hard to overestimate the importance of Greece in Byron's life, as in Juan's. Byron really came of age there. The country suited him emotionally, artistically, physically, and its political problems from the start engaged his best thought and his most serious sympathy. When he set out for Greece, he knew the assorted conventional attitudes of Englishmen toward it: the schoolroom attitude, for example, expanded sometimes into a lifetime of arduous study of the language and literature of ancient Greece. He was himself motivated by romantic enthusiasm, seeking beauty with strangeness in the gorgeous Levant, and indeed he found in the east all the elements of romance presented to him in actuality. It was poetically fortunate that the very name of Greece meant more than ever to Europeans at this time, and that the searchers after primitive societies had made the Levant the object of fashionable curiosity.

But Byron's experiences in Greece made him a phil-Hellene without any of the romantic trimmings. Without losing any of his schoolboy attitude toward the virtues of ancient Greek civilization, or replacing it with neo-Hellenic notions, and without romanticizing about the primitive virtues of the modern Greeks, he came to know Greece as it was, to see it politically as a nation, with a past, but especially with a future. If he marveled at Greek primitivism, at the Albanians and the Suliotes, for example, it was that they had retained so many rugged virtues, especially the passionate love of freedom, through so many centuries of degradation and oppression. As usual, he was on the side of the underdog, of the oppressed minority. For Byron, the modern Greek illustrated indestructible human nature, since all that was good in him was there in spite of overwhelming odds. The pirate-infested islands and the west coast of Albania and Epirus showed Byron a kind of barbaric civilization, rudely "natural" enough for contrast with more polished societies.

In a travel story, whose hero is to die as a champion of freedom, it is highly appropriate that Juan should find his highest emotional satisfaction and his first brutal acquaintance with tyranny and slavery in Greece, the cradle of beauty and freedom, and the most downtrodden of modern slave nations.

As a partisan of Greek freedom, Byron had a motive for being anti-

Russian even stronger than his detestation of the Holy Alliance.[10] His
fascinated disgust at Catherine, when he had read her praises in the
works of Voltaire and Grimm and the other French *philosophes* whose
opinions on all things he usually admired, is surprising, until we remember that his view of the empress's morals was colored by his politics.
Catherine was an unchaste woman, but in a double sense she was the
"teterrima causa" of all *"belli"* — as woman and as treacherous tyrant.
Writing of the Graeco-Turkish world of 1790–91, he made a natural
transition to Russia, for Catherine had twice fed Greek hopes of freedom, offering an alliance against Turkey, and had twice betrayed
them: [11]

> "I know [her] mighty Empire now allures
>   Much flattery — even Voltaire's, and that's a pity.
> For me, I deem an absolute autocrat
> *Not* a barbarian, but much worse than that.
>
> "And I will war, at least in words (and — should
>   My chance so happen — deeds), with all who war
> With Thought; — and of Thought's foes by far most rude,
>   Tyrants and sycophants have been and are."

Catherine and Russia are to represent a superficial civilization whose
actualities are worse than barbaric Greece or Turkey, and lest the reader
of 1822 should miss the satiric point, Byron has already reminded him
by way of an apostrophe to Catherine's grandson, the "grand legitimate
Alexander," in Canto V, that the present Russian member of the Holy
Alliance belongs to this tradition of tyranny.

There may well be in the Russian episode of *Don Juan* a veiled attack
on George IV, royal licentiousness, Wellington, and Castlereagh, as well
as a direct attack on war and tyranny. Moore had turned out recently
some very good hits at the grand tyrant on the Neva as well as at George
IV, and Byron may have been following him in coupling the two. That
the parallel in subject matter existed in Byron's mind is suggested by
his insertion of the dedicatory stanzas to Wellington at the head of
Canto IX, instead of Canto III for which they were first intended. In
1819, when he wrote these stanzas directed against war and conquerors,
Byron expected to canter right through *Don Juan*. But delays inter-
vened, and political changes took place. As a Whig, he took Queen Caroline's part during her trial, though he and Moore may have let their
"wits run away with their sentiments" on this occasion so happy for
puns and epigrams. When the Carbonari revolutions came to nothing
early in 1821, Byron, frustrated as a leader in Italian politics, began
to take a more active interest in English. He published the *Irish Avatar*

in Paris, and began the project for a magazine to stand for Pope and the Liberals. By the time he reached the composition of Canto IX in August–September 1822, the *Liberal* was organized, and he had had much opportunity for reflection on the current state of British politics. It would not do for him to write directly on British royalty — Murray had had enough trouble, and there was no reason to bring still more upon John Hunt. Besides, the historical framework of *Don Juan* must be maintained, and the cantos on England should be reserved for satire on high society. The cantos on Russia, then, were allowed to have an undertone of rich meaning for contemporary Liberals in England.

But these matters were between Byron and his immediate reading public. They do not, at least ostensibly, touch Don Juan as far as his story has been carried.

3

The Greek War of Independence really began as far back as 1770 in preliminary skirmishes between the Greek highlanders and the Turks. It flared up again, simultaneously with the French Revolution, during the Russian-Turkish war of 1787–91. Major Lambro Katsones, the original of Byron's Lambro,[12] joined with Captain Andrutsos, a famous klepht, in campaigns by land and by sea with the Turks during 1790–92.[13] The conflicts between the Greeks and the Turks on the one hand and the Russians and Turks on the other were therefore an historical ingredient of the world that Juan entered when he was washed up on Lambro's island.

We begin to hear rumblings from the great world of political warfare from the moment Lambro appears on the scene — a pirate from choice, but also as a patriotic rebel against the Turks. At Constantinople, the soldier of fortune Johnson is being sold into slavery as a prisoner of war; he had been captured in the battle of Widdin between the Russians and the Turks. The Sultan is preoccupied by "his daily council" on the war against Catherine, and the Russian victories, which had recently increased. When Juan and Johnson escape, they therefore naturally head for the Russian encampment on the banks of the Danube. Juan is following out the text that Man may supplement, or substitute for, Love by seeking Glory in the Camp and the Court. In the introduction of the theme of war, Byron's epic satire departs widely from the simple unity of the Don Juan legend, but it is still concerned with the central moral problems of the legend, honor and the ends for which men live.

Nowhere else in *Don Juan* did Byron deal a stronger blow for progressive and liberal thought than in Cantos VII–VIII, condemning wars of conquest. With all the Napoleonic world, he had been meditating furiously on war and conquest through the whole span of his adult life. This

was the period when the ideas of isolated philosophers, poets, and groups, who for centuries past had inveighed against war, began, under the stress of current events, to spread to the multitudes and to take shape in political and social organizations for world peace, and the outlawing of war.

In 1812–13, a series of letters by Edward Sterling (signed "Vetus") had appeared in the London *Times*, dilating on the horrors of the French wars, especially the battle of Leipzig. To make the sickening effect of these letters more complete for Byron, the Whig, the partisan of Napoleon, and therefore the opponent of any continental war, their purport was to inflame English popular feeling against the French, and to advocate "war to the knife" with Napoleon.[14] The letters were reviewed in *The Morning Chronicle* during the first two weeks of December 1813, and on December 9, Byron put a period to his poem *The Devil's Drive*, inspired by the *Morning Chronicle* articles.[15] In Byron's ballad, Satan, flying to London to see how his work is getting on there,

> ". . . hovered a moment upon his way,
>   To look upon Leipsic plain;
> And so sweet to his eye was its sulphury glare,
> And so soft to his ear was the cry of despair,
>   That he perched on a mountain of slain;
> And he gazed with delight from its growing height,
> Nor often on earth had he seen such a sight,
>   Nor his work done half as well:
> For the field ran so red with the blood of the dead,
>   That it blushed like the waves of Hell!
> Then loudly, and wildly, and long laughed he:
> 'Methinks they have little need here of *me!*' . . .

> "But the softest note that soothed his ear
>   Was the sound of a widow sighing;
> And the sweetest sight was the icy tear,
> Which Horror froze in the blue eye clear
>   Of a maid by her lover lying — . . .
> And stretched by the wall of a ruined hut,
> With its hollow cheek, and eyes half shut,
>   A child of Famine dying:
> And the carnage *begun,* when *resistance* is done,
> And the fall of the vainly flying!

> "Then he gazed on a town by besiegers taken,
>   Nor cared he who were winning;
> But he saw an old maid, for years forsaken,
>   Get up and leave her spinning;
> And she looked in her glass, and to one that did pass
>   She said — 'pray are the rapes beginning?' "

The combination of horror, wickedness, pathos, folly, and ridiculousness in the carnage of war had lain together in Byron's mind a good nine years before he undertook to write the Siege of Ismail.

In May 1816, he visited Waterloo, one year after its soil likewise had run red with blood. The famous passage in *Childe Harold*, Canto III, was the result, with its introductory stanzas on the futility of a war which has eclipsed the glory of Napoleon in vain, for it has brought no freedom from oppression. The conclusion of this passage, while celebrating those gallant men who fought and fell there in what they thought to be the cause of liberty, denies that their brief glory and the lasting fame of Waterloo equally compensate for the destruction caused by their loss:

> "Their children's lips shall echo them, and say —
> 'Here, where the sword united nations drew,
> Our countrymen were warring on that day!'
> And this is much — and all — which will not pass away." [16]

To the futility of wars of conquest that accomplish no good but only destruction, Byron added the folly of setting any store by military glory. Applying his Aristotelian ethics to Napoleon's career, he moralizes on the Napoleonic wars, begun with such fair promise for the freedom of Europe, and evolving, through Napoleon's unbridled lust for war, into the worst type of conquest:

> ". . . There is a fire
> And motion of the Soul which will not dwell
> In its own narrow being, but aspire
> Beyond the fitting medium of desire. . . .

> "This makes the madmen who have made men mad
> By their contagion. . . ."

Not only at Waterloo, and in the eager following of the post-mortems and the myths of Napoleon's career (fed to Byron by such people as Stendhal and Hobhouse), but also in the preparations for Italian rebellion, Byron continued to meditate upon war. "Revolutions," he recognized, "are not made with rose-water." Though he had not yet experienced battle himself, he had been near enough to it in imagination. By the time he wrote *Don Juan*, Cantos VII–VIII, his ideas had settled into a creed.

All wars, he thought, are terrible, hells upon earth, but wars in support of freedom are justifiable, even praiseworthy. He had indeed perceived that "Revolution alone can save the earth from Hell's pollution." War, however, embodies every human crime conceivable, but the worst is that it breeds a colossal hypocrisy, a blindness of ignorance and party prejudice. War hypocrisy induces hero worship for a general, a "butcher in large business," who has enriched himself by war, while it forgets the miseries and murders of untold anonymous millions. It allows a poet, who should know better, to call "Carnage God's daughter." "War cuts up not only branch, but root." It destroys in one hour, at the command of one mad leader, what nature can scarcely rebuild in thirty years. The pursuit of the hollow glory of individual fame, alive only in the throat of quickly forgetful mobs, is the worst folly and hypocrisy of all. This is the will-o'-the-wisp that keeps up the spirit of militarism and glorifies martial prowess.

History, Byron thought, ought to be written to divest war of its charm. The public should be let in on the facts behind the headlines in their morning papers, behind the long casualty lists, where names as often as not are misspelled:

> "History can only take things in the gross;
> But could we know them in detail, perchance
> In balancing the profit and the loss,
> War's merit it by no means might enhance,
> To waste so much gold for a little dross,
> As hath been done, mere conquest to advance.
> The drying-up a single tear has more
> Of honest fame, than shedding seas of gore.
>
> "And why? — because it brings self-approbation. . . ."
> (VIII, 3–4)

From the public standpoint, war is wasteful; and from the private, war does not give the individual the meed of honor and glory he is seeking. The momentary fame of military glory is "nothing but a child of Murder's rattles."

Byron uses his theme of war in civilized Europe to illustrate again his general theme of nature and civilization. One extraordinary digression occurs in Canto VIII at the height of the battle, when Ismail had been entered but not taken, — the stanzas on Daniel Boone, 61–67:

> " 'God made the country, and man made the town,'
> So Cowper says — and I begin to be
> Of his opinion, when I see cast down
> Rome — Babylon — Tyre — Carthage — Nineveh —
> All walls men know, and many never known;
> And pondering on the present and the past,
> To deem the woods shall be our home at last: — . . ."

Byron, who was an admirer of Americans and American freedom, had received a caller in Ravenna, "a young American, named Coolidge," early in 1821.[17] Coolidge and Byron talked about civilization and savagery and the pursuit of happiness. "The greatest (said **Byron**) of all living puzzles is, to know for what purpose so strange a being as man was created." He pumped Coolidge for tales of the American wilderness, and among other narratives, the young man related "that of Daniel Boon, the backwoodsman of Kentucky, which made a strong impression upon him." [18] Boone, then, was chosen as the good modern hero, the natural man, to counterbalance bloody Suvaroff (*videlicet* Wellington, and other military heroes of civilization):

> Boone "left behind a name
>   For which men vainly decimate the throng,
> Not only famous, but of that *good* fame,
>   Without which Glory's but a tavern song —
> Simple, serene, the *antipodes* of Shame,
>   Which Hate nor Envy e'er could tinge with wrong;
> An active hermit, even in age the child
> Of Nature — or the Man of Ross run wild. . . .

> "So much for Nature: — by way of variety,
>   Now back to thy great joys, Civilization!
> And the sweet consequence of large society,
>   War — pestilence — the despot's desolation,
> The kingly scourge, the lust of notoriety,
>   The millions slain by soldiers for their ration,
> The scenes like Catherine's boudoir at threescore,
> With Ismail's storm to soften it the more."

But this pessimism, even cynicism, is not Byron's final comment. He did not utterly despair of civilization, for he was at pains to lash its follies and crimes in this protracted satire, and the reforming satirist must always hope in his heart that his words will take effect. Moreover, Byron foresaw, though ironically only in a distant millennium removed by geological ages from the present, that happy period when wars, cutthroat conquerors, and tyrants will be as strange relics of an earlier civilization as the bones of mammoths seem to us.

"Conquest and its consequences," as Byron points out, are "what make Epic poesy so rare and rich." As in the love theme he refuted the popular notion of a Satanic Don Juan, and as in the travel theme he rejected the descriptions and rhapsodies of the travel books, so in the theme of war his epic satire dealt with war only to condemn it.

4

In the broad sense, all of Byron's *Don Juan* deals with society, the modern European world both east and west. But the last six cantos are especially concerned with the state of society in England, and the field of thought embraces both society at large and the *haut monde* of London's West End. The latter ranked foremost in Byron's thought, for he considered the "grand, *grand monde*" as a kind of tail that wags the dog. But he never lost sight of the nation as a whole, and its position in European society, while concentrating on the manners and characters of the "four thousand." The keynote is sounded in Canto X, with Juan's first sight of the white cliffs of Dover, a lament for Britain, no better than a slave gaoler of other slave nations, when it "*might have been*" the noblest in history.[19] At the conclusion of the canto, pausing with Juan to contemplate the view of London,

> "a wilderness of steeples peeping
> On tiptoe through their sea-coal canopy,"

Byron deplores the mistaken activity of Mrs. Fry. Why should Mrs. Fry waste her time preaching in Newgate? She ought to go to work on hardened and imperial sin in the houses of the great:

> "Tell them, though it may be, perhaps, too late —
> On Life's worn confine, jaded, bloated, sated —
> To set up vain pretence of being *great*,
> 'T is not so to be *good*. . . . ."

In general, Byron condemns English society for its materialism, its selfish irresponsibility, its frigidity, and its unnaturalness. He deals in Canto XII with the power of money, as it is specifically exercised in "the marriage mart." He ridicules abstract theorists, like Malthus, who set up new philosophical codes for an already artificial society, living by unnatural conventions. In Canto XIII, he deals with the ennui of the members of Society, where the acme of polish is represented by Horace's *nil admirari*, and a country house party is made up of "two mighty tribes, the *Bores* and *Bored*." Hunting, matchmaking, intrigues, and French cookery (the last word in artificiality), form the outer trimmings of Lord Henry's real reason for being in the country, political fence mending in the interests of maintaining the grand principles, Place and Patronage. Even the native ghost is treated by all except Juan as a subject of no importance, or an occasion for pastime and jest.

Seeming, not being, cant, hypocrisy, and heartlessness are the qualities Byron most deplores in English society. He reveals them, with exquisite lightness of touch, in action in the shifting tides of fashion, fads, and conventional pleasures. For success in this society, Juan must cling to the precepts, "*carpe diem*" and "be not what you seem but what you see."

The questions how far Byron's view of English society is true and trustworthy, and how valid his criticism of it may be, are illuminated interestingly by the Countess of Blessington. Her *Conversations with Lord Byron*, which should certainly be read in conjunction with *Don Juan*, Cantos XI–XVI, took place, however, after he had completed Canto XV. Her point of view can have had no substantial effect on the poem. But it is interesting that Byron's talks with her and his reading of the Count D'Orsay's Journal (destroyed without ever being published) seem to have stimulated him into hurrying the poem through the press. On the day that he warned D'Orsay through the Earl of Blessington that there were remarkable coincidences between the Journal and *Don Juan*, Byron wrote off to Hunt for proofs of the remaining cantos urgently needed for correction. The corrections, however, as they are noted by E. H. Coleridge, took the form only of the usual improvements in diction and phrasing and the addition of two or three stanzas. Perhaps the quality of the Blessingtons' conversation saved Byron from a few errors of taste and rapport which he might have made, had he not had that timely contact with people who were more recently acquainted with the high society he was describing. The Countess, and even Trelawney and other visitors, noticed how old-fashioned Byron's manners and speech had become during his exile from England. He impressed Trelawney as not having realized that the Regency Buck had become passé. Lady Blessington declares that Byron's knowledge and understanding of English society were very imperfect. "Byron sees not, that much of what he calls the usages of cant and hypocrisy are the fences that protect propriety. . . ." [20] Ultra-feminine as her comment doubtless is, nevertheless it is the answer of the latest fashion, the Victorian, to Byron's indictment of society.

Some cancellations, therefore, have to be made by the careful reader of Byron's cantos; something must be subtracted both for his imperfect and perhaps self-deceiving view, and for the change in manners from the eighteenth to the nineteenth century that he never understood, though he felt it keenly. A strong and ample residue of permanent good sense remains, however, and the best proof of that is the use that later Victorian satirists of society made of his poem — Bulwer Lytton, Disraeli, Thackeray, Meredith, and Trollope, to name only the most prominent.

No complete verdict can be passed on Byron's picture of English society, since it is an unfinished fragment. But that it is quintessential, a mine for future writers on the subject, and the most diverting and sparkling passage of *Don Juan*, no reader can deny. The story of Don Juan and his love affairs, expanded to include the whole of Europe, tempest and travel, war and peace, is at last brought home to the responsible apex of European society, its most privileged class, the British aristocracy.

CHAPTER SIX

Byron's Library and His Reading

In the sensational drama of Byron's life, biographers are excusably inclined to underemphasize his reading. When one may truthfully describe such arresting and amusing matters as Byron being made love to by fashionable ladies, or sparring at pugilist Jackson's gymnasium, or rattling over the roads of Europe with his incredible menagerie of animals, one has little room left for the picture of Byron in solitude turning over books in his "much-tumbled library." Yet Byron in his library is an equally true picture, to say the least, and has rather more to do with the production of his poetry.

Not only in Byronic biography, but in criticism, the same underemphasis may be observed. The custom of critics has been to pay more attention to the autobiographical content of Byron's poetry than to its literary background. But there is a puzzle here that comes to light as soon as one has grasped the full details of that extraordinary life. Byron, like all poets, had the power of selecting from his experiences those which have universal appeal, objectifying and generalizing them so that they pass from the particular to the universal. But when we know the full story of his life, we may well be surprised that the autobiography in his poetry is as restrained and as universally applicable as it is. What power preserved his sanity and balance in poetic expression if it was not the force and light that he derived from reading?

Wordsworth relates an incident in the fifth book of *The Prelude* to illustrate his own experience of the steadying power of poetry. He watched from the shore while men were dragging Lake Esthwaite for the body of a drowned bather:

> "At last, the dead man, 'mid that beauteous scene
> Of trees and hills and water, bolt upright
> Rose, with his ghastly face, a specter shape
> Of terror; yet no soul-debasing fear,
> Young as I was, a child not nine years old,
> Possessed me, for my inner eye had seen
> Such sights before, among the shining streams
> Of faery land, the forest of romance.
> Their spirit hallowed the sad spectacle

> With decoration of ideal grace;
> A dignity, a smoothness, like the works
> Of Grecian art, and purest poesy."

Such was the sustaining, shaping effect of art on the experiences of a sensitive mind.

Byron's mind was steeped in literature. His world, and the world of his friends, was made up as much of books as of society. Even the actual "autobiography" in Byron's poems cannot be fully understood without reference to its literary background, for experience came to Byron from books as well as from life. A good part of his life was spent in reading.

It will be fruitful to dwell for a while on the contents of Byron's library and his manner of reading, in order to understand what part literature played in the composition of *Don Juan*. In piecing together these facts from Byron's correspondence and other sources, I have looked beyond the scope of *Don Juan* alone, hoping that by setting before the reader a coherent description of Byron's library and reading habits, he will receive a new impression, full of implications, of the mind of Byron, the poet.

1

As a schoolboy, Byron soon discovered the pleasures of neglecting his lessons and reading what he liked. Dr. Glennie, the headmaster of Dulwich, where Byron was enrolled from 1799 to 1801, allowed him the run of his library. "In my study," Dr. Glennie wrote to Moore, "he found many books open to him; among others, a set of our poets from Chaucer to Churchill, which I am almost tempted to say he had more than once perused from beginning to end." [1] Byron later characterized the Chaucer-to-Churchill poets, with some obligatory exceptions, as "*voces et praeterea nihil*," [2] and claimed that until several years later he read poetry of any kind only with the utmost reluctance. His contemporaries, however, believed that his remarkable English vocabulary and dexterity of style were laid down on the foundation of this early acquaintance with English poetry. But Byron found in Dr. Glennie's library the adventure stories of the sea that were among his early favorites — Smollett's *Roderick Random*, the *Narrative of the Shipwreck of the Juno*, which he made use of years later in *Don Juan*, and his grandfather Foulweather Jack Byron's seagoing narratives.

Byron, of course, was not reading with any view to becoming a writer. The "Old English Baron" felt himself called by his station to a life of action. He was above the discipline of school studies, and though he read voraciously, he did so for the sheer pleasure of reading. His pocket money was limited, but curiosity and love of display combined to make him invest in the beginnings of his own library, and then to donate some of the less-wanted volumes to Harrow. Moore, in his researches for his life of Byron, saw some of the books, pompously inscribed, that he bequeathed to the Harrow library.[3]

At Newstead in the summer of 1803, visiting his tenant, Lord Grey de Ruthin, Byron made the acquaintance of Strangford's "translations" from Camoëns, and the Poems of Thomas Little.[4] But he was in ampler literary company by September, when he settled in Southwell at Burgage Manor with his mother, and refused to go back to school at Harrow. Their landlord, Moore wrote, had left in the house "a library of some extent, which the young poet, he says, ransacked with much eagerness. . . ." The Life of Lord Herbert of Cherbury particularly interested him.[5]

The libraries of Byron's new friends, the Pigots and the Rev. Mr. Becher, must also have been godsends. "My resources of amusement," Byron wrote in March 1804, "are Books, and writing to my Augusta. . . ."[6] Reading "for escape," he went through the amazing number of books noted in the Memorandum of 1807, especially the some "thousands of novels." Reading led to writing, which in turn brought him social success. Becher tried in vain to guide him away from romance and light verse to more solid fare. "The light and miscellaneous literature of the day" prevailed.[7]

Whatever Byron's reading may have been at the library of Trinity College, Cambridge, where he resided intermittently from 1805 to 1808, his curiosity about current literature persisted. He recollected years later the pleasure he had had in reading Scott's poetry for the first time with William Bankes in his rooms, and buying and devouring with Edward Long the 1806 edition of Moore's poems.[8] In November 1807, however, he made the inventory of his reading to date in the memorandum book quoted by Moore,[9] and in January 1808, repeated it in substance in a delightfully impudent letter to Dallas, who was concerned about Byron's intellectual frivolity.[10] The ostentatious list was to prove to his own conscience and the world that he was neither ignorant nor neglectful of solid learning. It contained one hundred works mentioned by title and many others lumped together as "all the British classics," "little Italian," "some French," etc. At least forty of the identifiable works he owned himself, judging from their appearance in the 1816 Sale Catalogue of his library. After he had moved to Newstead in the autumn of 1808, he described his library to Augusta as "rather extensive." It included at least all the books he was consulting for the *English Bards and Scotch Reviewers*. Reading is listed as one of the daily diversions of the house party at Newstead the following spring.

But when Byron set off with Hobhouse for Spain and the East, he

took only a few books with him. Hobhouse, to be sure, had books, and a
plentiful supply of pens, ink, and paper to write his Travels; but Byron
had renounced scribbling (for the first time) and jotted down *Childe
Harold* on odd scraps of paper with the gold pen given him by Dr. Butler. The reading habit, however, was in his bones. Galt's first sight of
Byron was in the garrison library at Gibraltar, where Byron had come
in the hot sultry noon to read and scowl. At Malta, Galt says, he made
straight for the public library and began taking Arabic lessons from
one of the librarians; "his whole time was not, however, devoted to study;
for he formed an acquaintance with Mrs. Spencer Smith. . . ." [11]

When Hobhouse left Byron to winter at Athens — a delightful year of
horseplay and study with the young Italians and Greeks at the monastery, of swimming off the rocks at Piraeus, and sight-seeing jaunts with
Lord Sligo — Byron took up Italian and modern Greek, collected a
small library of books in those languages, and began to feel homesick
for his books at Newstead. He had been away for more than a year, and
he worried about their condition, probably unused and uncared for by
his mother. His letters to her frequently end with an appeal, "Pray take
care of my books," and he wrote to Hodgson that he wished to be sure
that he had a few of them, "one's own works for instance, any damned
nonsense on a long Evening. I had a straggling number of the E. Review given me by a compassionate Capt. of a frigate lately. . . ." [12]
He especially wished that he had not omitted to bring Bland and Merivale's Greek Anthology. [13]

At last driven by ambition and a lack of cash, he packed up his collection of Greek and Italian plays, Romaic dictionaries, and stray volumes, such as Fougeret de Monbron's *Le Cosmopolite*, which he had
picked up in the Archipelago and from which he drew the motto for
Childe Harold, and returned to England. Once in the hands of John
Murray, the publisher, and settled in his new lodgings in St. James's
street, London, Byron was drawn irrevocably into the bookmaking and
bookselling world.

This was the heyday of bookcollecting, and Byron did not escape the
fever. He frequented the auction rooms, where he used to meet Sheridan
and other book lovers in search of a bargain. Murray became a kind of
librarian for him, supplying him with books from his own shop or buying them for him elsewhere. Moreover, Byron's new fame as the author
of *Childe Harold* brought him scores of books through his publisher.
Murray's packets included presentation copies of new works and the
manuscripts of aspiring poets together with the letters from Byron's
admiring public. Murray also submitted manuscripts for Byron to criticize, for instance, Gally Knight's *Persian Tales*, and Byron was intensely
flattered by the request of his former publisher Cawthorn that he read

and criticize the manuscript of Mme. D'Arblay's new book. The authors and journalists associated with Murray were eager to lend books to Byron, some of them wanting to change his political views, others like J. W. Ward, who lent him the unpublished *Oedipus Judaicus* of William Drummond, to support or refute his religious opinions. Mackintosh sent him a work on Turkish literature, and Edward Griffiths contributed books for Byron to review in the *Monthly Review*.

Murray's habit of supplying his authors with books was both generous and well-founded as good business policy. All books or papers necessary for the composition of a work he furnished the author gratis, and in celebration of the publication he would make the author a generous gift of copies of his newest and choicest issues. He never neglected in his correspondence to list with enticing comments what was new on his shelves, and his authors bought from him at a great rate. These books would suggest new literary projects, and this year's publications sown in the libraries of authors would spring up in next year's literary crop. It is not surprising to find among Byron's books a substantial number with the John Murray imprint.

In 1813, Byron had to move the bulk of his library from Newstead to London. The move was occasioned by the necessity to strip Newstead preparatory for its sale to pay off the enormous debts contracted in his minority and in the Rochdale law-suit. Byron intended to sell the books, and the furnishings also, in London and set off again for the Mediterranean. Since his rooms in Bennet Street were too small to receive them, he had the books sent to Murray for sorting and cataloguing, adding his London collection to them. The project went as far as preparing the catalogue for the auction.[14] But finally the purchaser withdrew from the negotiations over Newstead, forfeiting a large deposit, which temporarily eased Byron's financial straits. Byron came back to London for the season, the Dandy's Ball, dinners with Sheridan and Rogers, the liaison with Augusta, Caro Lamb's persecutions, and Lady Melbourne's conversation. The plan for going abroad was postponed, and Byron could not make up his mind what to do.

Meanwhile, his library remaining in storage at Murray's, all but the books he had reserved for taking abroad with him, Byron began to make a new collection. He could not get along without books. Even with Augusta for company, he could not face the prospect of Newstead without a library, when they withdrew to the country in the heavy winter weather of January 1814, to avoid the gossip about their connection. Taking some books with him, "a great consolation for the confinement," he bought more on the way in Nottingham.[15] In London, once again, in the midst of the furore raised by the appearance of "To a Lady Weeping" in the second edition of the *Corsair*, Byron kept close to his rooms. On March 15, looking over a catalogue of a forthcoming sale, he wrote Murray "to secure for me Bandello's Italian Novels at the sale tomorrow. To me they will be nuts." [16]

At last in April 1814, when he had settled in new rooms in the Albany, he was able to retrieve his library from Murray's, having been without it for nearly a year:

"March 28, 1814: This night got into my new apartments. . . . Spacious, and room for my books and sabres. . . . Redde a little of many things,—shall get in all my books tomorrow. Luckily this room will hold them — with 'ample room and verge, etc., the characters of hell to trace.' " [17]

It took Murray two weeks to recover them, while Byron fretted with impatience over the delay. Napoleon had been exiled to Elba and the Tories were riding high. With the *Corsair*, Byron had publicly renounced scribbling (for the second time), but this was no time for a Whig author to remain silent. As he wrote to Moore in defense of his anonymous publication of the Ode to Napoleon Bonaparte:

"the provocation was such as to make it physically impossible to pass over this damnable epoch of triumphant tameness. 'T is a cursed business; and, after all, I shall think higher of rhyme and reason, and very humbly of your heroic people, till — Elba becomes a volcano, and sends him out again. I can't think it all over yet. . . . In the mean time, I have bought a macaw and a parrot, and have got up my books." [18]

He began to sort them over and reduce them to order, with a more serious literary purpose than before. Reference books, which he had formerly consulted at Murray's, he now bought for himself. He already had Bayle's Dictionary, and added to them "a *Moreri*" (a biographical dictionary) and an "*Athenaeus*" (Isaac Casaubon's edition of the *Deipnosophistae*).

During the hectic years from the publication of *Childe Harold* to this date in 1814, Byron had had opportunities to browse in other libraries. In London, there was the Alfred, a stuffy club indeed, but always affording the consolations of "books and quiet." [19] At Holland House he was in intimate touch with the aristocratic literary traditions of the eighteenth century. Lord Holland wrote a life of Lope de Vega, and edited the memoirs of Lord Waldegrave and Lord Orford. Dr. John Allen, "a devourer, a *Helluo* of books," as Byron called him, presided over the Holland House library and took a prominent part in its social life.[20]

Even when Byron was immersed in a love affair, literature formed one of the delights of "the gods in Lucretius." Lady Melbourne and Lady Oxford notably blended literary guidance with the affairs of the heart. Byron read Lucretius with Lady Oxford, and inspected the remnants of the Harleian Library at their place in Herefordshire.[21] The Websters, on the other hand, though Sir James dabbled in literature and insisted on publishing against the better judgment of all his friends, were not so well furnished with a library. Byron relied there on the books he brought with him, perhaps the set of British poets in a traveling case, listed in the 1816 Sale Catalogue, but especially his Italian books — "Dante, and Alfieri, and some others as harmless as ever wrote" — until Sir James begged him to suppress them as not fit reading for the ladies.[22]

In August and September 1814, Byron was again at Newstead with Augusta, waiting either to sail for Italy or to be accepted by Annabella Milbanke. "Books I have but few here, and those I have read ten times over, till sick of them." [23] At length Annabella accepted him, and he returned to London to attend to business, the tailor, and the theater with Moore. On the way to Seaham, protracting the journey towards the wedding as long as he decently could, Byron was delighted with a wedding gift from Murray of a new edition of Gibbon — "all the additions are very great improvements" — and begged Murray to make "an occasional inquiry in Albany, at my chambers, whether my books &c. are kept in tolerable order." [24] Murray continued fresh supplies of books through the honeymoon, including the earnestly desired *Guy Mannering.* Byron wrote to Lady Melbourne from the Milbanke place at Halnaby in Yorkshire: "it is just the spot for a moon; there is my only want, a *library*, and thus I can always amuse myself, even if alone." [25]

The new house in Piccadilly Terrace received the Byrons and their debts in July 1815. During the ten months of his residence there, before his self-exile to Europe, Byron could take little comfort in his library. The bailiffs time and again were established in possession, and in November Byron sent the whole library to Crook and Armstrong's to be out of harm's way.[26]

In the meantime, he spent a good share of his days and nights at Drury Lane Theater. One of his duties as a sub-committee member was to peruse, "himself or by proxy," the library of nearly five hundred plays on the green-room shelves, in search of presentable pieces.[27] None answered the purpose, but this review of the flotsam of sentimental comedy and tragedy fortified, by contrast, Byron's delight in the classics of British drama. In their effort to revive the stage, the committee turned to the best literary artists of the day, to Coleridge, Sotheby, Southey, and Scott, who introduced Maturin to them. Byron acquired a kind of despair at the present state of English playwriting.

In November, Murray was shocked to hear in a roundabout manner that Byron had had to give up his books, and instantly sent Byron £1,500, "with the assurance that another sum of the same amount should be at his service in a few weeks. . . ." [28] During the following trying months, Murray's financial assistance to Byron was most delicate and generous. Byron had been in the habit of giving away to worthy individuals the initial proceeds of his poems. Now Murray pressed him to take £1,000 for himself for *Parisina* and the *Siege of Corinth*. If he would not accept immediate payment for his new poems, Murray offered to sell the copyrights of all his past works for his use.[29] He further offered to buy Byron's library, and this offer Byron accepted. The books were appraised by another bookseller, Mr. Cochrane, at £450, and Murray dispatched £500 at once to Byron.[30] But before the deal could be closed, the books were traced and attached by the sheriff for another debt. Byron returned Murray's bills, "not accepted, but certainly not unhonoured," and made arrangements to redeem the books himself.

In March 1816, however, during another attempt to sell the books to Murray, Byron's creditors brought a fresh execution, — the tenth, said Byron, in as many months. He was "pretty well hardened," and the books "had much better be sold at once by public auction." [31] Accordingly, the auctioneer was engaged, a catalogue [32] drawn up and proofread by Byron himself, and the sale was held on April 5 and 6 at Evans's rooms, 26, Pall Mall. "Mr. Murray was present at the sale, and bought a selection of books for Mrs. Leigh, for Mr. Rogers, and for Mr. J. C. Hobhouse as well as for himself. . . ." The books, the screen, "with the portraits of actors and pugilists which is still at Albemarle Street," the silver cup, etc., brought £723 12s. 6d.[33] This sum, less costs, commissions, and Excise duty, went to Murray, to reimburse his £500 purchase and to settle Byron's account for books bought from Murray, which had been allowed to run on from January 1814. For Byron to keep any of the sale profits "would be a sort of swindling, more particularly with an account still owing to you. So there's an end of that matter; besides you bought many of the dearest bargains yourself." [34] One of the dear bargains was Burton's *Anatomy of Melancholy*, 2 vols. bound in russia, for which Murray gave £1 8s., and which he sent to Byron several years later as a present when Byron wanted another copy.[35]

2

The 1816 Sale Catalogue affords a good opportunity to summarize the contents of Byron's library. It stands to reason that the list does not represent all the works Byron owned. The fact that there are many duplicates suggests that Byron had followed, insofar as he was able, the magnificent policy of Richard Heber in bookcollecting: to have three copies of each work, one for show, one for use, and one for lending. Moreover, many books do not appear in the Catalogue which, from references to them in Byron's letters and journals, he must have possessed.

Major Pryce Gordon, who met Byron a month later in Brussels, reports that Byron's huge traveling coach, copied from one of Napoleon's, contained not only a *lit de repos*, a plate chest, and every apparatus for dining, but also a library.[36] Byron might have picked up some new books in the two weeks between the sale and his departure from England, but it is more likely that he kept back some favorites as a nucleus for a new library. Indeed, he expressly states that he will "reserve several" from the sale.[37]

An accurate estimate of the titles and the number of volumes at the sale is impossible, since the Catalogue sometimes lumps books together as "A Collection of odd Volumes" or "A Lot of Pamphlets," or concludes the description of a lot with the words "and 12 more," or "nine more." But there were more than seventeen hundred volumes on sale, representing over five hundred works. A considerable number may have been in Byron's possession for ten years, since they are identifiable in the 1807 Memorandum of his reading and are editions of 1807 or earlier. Many more are the major works of Murray's publishing house; some, like Langhorne's *Plutarch*, Mitford's *Greece*, Buffon's *Natural History*, Lavater's *Physiognomy*, and the works of Isaac D'Israeli, no doubt were willingly acquired to satisfy Byron's special interests; others, like the more than fifty travel books, perhaps indicate Murray's successful salesmanship. Still other volumes may be presentation copies (or duplicates) since they are the works of Byron's friends — for instance, Hodgson, Hobhouse, and Rogers. About seventy volumes, including some of this last group, may be written off as trash, "ephemerae," probably also "facetiae," everything from very minor poetry to novels like the *Miseries of Human Life* in 2 vols.

The largest block of works is in the field of English literature, over two hundred volumes of poetry, one hundred of plays, one hundred and twenty of novels, and nearly a hundred of essays and other types of nonfiction. There are several collections of the British poets, and everything by Scott and by Wordsworth published up to that time. Scottish poetry, including Burns, is well represented. The plays include the illustrated set of Shakespeare and Mrs. Inchbald's two collections of dramas and farces. Mrs. Barbauld's edition, 1810, of the great English novels, in fifty volumes, is flanked by separate editions of Fielding, Smollett, Mrs. Opie, and Miss Edgeworth. There is nothing, surprisingly, by Mme. D'Arblay or by Miss Austen. Several English translations should be listed, especially *de luxe* editions of *Don Quixote*, *Gil Blas*, *Vathek*, the *Arabian Nights*, Merivale's fragment of *Orlando Furioso*, and Gifford's *Juvenal*.

The nonfiction includes notably Bacon, Swift, and Burton. There are in addition a few works of criticism, for example, Warton *On the Genius of Pope*, Dunlop's *History of Fiction*, Sismondi's *Littérature du Midi*,

Kames's *Elements of Criticism*, and Payne Knight *On Taste*. Numbers of the *Critical Review* from 1795 to 1807, and of the *Edinburgh Review* from its commencement, accord ill with Byron's statement that he read no reviews until he was eighteen years old, in 1806; they may, however, have been purchased all at once in that year or later. There are eleven odd numbers of the *Quarterly Review*.

Of biography, letters, and memoirs, there are over two hundred and fifty volumes, besides several biographical dictionaries. Biography was a favorite type of reading with Byron, and the subjects range from Plutarch's *Lives* to Napoleon. Several special favorites are present: De Grammont, Grimm's *Correspondence*, Rousseau's *Confessions*, Boswell's *Johnson*, and Johnson's *Lives of the Poets*. These must be duplicates, since Byron continued to read and quote from them during his continental sojourn.

Nearly two hundred volumes of history range from Gibbon, Herodotus, Polybius, Sallust, etc., to oriental histories of Turkey, Persia, and Bengal. About half are on English and Scottish history, including Parliamentary history and debates. Twenty-five or more deal with French history, ranging from Davila's Civil Wars to many books on the Revolution and Napoleonic wars. Several books deal with the history of Prussia and especially of Frederick the Great.

Greek and Latin classics are rather scantily represented; some obvious textbooks and a number of dictionaries help to swell the total to more than eighty volumes. They include a complete set of Lucian, fine editions of Homer, Virgil, Cicero, Horace, etc., and a few plays of Aeschylus, Sophocles, and Euripides.

Byron apparently dumped all his collection of Italian literature, since he was on his way to Italy anyway. There are the works of Machiavelli, two copies of Ariosto's *Orlando Furioso*, five of Tasso, three of Dante, two of Petrarch, and the Bandello. The volumes of French literature consist of the memoirs already mentioned, a complete set of Voltaire (edited by Smollett), Montaigne's essays, Rabelais, Rousseau, Marmontel, etc.

Besides Buffon, there are a few other natural histories, an astronomy, a chemistry, a Euclid, a book on mechanics, and several on medicine and hygiene; some of these are perhaps school textbooks. Religion is represented by controversial works on Christian theology and a copy of the Greek New Testament. Byron took with him a pocket Bible, the parting gift of Augusta. Sporting interests are shown in works on boxing, fencing, and walking. Some miscellaneous works on oratory and elocution reflect Byron's parliamentary ambitions. Finally, reference books abound, particularly historical dictionaries, geographies and atlases, gazettes and guidebooks, and two works on costume, one oriental and one ancient.

Sir Walter Scott gave his opinion to Moore in 1829 that Byron was not particularly well read either in history or poetry, but this judgment must be taken as what an expert older reader, with a library of 15,000 to 20,000 volumes, would think of a younger man equipped with a much smaller, though compact and rich, collection of books. Byron seldom made an effort to appear bookish or well read; on the contrary, he affected the dilettantism of the noble and the dandy. As D'Israeli observed of him, though he was really studious, he preferred to appear indolent, as being more dashing.

3

Almost at once Byron began to collect books again on the continent. Major Gordon gave him the welcome present of Casti's *Novelle Amorose* in three volumes. The bookstores of Geneva and Lausanne were ransacked. Byron's letters to those of his friends who were planning to visit him on their continental tours began to contain the amusing shopping lists, with which he continually charged Murray, for everything from tooth powder to books. Shelley, by some strange accident, had never read the *Nouvelle Héloise*, to which Byron now introduced him. They were in raptures over it, as they traversed the sacred ground where the action had occurred. Even the tiny inns where Hobhouse and Byron rested on their Jungfrau tour in September were eagerly examined for stray books, — at Clarens, a Bible and a translation of Mme. D'Arblay's *Cecilia*, and at the inn of the following night, a French translation of Schiller.

The daily exchange of books and book lore between Byron and the Shelleys during the summer on Lake Leman is part of the familiar story of that poetic house party. Monk Lewis's reading to Byron from Goethe's *Faust* is also well-known. But in the midst of the French and German literature — ghost stories, ballads, *Faust*, and all the good literary talk at Coppet with Mme. de Staël and her household, Italian literature was not neglected. Dr. Polidori acted as a tutor in Italian to Mary Shelley and Jane Clairmont, reading Tasso with them regularly in the mornings. "Corinne" and her guests, A. W. Schlegel and Charles Victor de Bonstetten, furnished Byron and Hobhouse with much literary gossip about the *literati* of Milan and some valuable letters of introduction for their visit in the autumn.

Armed with Rousseau's *Confessions* for entertainment, Byron and Hobhouse journeyed from Geneva over the Simplon, past Lake Maggiore, down to Milan. For several weeks there, they were fêted by the

Abbé Brême and his friends among the literary great of Italy, including Monti, now past his prime, of whom S. Brême said, "Je le revère
comme son portrait." The classicism-romanticism debate shared the
conversation with post-mortems on the recent political troubles, and the
two subjects, among the Italians at least, were somewhat involved in
each other.[38] At a dinner party with S. Brême on October 17, Byron
and Hobhouse met M. de Beyle (Stendhal), Silvio Pellico, and Monti:

"Monti was for imitating Homer, and the ancient originality was impossible;
nothing was left for the moderns but following the old models. He quoted
Shakespeare in proof. We all thought very much to the contrary. . . . The
whole party seemed to delight in making him angry, and he poured forth
torrents of dogmas; when at last he had finished he talked quietly with Lord
Byron." [39]

Stendhal, to whom Byron was attracted as a fellow admirer of Napoleon, records the fact that Silvio Pellico told Byron about the satires
of Buratti, the Venetian poet, and that Byron eagerly inquired the name
of the bookseller where he might buy Buratti's works. The company
laughed at his naïveté in supposing that such subversive literature could
be printed in Italy, but the next day they introduced him to Buratti's
poems in manuscript, and taught him to puzzle them out in the Venetian
dialect.[40]

Evenings were spent at the theater, and mornings in sight-seeing at
the libraries and galleries.[41] Byron wrote to Murray:

"I have been to the Ambrosian Library — it is a fine collection — full of MSS.
edited and unedited. I enclose you a list of the former recently published.
These are matters for your literati. For me, in my simple way, I have been
most delighted with a correspondence of letters, all original and amatory,
between *Lucretia Borgia* and *Cardinal Bembo*." [42]

On another visit to the Ambrosian, he and Hobhouse met Mai, the
librarian there before he went to the Vatican, and purchased Mai's
works.[43]

In November, Byron settled for the winter in Venice. He wrote to
Kinnaird, his friend and banker in London, on the 27th:

"If I could but remain as I now am, I should not merely be happy, but
contented, which in my mind is the strangest and most difficult attainment of
the two — for any one who will hazard enough may have moments of happiness. I have books — a decent establishment — a fine country — a language
which I prefer — most of the amusements and conveniences of life — as much
society as I choose to take — and a handsome woman, who is not a bore and
does not annoy me with looking like a fool, setting up for a sage." [44]

Books came first on the list of sources of contentment. They had accumulated at such a rate during the summer that he had written to Murray from the Villa Diodati not to send him out any more — "I have too many." Now the overflow from the traveling coach library could be settled on shelves at the Segatis.

In return for Canto III of *Childe Harold*, Murray had sent Byron Coleridge's *Christabel*, Scott's *Antiquary*, and some other volumes, — Mrs. Hemans' *Restoration of the Works of Art to Italy*, the latest *Edinburgh Review*, Gally Knight's *Ilderim*, etc. Now Murray wished to furnish him with Gifford's Ben Jonson, and "very many new important and interesting works of all kinds in the press, which I should be happy to know any means of sending." [45] Means were found, in the post and in the luggage of travelers to Italy, though for some time Byron could not dissuade Murray from the vexatious habit of entrusting the parcels to the Foreign Office for forwarding.[46] No good could ever reach Byron from the hands of Castlereagh or any of his Tory colleagues.

Every visitor to Byron from London brought a consignment of books — Hobhouse, the Kinnairds, Rose, Croker, Moore, Shelley; Hanson, the lawyer, should have brought some, when he came out in 1818 with the papers to be signed for the sale of Newstead, but "the monster left my books, everything. . . ." He "swore the books were a 'waggon-load.' If they were, he should have come in a waggon — he would in that case have come quicker than he did." [47] Byron wrote off to Hobhouse immediately to retrieve them:

"You must send off a *man* on *purpose* with them on the receipt of this. I will pay any thing within *three hundred pounds* for the expense of their transportation. . . . They are all in Chancery Lane . . . with young Spooney [Hanson]; extract them, and send a man by chaise on purpose; never mind expense, nor weight. I must have books, and magnesia, particularly 'Tales of My Landlord.' " [48]

This was the ecstasy of disappointment.

But there were other sources of books more near at hand. Byron took up Venetian literature, and studied the Venetian dialect, not only to understand Mmes. Segati and Cogni, but also to enjoy the Venetian theater, which he visited almost daily. He made progress in Tuscan at the *conversazione* of Mme. Albrizzi and the Countess Benzone, and for a while delved into Armenian at the convent on the island of San Lazzaro, whither he rowed himself every morning for his lesson and studies. Murray and his synod were intensely interested in what he could report about manuscripts and books in the convent library, "translations also from Greek originals, now lost, and from Persian and Syriac, &c." But their efforts to encourage Byron's scholarship were of no avail.[49]

Byron also sent Murray books from time to time by returning travelers, and arranged a business connection for his Venetian bookseller, Missiaglia, "proprietor of the Apollo Library," with Murray. By Missiaglia, Byron dispatched to Murray, besides some books and periodicals, Dr. Aglietti's collection of letters written to Algarotti by English grandees of the eighteenth century.[50] From 1818 on, Missiaglia therefore represented the Murray house in Venice, a great convenience to Byron after he left Venice, and parcels and letters from England directed to the Carbonaro English nobleman began to be tampered with by the police. Through Missiaglia, also, Byron subscribed to Galignani's library and *Messenger*. In his journal at Ravenna, January 1821, Byron records the arrival of packets of books "from England and Lombardy — English, Italian, French, and Latin." [51]

Shelley continued his correspondence with Byron and sent him books — Peacock's *Melincourt*, Godwin's *Mandeville*, his own latest work, *The Revolt of Islam*, and some newspapers, "if I find they will escape the embargo." [52] When he came to Italy, he wrote that he had brought Byron some books "packed up at the bottom of a large box of my own." They included Hunt's latest publications and *Frankenstein*.

In 1817, Byron made the acquaintance of Richard Belgrave Hoppner, the English Consul in Venice. Hoppner, son of the painter John Hoppner, was also a godson of Gifford, whom Byron considered to be his own father in poetry. The acquaintance began in business, but after Hobhouse left Venice, Byron asked Hoppner to go riding with him every day on the Lido, and their store of common acquaintances drew them together into a mutually agreeable friendship.

Byron took along books on the Lido excursions, the latest acquisitions, and read aloud passages that struck his fancy as they rode over in the gondola. Hoppner says he would often

"repeat whole stanzas of the poems he was engaged in writing, as he had composed them on the preceding evening; and this was the more interesting to me, because I could frequently trace in them some idea which he had started in our conversation of the preceding day, or some remark, the effect of which he had been evidently trying upon me." [53]

This is valuable evidence on the mingling of reading, conversation, and composition in Byron's daily routine.

Byron made use of Hoppner to secure him translations of anything in German which he needed, and in return, when Byron was away from Venice, he gave Hoppner the use of his library at the Palazzo Mocenigo.[54] Hoppner frequently executed book buying and shipping commissions for him.

The great library of St. Mark's does not seem to have attracted Byron as a reader, though Hobhouse spent toilsome hours there working up the notes to *Childe Harold,* Canto IV. Byron may have used it early in 1817, when he commenced studying for *Marino Faliero,* for he turned over "all the histories" of Venice in search of the facts. But he bought the Venetian histories which he principally used in constructing *Marino Faliero* and the *Two Foscari*.[55] Byron bought books liberally at this time, for example, a ninety-two volume set of Voltaire, which entertained him through 1817, though Voltaire's "inaccuracies" annoyed him.[56] Finally, Kinnaird objected that he was exceeding his income, and charged him with commencing again the "Epicurean system" of living. Byron replied that "furniture, books, and a horse or two," frequent journeys, "living at a distance from Venice, and being obliged to keep up two establishments" amply explained the draughts.

Toward the end of 1819, Byron's unsettled way of life came to a crisis. It rested with Count Guiccioli, the Countess and her family, and finally with the Pope, whether he should become permanently attached to Countess Guiccioli. He sojourned in Ravenna, in Bologna, finally in La Mira again near Venice, going in to the city daily during the week Moore was visiting him. Meanwhile most of his books stayed at the Palazzo Mocenigo. At last with the new year, Byron was summoned to Ravenna, gave up all plans of emigrating to America, and resigned himself to *"serventismo."* By the middle of January, he wrote to Venice and Bologna to have his "movables" shipped to Ravenna, and moved into a part of the Guiccioli mansion. Most of the books came with the furniture.[57]

Ravenna was remote and less well provided with bookstores than Venice. It had a small library, but the inhabitants customarily shopped at Bologna or had things sent from Venice. Byron kept his courier Vincenzo plying back and forth. With every trip to Venice, he sent books to Hoppner, — "though the latter arrivals have not been very interesting you shall have the best of them," especially the recent novels for Mrs. Hoppner; and Vincenzo brought back the Murray shipments from Missiaglia.[58]

Byron, increasing in literary independence and belligerency, was also economizing and began to be more critical of Murray's selections:

"Aug. 12, 1820: . . . no *more modern* poesy, I pray; neither Mrs. Hewoman's, nor any female or male Tadpole of Poet Wordsworth's, nor any of his ragamuffins. Send me . . . Scott's novels — the *Monastery*."

"Sept. 8, 1820: . . . Thanks for books — but as yet no *Monastery* of Walter Scott's, the only *book* except *Edinburgh* and *Quarterly* which I desire to see. Why do you send me so much *trash* upon Italy?"

"Oct. 12, 1820: By land and Sea Carriage a considerable quantity of books have arrived; and I am obliged and grateful. But *Medio de fonte* . . . which, being interpreted, means,

> I'm thankful for your books, dear Murray;
> But why not send Scott's Monast*ery?*

the only book in four *living* volumes I would give a baiocco to see — abating the rest by the same author, and an occasional *Edinburgh,* and *Quarterly,* as brief chroniclers of the times. Instead of this, here are Johnny Keats's *p-ss a bed* poetry, and three novels by God knows whom. . . . Crayon is good; Hogg's Tales rough, but *racy,* and welcome. . . . Books of *travels* are expensive, and I don't want them, having travelled already; besides, they lie. Thank the Author of *the Profligate,* a comedy, for his (or her) present. Pray send me *no more* poetry but what is rare and decidedly good. There is such a trash of Keats and the like upon my tables, that I am ashamed to look at them. I say nothing against your parsons, your Smedleys and your Crolys: it is all very fine; but pray dispense me from the pleasure, as also from Mrs. Hemans. . . . I am in a very fierce humour at not having Scott's Monastery. You are *too liberal* in quantity, and somewhat careless of the quality, of your missives. . . . Rose's work I never received: it was seized at Venice."

"Nov. 4, 1820. W. Scott's *Monastery* just arrived: many thanks for that Grand Desideratum of the last Six Months." [59]

Byron's petulance over the books that Murray sent him or did not send him was only part of the strained relations between him and his publisher caused by the *Don Juan* row. The strain increased during the following year, and in September, still under the influence of Shelley's visit, his books and furniture packed to move to Pisa, Byron made his list of proposals to Murray including instructions on future book shipments. No more English publications were to be sent except the undoubted works of Scott, Crabbe, Moore, Campbell, Rogers, Gifford, Miss Baillie, Irving, Hogg, Wilson, and voyages other than those in the Mediterranean countries. He asked further that all reviews and magazines and private opinions of himself be omitted. "Walter Scott has not read a review of *himself* for *thirteen years.*" Thus Byron cut himself loose from the feverish stream of ephemeral literature.[60]

However, within a fortnight Byron was ordering more books from Murray. He added D'Israeli to the list of acceptable authors; he wanted Sophia Lee's "German's tale" for his *Werner,* Faber's Treatise on the "Cabiri," Sainte-Croix's "Mystères du Paganisme" (referred to in Mitford), a common Bible of good legible print bound in russia (to spare wearing out the one given him by his sister), Plutarch's Morals "in the *old* English translation," Gillies' "Greece," the "Life of Apollonius of

Tyana," "Leslie's Short and Easy Method with the Deists," and Burton's "Anatomy of Melancholy." "I want a Bayle, but am afraid of the carriage and the weight, as also of folios in general." [61] These caught up with him in Pisa and were established in the combined library and billiard room, where Byron used to receive Trelawney, Shelley, Medwin, and other visitors.

Leigh Hunt, who occupied the ground floor of Byron's house in Pisa in 1822, had a good opportunity to become acquainted with Byron's library and reading tastes. He comments on Byron's fondness for Gibbon, but continues in the disparaging tone he adopted in *Lord Byron and Some of His Contemporaries:*

"Lord Byron's collection of books was poor, and consisted chiefly of new ones. I remember little among them but the English works published at Basle, (Kames, Robertson, Watson's History of Philip II, &c.) and new ones occasionally sent him from England. He was anxious to show you that he possessed no Shakspeare and Milton; 'because,' he said, 'he had been accused of borrowing from them!' . . . Spenser he could not read; at least he said so. . . . I lent him a volume of the 'Fairy Queen,' and he said he would try to like it. Next day he brought it to my study-window, and said, 'Here, Hunt, here is your Spenser. I cannot see any thing in him.' . . . When he found Sandys's 'Ovid' among by books, he said, 'God! what an unpleasant recollection I have of this book! I met with it on my wedding-day; I read it while I was waiting to go to church.'

"The only writer of pastimes, whom he read with avowed satisfaction, was Montaigne. . . . Franklin he liked. He respected him for his acquisition of wealth and power. . . . Franklin's Works, and Walter Scott's, were among his favourite reading. His liking for such of the modern authors as he preferred in general, was not founded in a compliment to them; but Walter Scott . . . he read . . . over and over with unaffected delight. . . .

"It was a jest between us, that the only book that was unequivocally a favourite on both sides was Boswell's 'Life of Johnson.' " [62]

In the winter of 1822–23, Byron's library began to diminish. The ban on current literature was partly responsible, though in Genoa Byron still saw the latest books from England through his membership there in the "Reading Association" [63] and his exchange of books with the Blessingtons. But he was considering the expedition to Greece and gathering all his resources in ready cash. As soon as he reached Genoa, he began disposing of unwanted possessions, including "various useless books," [64] and in June 1823, he arranged to sell all his furniture, most of his books, and all but one carriage, through the agency of his bankers, Webb and Barry.[65] From time to time, he amplified his instructions to them on which books to withhold from sale, principally presentation copies. Some books he took with him when he sailed for Cephalonia, especially

Scott's novels, for reading these and other favorites continued to be his
chief solace up to the day of his death.

But what books he had with him, and what were sold in Genoa, it is
impossible to determine without access to other than printed records.[66]
His possessions were shipped home with his body in 1824, but they were
not sorted and disposed of, except the Memoirs which were promptly
burned, until the spring of 1827. Then, in collecting and sorting docu-
ments for Moore's proposed *Life, Letters, and Journals*, the executors,
Hobhouse and Kinnaird, and Murray destined Byron's remaining books
for the auction rooms. On July 7, 1827, and the days following, Evans
held the sale. Moore records on July 11 that he went to look at the books
— "nothing remarkable among them. There are some pencil marks of
his on the Prometheus of Aeschylus . . . about 'dethroning Jove,' which
I must refer to." [67]

4

The 1827 Sale Catalogue [68] amply justifies Moore's disparaging comment, though the titles provide valuable hints and corroborations about
Byron's reading in Italy. It seems likely that the nine hundred or more
volumes comprise what could not be sold in Genoa, but were shipped to
London by Webb and Barry upon the news of Byron's death. They do
not, for example, include many of Byron's favorite books that he must
have taken with him to Greece. Many of the sets are broken, lacking
volumes, or are described as damaged. The list includes half a score of
the presentation copies which the bankers were instructed to withhold
from sale. The whole collection looks like the remnants of a library.

About one hundred volumes may be laid at Murray's door, including
the shoals of travel books and the "trash of Keats" and other contemporary poets. Here also are Crabbe, Rogers, Hogg, Barry Cornwall,
Croly, Luttrell, Miss Baillie, Mitchell's Aristophanes, and Whistlecraft
(three copies). Campbell's *Specimens* and a Warton edition of Pope are
the only English classic poets. Memoirs and biographies, to the extent of
more than fifty works, many from Murray's press, include the old favorites Grimm and Rousseau, though not de Grammont and Boswell's *Johnson*, and add new favorites — de Retz, the Duc de Richelieu, and Spence's
Anecdotes.

Hunt's observation of the lack of Shakespeare and Milton is confirmed, though there is a Hayley's *Life of Milton*. A number of the Basle
editions Hunt noted include Sterne's *Tristram Shandy*, Smith's *Philosophical Essays*,[69] and Gibbon's *Life and Miscellaneous Works*. Galignani seems to have supplied a goodly number of Paris editions: the works
of Beaumarchais, Regnard, Chénier, Mirabeau, La Fontaine, Mar-

montel, Nodier, Prévost, and many additional French novels of the kind
Byron so justly pointed out as being more objectionable than his *Don
Juan*, — Cottin, Crébillon Fils, and Pigault le Brun (more than sixty
volumes of this last). Novels, indeed, abound, but are indiscriminately
chosen. There is *Antar*, the oriental curiosity of the period, but *Anastasius*, a book that Byron greatly admired, is not present. Voltaire's tales,
Gil Blas, and the *Nouvelle Héloise* are listed, but no Fielding or Smollett,
and of Scott, only the presentation copy of *Halidon Hill*.

The classics are again very scanty, but they include two translations
of the works of Lucian, one in French, the other in Italian, and a Petronius Arbiter, besides translations of almost every known Greek romance.
Italian translations of the *Iliad* by Monti, of Pindar by Mezzanotte,
and of Herodotus by Mustoxidi probably are present because of Byron's
acquaintance with the translators. A folio Horace with commentaries,
Venice 1509, is one of the few antique books in the collection. The Greek
tragic theater with the marginal pencillings, is flanked by Seneca's
tragedies, and the favorites Tacitus and Suetonius are supplemented by
Xenophon, Aulus Gellius, and Diodorus Siculus. But Mitford's *Greece*
and Gibbon's *Decline and Fall* do not appear.

Italian literature and history are naturally much more heavily represented than in 1816, — Franceschini, Morelli, Foscolo, Guidi, Ricci,
Foscarini, etc. There are Lord Glenbervie's translation of *Ricciardetto*,
Canto I, and three cantos of Ossian translated into Italian. Of Renaissance Italian literature there is very little: the works of Firenzuole, a
quarto Pulci, Sannazaro's poems, Fairfax's translation of Tasso's *Gerusalemme Liberata;* but the Ariosto which Moore brought to Byron is
missing, though there is a life of Ariosto. Neither do we find the three
small volumes of Dante which Byron carried about with him habitually
at Ravenna, but there is a commentary on Dante. Five histories of Venice, by Diedo, Daru, Laugier (two copies), Giannotti, and Sandi, are
those from which Byron drew for his Venetian tragedies.

Other volumes remain as traces of Byron's interests during these
years. The Russian histories, biographies, and travel books — Castéra,
Tooke, Karamsin, Macmichael, and others, — supplied him with information for *Don Juan*. Two copies of Warton on Pope, "much damaged," record traces of the controversy with Bowles. Schlegel's *Lectures on the History of Literature* recall Byron's acquaintance with
A. W. Schlegel, and his struggles in 1821 to understand and appreciate
the Schlegelian ideas. The period of Armenian studies is represented by
Armenian dictionaries and a Biblica Sacra Armena. Historical guidebooks to Florence and Rome are probably the débris of *Childe Harold*,
Canto IV, and the 1817 sight-seeing tour. Finally, a number of books
about colonizing in North and South America, not all from Murray's

press, record the project to emigrate, with or without Countess Guiccioli, and become a citizen of the New World.

5

Aside from what Byron read (and I do not mean to imply that the mere presence of a book in Byron's library is a guarantee that he read it or that it made any lasting impression on him) — how Byron read, how books affected him, and what use he made of reading in his writing are questions to be considered.

Throughout his life books were always an escape from himself and his miseries. He seldom read with any preconceived purpose or direction. The impersonal companionship of the printed page was a solace that no human being could give him, not even Augusta. Next to reading, a tête-à-tête conversation pleased him best, for from it, as he confessed about his daily conversations with Hoppner, he could "go home with a new idea. . . . It sets my mind to work; I enlarge it, and it often gives birth to many others. . . ." [70] This was his method with books also. The daily and nightly hours of reading became, as he said, a habit of his life, like riding, swimming, and writing — his other methods of release. When he was a young boy, he read during every waking hour of solitude — to avoid being alone with himself, as much as for any other reason. The last time he rose from his bed was to be carried into the next room to turn over the pages of his books.

Though the 1813–14 Journal is full of affectation, it gives a characteristic picture of his reading. The fact that this was the era of the first consignment of his library for sale may somewhat excuse the "desultoriness," the reading "to no purpose," "to while away the time." Besides, it was a period of unusual emotional upheaval; hence the existence of the Journal itself, as a relief for his feelings. The irritated confession that his head is "full of useless lumber," and resolutions "to begin a more regular system of reading soon," chime in with his self-accusations of idleness and uselessness. The passage of time haunts him, as it always did, especially near his birthday, without any worthwhile accomplishment. Driven by ambition, impatient with himself and dissatisfied with his world, Byron reads in snatches, subject to whim and circumstance and his pervading egoism. His attention flits from book to book and mingles with reverie and the darting associations of memory. The observations recorded in the journal on his reading are charged with comparisons between what he reads and his own experiences and opinions.

Byron, however, could really lose himself in a book, especially a novel. There were reasons, characteristically personal ones, for his attachment to the Waverley Novels — his admiration of Scott's generous frank heart, and his gratitude for the way Scott had befriended him in adversity. But even if they had not been Scott's work, the "Scotch novels" would have appealed powerfully to him with their combination of a commonsense viewpoint and romantic adventures in a vividly real and factual world of history. Nothing is more striking in Byron's remarks on his reading than the frequency and fervor of his mention of Scott's novels and his dependence on them for daily comfort.[71] Other novels besides Scott's were equally gripping, though probably *Vathek* was the only one that had so enduring a reign. With the *Arabian Nights* and the books of eastern travel and history, *Vathek* was a boyhood enthusiasm, and he reserved a copy of it at Genoa to take with him to Greece.[72] Schiller's *Armenian, or the Ghost-Seer* also took great hold of his imagination. "I never walked down St. Mark's by moonlight without thinking of it, and '*at nine o'clock he died!*' — But I hate things *all fiction.* . . . There should always be some foundation of fact for the most airy fabric, and pure invention is but the talent of a liar." [73]

His reading of novels indeed, was not uncritical, even of Scott's novels, whose errors and signs of haste he deplored while yearning for at least four new novels every year. Feminine sentimentalism repelled him; he abhorred the very word sentiment. Among women novelists he liked Miss Edgeworth and Madame D'Arblay best, because they were full of strong good sense. All the Countess Guiccioli's hysterics and changeableness were due, he was sure, to reading "Corinne." (One would like to know what the Countess said to that, for her *Recollections* give no hint.) He despised "clap-trap" and an air of horrid mystery, and admired Walpole's *Castle of Otranto* chiefly because it was the first of its kind and the work of a nobleman. Sensationalisms, like those in Lewis's *Ambrosio, the Monk*, were "the philtered ideas of a jaded voluptuary" — "they have no nature." Richardson's *Clarissa* he could not read, though he knew that heroine by reputation and suspected Annabella of being very much like her.[74]

The great eighteenth century novels were his favorites next to Scott, and represented to him the peak in English fiction, like Pope in English poetry.[75] Smollett's novels, particularly *Roderick Random*, were among his earliest favorites. Fielding's novels he read repeatedly, and Schlegel's *Lectures* became wholly acceptable only when they nominated Goldsmith's *Vicar* as the best short novel of all time. *Don Quixote* and *Gil Blas* stood at the summit with these great classics.

Trelawney complained that Byron drew most of his notions about human nature from books. "From reading Rochefoucault, Machiavelli, and other soured cynics, he learnt to distrust people in general. . . ." [76] But it would be nearer the truth to say that books contributed to Byron's

understanding of human nature; he read only to confirm and find instances of his own experience of people, especially of women. He studied
feminine character as if he were in the laboratory, using books as commentaries rather than texts. We can see the process in his letters to Lady
Melbourne, his teacher in this course of study: Annabella Milbanke
"always reminds me of 'Emma' in the modern Griselda." [77] Fielding frequently supports his observations on "the fair sect" and the way the
feminine mind works. Lady Caro's "manners and language are *Del-
phine*," and the closing sentence of one of her letters "is awfully amiable
. . . very like the style of Miss Matthews in 'Amelia' and Lucy in the
'Beggar's Opera.' . . ." His relations with Lady Frances Webster remind him of passages in Jonson's and Arthur Murphy's comedies, but
"there is no comedy after all like real life." Her attempt to rationalize
her unfaithfulness is better than Mr. Square's philosophizing, but "has
enlivened my ethical studies on the human mind beyond 50 vols." "In the
first vol. of Marmontel's Memoirs," he wrote, "towards the end, you
will find my opinion on the subject of women in *general* in the mouth of
Madame de Tencin. . . ." She advised Marmontel to make friends with
women rather than with men, "for by means of women one does what one
wishes with the men"; but to guard against a love affair with any woman
who he thinks could be useful to him.[78]

As for more serious reading and study, enough has been said to indicate Byron's fondness for history. Roman history ranks with fiction and
the Orient among his first loves, and Greek history was soon added to
it. Hallam's *Middle Ages* was a favorite; also Robertson's "State of
Europe" in *Charles V* — "it contains an epitome of information." [79]
The new conception of the evolution of empires, developed in Gibbon,
provided the intellectual background for *Childe Harold*. But the large
number of biographies in Byron's library attests likewise his adherence
to the older attitude towards history, that it is the record of the heroic
deeds of great men, a theory also applied in the materials of *Childe
Harold*, and the tragedies. Goode remarks that Byron's principal interest seems to have been in the great clashes between East and West.

But Byron was no systematic student. Moore, commenting on Byron's
conversations with Dr. Kennedy, when Byron confounded the doctor
with his wide, accurate knowledge of the Bible and theological writings,
says:

". . . the alleged familiarity of Lord Byron with [Stillingfleet and Barrow]
must be taken with a similar abatement of credence and wonder to that which
his own account of his youthful studies, already given, requires: — a rapid eye
and retentive memory having enabled him, on this as on most other subjects,
to catch, as it were, the salient points on the surface of knowledge, and the
recollections he thus gathered being, perhaps, the livelier from his not having

encumbered himself with more. . . . Of the Scriptures, it is certain that Lord
Byron was a frequent and almost daily reader. . . . How much, in addition
to his natural solicitude on the subject of religion, the taste of the poet
influenced him in this line of study, may be seen in his frequently expressed
admiration of 'the ghost-scene,' as he called it, in Samuel, and his comparison
of this supernatural appearance with the Mephistopheles of Goethe." [80]

Byron, indeed, had no training in study, or at least did not profit
from what he might have had. His disgust at the enforced, pedestrian
study of the classics at Harrow, and at the shams and negligence of
learning at Cambridge, is forcibly recorded in *Childe Harold* and *Don
Juan*.[81] But the breadth of his interests, his excellent common sense,
strong memory, rapid wit, and sensitiveness to impressions — the natural endowments of genius — enabled him to arrive at just and well-
proportioned views under his own tutelage. Book learning was supplemented by the unusual experiences afforded him in the very circumstances
of his life and his travels. Moore notes rather enviously the variety of
his acquaintances and modes of life, in England and especially abroad,
— "to-day in a palace, to-morrow in a cowhouse — this day with the
Pacha, the next with a shepherd," — and concludes that Byron attained
a much wider and more just perspective on life than a nobleman usually
enjoys.[82]

Byron's comment to Scott on Scott's dislike of Lord Orford's *Memoirs of the Last Ten Years of George II*, though fundamentally a
Whig-Tory difference of opinion, shows his sense of historical proportion:

"Recollect that those 'little factions' comprised Lord Chatham and Fox, the
father; and that *we* live in gigantic and exaggerated times, which make all
under Gog and Magog appear pigmean. After having seen Napoleon begin
like Tamerlane and end like Bajazet in our own time, we have not the same
interest in what would otherwise have appeared important history." [83]

To Lady Blessington, he said, "He who would take a just view of the
world must neither examine it through a microscope nor a magnifying-
glass. . . ." [84]

Byron's Ravenna Journal, 1821, shows him at work in his library:

"Jan. 5, 1821: Read the conclusion, for the fiftieth time (I have read all W.
Scott's novels at least fifty times), of the third series of *Tales of My Landlord*
— grand work — Scotch Fielding, as well as great English poet — wonderful
man! I long to get drunk with him. . . . Read Mitford's *History of Greece* —
Xenophon's *Retreat of the Ten Thousand*. . . . Visited La Contessa. . . .
Talked of Italy, patriotism, Alfieri, Madame Albany, and other branches of
learning. Also Sallust's *Conspiracy of Cataline,* and the War of Jugurtha.
. . . Came home — read the *Ten Thousand* again, and will go to bed."

"Jan. 6, 1821: Read Spence's *Anecdotes*. Pope a fine fellow — always thought
him so. Corrected blunders in *nine* apothegms of Bacon — all historical —
and read Mitford's *Greece*. Wrote an epigram. Turned to a passage in Ginguené — ditto in Lord Holland's *Lope de Vega*. Wrote a note on *Don Juan*.
At eight went out to visit. . . . Came home, and read Mitford again."

"Jan. 7, 1821, Sunday: Read Spence, and turned over Roscoe, to find a
passage I have not found. Read the fourth vol. of W. Scott's second series of
Tales of My Landlord. Dined. Read the Lugano Gazette. Read — I forget
what. . . . Turned over and over half a score of books for the passage in
question, and can't find it. Expect to hear the drum and the musquetry
momently. . . . In the mean time, I may as well read as do any thing else,
being alone." [85]

So the entries continue, weaving together reading, writing, comments,
and conversation, following his fancy or the needs of the verse writing
in hand.

The correction of Bacon's apothegms — a feat of which Byron was
extremely proud — is typical of his attachment to fact and accuracy
in details. He did not care how much people objected to the morals of
the *Bride of Abydos*, for example, but he would not have his accuracy of
"costume" impugned. In the series of notes to Murray that accompanied
its passage through the press, as with all his other spasms of proof-
reading, we find him sifting pedantically for errors: "Look out in the
Encyclopedia" whether Mahomet was buried at Medina or Mecca. "I
have no book of reference by me." For authority to call Potiphar's wife
"Zuleika," Byron refers Murray to Jones, D'Herbelot, *Vathek*, or the
notes to the Arabian Nights. He wants a line changed to read, "He
makes a solitude, and calls it peace." " 'Makes' is closer to the passage
in Tacitus, from which the line is taken." Byron took pains to send Murray three tactfully phrased corrections to Campbell's *Specimens of the
British Poets;* the errors were blemishes that should not mar an otherwise satisfactory work.

Byron had the habit of annotating his books in the margins, injecting
his own ideas into the silent tête-à-tête with the author.[86] The story of
his marginal comments on the first edition of D'Israeli's *Literary Characters* is well known.[87] One of these marginal notes is the list of his earliest tastes in literature. Others are likewise personal reflections, confirma-
tions of or objections to the ideas in the text, based on Byron's personal
experience. Lady Blessington thought that she could trace through such
marginal notes Byron's unconscious plagiary of ideas. He was never
willing to acknowledge the similarity of his ideas with those of any individual author, and her charitable conclusion was that the desultoriness
of his reading had made him forget the identity of "the original crude
embryos he had adopted":

". . . a book that he was constantly in the habit of looking over fell into my hands, and I traced various passages marked by his pencil or by his notes, which gave me the idea of having led to certain trains of thought in his works. He told me that he rarely ever read a page that did not give rise to chains of thought, the first idea serving as the original link on which the others were formed. . . ." [88]

The combination of an astonishing verbal memory and the rapid association of ideas is probably at the bottom of the reminiscences and echoes to be found in all of Byron's poetry. Every critic has noticed the abundance of these, and sometimes the observation has been magnified into charges of plagiarism.[89] Byron was unduly irritated by such charges, and it will be well to examine briefly how far they are true.

The vividness of Byron's verbal memory needs no further attestation than the frequency and range, not to mention the happiness, of quotations in his letters and works.[90] Everyone who knew him remarks on his extraordinary skill in this particular in his conversation. Trelawney and Medwin, nonliterary men, were deeply impressed, but the more literary Countess of Blessington also found his memory "extraordinary, for he can repeat lines from every author whose works have pleased him; and in reciting the passages that have called for his censure or ridicule, it is no less tenacious." [91]

In both his letters and his poetry, Byron is often careful to indicate, by quotation marks or direct reference to his source, that he is aware of his indebtedness. But sometimes he adopts a whole sentence without acknowledgment, for example, the witticism in Gibbon about the young Persians, who "were taught to speak truth, to shoot with the bow, and to ride." [92] Byron's use of quotation is almost invariably decorative, a trick of style; it is not an indication of wilful plagiarism, but rather of the depth of impression made on his mind by various authors.[93] The early accusation that he had borrowed Goethe's "*Kennst du das Land*" without acknowledgment for the opening lines of *The Bride of Abydos* taught him to be more circumspect, for example, in his imitations of *Christabel* and of *Vathek* in the *Siege of Corinth*. Even on the score of borrowing his opinions, Byron was not seriously worried by charges of plagiarism.[94] À propos of Montaigne's "plagiaries," Byron said to Lady Blessington:

"Who is the author that is not, intentionally or unintentionally, a plagiarist? . . . for if one has read much, it is difficult, if not impossible, to avoid adopting, not only the thoughts, but the expressions of others, which, after they have been some time stored in our minds, appear to us to come forth ready armed, like Minerva from the brain of Jupiter, and we fancy them our own progeny, instead of being those of adoption. . . . To be perfectly original, . . . one should think much and read little; and this is impossible, as one must read much before one learns to think; for I have no faith in innate ideas, whatever I may have of innate predispositions. . . ." [95]

The pamphlet attack, signed "Oxoniensis," for example, charging that *Cain* is "nothing more than a canto [*sic*] from Voltaire's novels, and the most objectionable articles in Bayle's Dictionary," left Byron cold.

The type of plagiarism sometimes charged against Byron about which he was indeed sensitive, is that in which the ground plan of a scene or action, or the turn and manifestation of character are borrowed, and especially when the borrowing has been from a contemporary author.[96] Galt was the first to complain that the plot of *The Bride of Abydos* was borrowed from one of his tragedies.[97] The accusation that most nettled Byron was that he had leaned heavily upon both Marlowe's *Dr. Faustus* and Goethe's *Faust* in his *Manfred*.[98] Eventually, he had to retract some of his obviously untrue remarks about Goethe's influence, and allowed that *Prometheus* (a respectable classical source), "if not exactly in my plan, has always been so much in my head, that I can easily conceive its influence over all or any thing that I have written; — but I deny Marlow and his progeny. . . ." [99]

From then on, he carefully prefaced *Beppo*, all his plays, and the cantos of *Don Juan* (after he was acknowledged to be their author) with references to his sources. He was desperately worried that Murray, the forgetful publisher, might omit his preface to *Werner*, acknowledging his dependence upon Miss Lee's *German's Tale*. When the storm of criticism against the brutality of *Don Juan*, especially the shipwreck scene in Canto II, coincided with Watts's articles on Byron's plagiarism, Byron wrote Murray:

"I think that I told both you and Mr. Hobhouse, years ago, that [there] was not a *single circumstance* of it *not* taken from *fact;* not, indeed, from any *single* shipwreck, but all from *actual* facts of different wrecks. Almost all *Don Juan* is *real* life, either my own, or from people I know. By the way, much of the description of the *furniture,* in Canto 3d., is taken from *Tully's Tripoli* (pray *note this*), and the rest from my own observation. Remember, I never meant to conceal this at all, and have only not stated it, because *Don Juan* had no preface nor name to it. If you think it worth while to make this statement, do so, in your own way. *I* laugh at such charges, convinced that no writer ever borrowed less, or made his materials more his own. Much is coincidence. . . ." [100]

The back tracking, even within this impassioned statement, is noteworthy.

Moore endorses Byron's stand on the rights of the poet to borrow all the technical details he needs, quoting Tasso's example on the arts of war.[101] But he appears to have been confused on the question whether

Byron wrote wholly from his own experience in everything he produced. Moore had once suggested to Byron that he write something about "a melancholy event which had just occurred in my neighborhood," and in rejecting the suggestion, Byron replied: "I could not write upon any thing, without some personal experience and foundation: far less on a theme so peculiar. Now, you have both in this case; and, if you had neither, you have more imagination, and would never fail." [102] This confession and Byron's obvious practice of making use of his experience convinced Moore; yet they did not satisfy his conception of the methods of a great poet. [103] Besides, Moore noticed at Venice in 1819 Byron's practice of poring over books to stimulate his imagination when he was writing:

"Observing a volume in his gondola with a number of paper marks between the leaves, I enquired of him what it was? — 'Only a book,' he answered, 'from which I am trying to *crib*, as I do wherever I can; — and that's the way I get the character of an original poet! On taking it up and looking into it, I exclaimed, 'Ah, my old friend, Agathon! — 'What!' he cried, archly, 'you have been beforehand with me there, have you?'

"Though in imputing to himself premeditated plagiarism, he was, of course, but jesting, it was, I am inclined to think, his practice, when engaged in the composition of any work, to excite thus his vein by the perusal of others, on the same subject or plan, from which the slightest hint caught by his imagination, as he read, was sufficient to kindle there such a train of thought as, but for that spark, had never been awakened, and of which he himself soon forgot the source." [104]

In the preface to the *Life, Letters, and Journals*, Moore, comparing Byron to Petrarch, gave his considered judgment:

Byron's "literary and personal character were so closely interwoven, that to have left his works without the instructive commentary which his Life and Correspondence afford, would have been equally an injustice both to himself and to the world."

Pursuing this principle, in presenting Byron's stanzas "To My Son," Moore, though acknowledging his ignorance of any liaison which at that time could have brought Byron a son, continues:

"On the other hand, so entirely was all that he wrote, — making allowance for the embellishments of fancy, — the transcript of his actual life and feelings, that it is not easy to suppose a poem, so full of natural tenderness, to have been indebted for its origin to imagination alone." [105]

But the necessity he was under to give Byron a light coat of whitewash, sufficient to satisfy Hobhouse and Kinnaird, joined with his own doubts on the subject to make him qualify these statements. Though "a certain

degree of foundation in *fact* seemed necessary to Byron," it might be so
small, perhaps visible only to Byron's own fancy, that it would be dangerous "to aim at tracing through his stories these links with his own
fate and fortunes." This remark, Moore says, applies to all Byron's
stories,

"in which, though the emotions expressed by the poet may be, in general,
regarded as vivid recollections of what had at different times agitated his own
bosom, there are but little grounds, — however he might himself, occasionally,
encourage such a supposition, — for connecting him personally with the
ground-work or incidents of the stories." [106]

Moore stands by his original principle as far as the emotions expressed
in any Byronic poem go, but makes an exception of "ground-work" and
"incidents."

Lady Blessington seems to have grasped the simple truth and actually
to have surprised it out of Byron himself, if what she reports is accurately stated. She writes:

"As Byron had said that his own position had led to his writing 'The De-
formed Transformed,' I ventured to remind him that, in the advertisement to
that drama, he had stated it to be founded on the novel of 'The Three
Brothers.' He said that both statements were correct, and then changed the
subject, without giving me an opportunity of questioning him on the unacknowledged, but visible, resemblances between other of his works and that
extraordinary production." [107]

Literature and life contributed simultaneously to Byron's poetry.
Old Isaac D'Israeli remarked to his son: "What is called originality
is little understood. New sentiments, thoughts, images seem each day
more difficult. Byron was always haunted with the fear and the necessity
of plagiarism. He need not have been alarmed. He is one of the most
original of writers. . . . A new style, based on truth, must carry everything before it." [108]

The reasons why Byron should have been extraordinarily sensitive to
charges of unoriginality in his poetry seem complicated, but they are
open to deduction. In the first place, stung by the *Edinburgh Review*
article criticizing his youthful imitations, he had announced to the world
his adherence to the poetical theories of Pope and the classicists, and
he had to maintain an attitude not only of authorized originality but of
superiority toward the contemporary romanticists. To be accused of
borrowing from them especially hurt his *amour-propre*. In the second
place, he had a deep sincere conviction that reality is more poetic than
fiction, that history is greater than romance, that art can never capture
in any medium an ideal that will surpass the actuality. He made his great
reputation on the basis of *Childe Harold*, Cantos I and II, a true story

of his travels and a transcript of the real world. The profound originality of this poem made it popular and fastened on Byron the legend that
he never wrote anything except from his own experience — an intriguing
but on the whole embarrassing legend when it came to the Oriental
tales.[109] Nevertheless, Byron would rather be accused of murder and
piracy, than destroy the great attraction of his work, that it was wholly
original with him. That point was his excuse to his own conscience for
not living up to his classicist poetical creed; theory might yield grace-
fully to truth, but only to truth.[110]

Finally, Byron became obsessed with the idea that he should provide
variety, at least in style. As far back as 1814, his letters to Murray refer
frequently to his variety in composition and meter, with the undertone
of suggestion that he resented complaints about the monotony of his
heroes and Oriental subject matter. But how to furnish variety on the
basis of a monotonous experience alone? He could not afford to borrow
from the experience of other poets. Any suggestion of the secondhand,
especially of the contemporary at secondhand, would break down at once
his best claim to fame, and would destroy his own artistic pride. There
was sound truth in this position. Byron knew himself, and his readers
knew him well enough, to recognize that, as Galt says, he "was only
original and truly great when he wrote from the dictates of his
own breast, and described from the suggestions of things he had
seen. . . ."[111]

But the time came when personal experience was not enough; it could
not be made to convey all the things that Byron wanted to say. To the
lonely reader in the Albany, as to the exile in Italy, the life of the printed
page was a satisfying supplement to his own experience. Fiction offered
a vehicle for his ideas, and fiction he found could not be a transcript of
his journal. He began using literary sources for the *Siege of Corinth,
Parisina, Mazeppa,* the plays, etc.:

> "No more — no more — Oh! never more on me
>   The freshness of the heart can fall like dew. . . .
> No more — no more — Oh! never more, my heart,
>   Canst thou be my sole world, my universe! . . .
> The illusion's gone for ever, and thou art
>   Insensible, I trust, but none the worse,
> And in thy stead I've got a deal of judgment,
> Though Heaven knows how it ever found a lodgment." [112]

Beppo could be an amusing anecdote he heard the other evening at the
Countess Benzone's. But for *Don Juan* he had to look further afield, and
my object will be to suggest some of the literary ingredients Byron used
in composing that satiric picaresque novel.

CHAPTER SEVEN

The Literary Background of Don Juan: Incidents

Don Juan is a compound of self-expression and literary reminiscence. We have seen that Byron wrote fundamentally from his own feelings and ideas, and that when he read, he was likewise habitually conscious of himself and his world at the center of the book. He identified himself with characters, and visualized scenes, making them his own. He associated scenes and ideas from one book to another, and from books to his own life. The details that appealed to him were those that corroborated his own experience and tastes. In all Byron's poetry, therefore, purely autobiographical elements are blended with echoes of the literature he had absorbed so deeply as to make it part of himself. Thus his poetry has both personal and cultural qualities to appeal to his readers. In the following analysis of each section of *Don Juan,* I shall endeavor to show how the personal elements are fused with the literary, and thus to restore the full literary flavor of the poem for modern readers.

1

The motto of the first and second cantos of *Don Juan* may perhaps be blamed for part of the public conviction that Byron was writing literal autobiography. He selected it from Horace's *Ars Poetica:* "Difficile est proprie communia dicere," "It is hard to treat in your own way what is common." Byron's friends took this to be a confession that he was writing about his domestic affairs, which were certainly common property. In Horace's context, *communia* means literary subjects which have been often handled by the poets and are well-known to the public, for he continues, "you are doing better in spinning into acts a song of Troy than if, for the first time, you were giving the world a theme unknown and unsung." [1] The motto was highly appropriate for a new version of the Don Juan legend. Byron was noted, however, not only for public confessions in his poetry, but for puns, and Hobhouse in his letter of January 8, 1819, advising Byron not to publish *Don Juan,* must have accused Byron of substituting in his mind for *communia* the words *domestica facta.*[2] Replying on January 25, Byron said:

"The motto 'domestica facta' merely meant *common life* which, I presume, was Horace's meaning — the *Julian* adventure detailed was none of mine; but one of an acquaintance of mine (Parolini by name), which happened some years ago at Bassano, with the Prefect's wife when he was a boy; and was the subject of a long case, ending in a divorce or separation of the parties during the Italian Viceroyalty. . . ." [3]

Byron's understanding of *communia* as common life, and his further interpretation of that phrase as what had actually occurred within his knowledge, throw light on his conception of the term Nature, an eighteenth century concept based in part on this very passage in Horace. As with *Beppo*, Byron was founding his story on an anecdote from real life, resolved to incorporate nothing in Juan's adventures except actual fact.

Although Parolini's story may have been uppermost in his mind, there is undeniable autobiography in his account of it, for example, the characterization of Donna Inez, who combines the features of both Byron's wife and his mother, and the resemblance of the whole plot to an affair of Byron's Southwell days, when he is supposed to have been allowed undue freedom with the daughter of a neighboring family who hoped thereby to entrap him for her husband. Perhaps there is autobiographical recollection in the closing scene of the Julia episode, when Juan becomes seasick while reading Julia's letter. The letter with its insistence on the singleness of Julia's love, now irrevocably lost, reminds us of Byron's sets of farewell verses to Mary Chaworth upon his leaving England in 1809. Yet the *Lines to Mr. Hodgson Written on Board the Lisbon Packet*, at the same time, though not then published, show Byron, the sufferer from love, in high spirits and surrounded by the seasick:

> "Hobhouse muttering fearful curses,
>   As the hatchway down he rolls,
> Now his breakfast, now his verses,
>   Vomits forth — and damns our souls.
>   'Here's a stanza
>   On Braganza —
>   Help!' — 'A couplet?' — 'No, a cup
>   Of warm water — '
>   'What's the matter?'
>   'Zounds! my liver's coming up! . . .

> "But, since Life at most a jest is,
>   As philosophers allow,
> Still to laugh by far the best is,
>   Then laugh on — as I do now.
>   Laugh at all things,
>   Great and small things,
>   Sick or well, at sea or shore. . . ."

If Parolini's anecdote and Byron's reminiscences are at the bottom of the Julia episode, it is a case of real life imitating art, for the plot is a commonplace of fabliau and comedy. Analogues abound, wherein a young gallant, innocent like Juan, or a scheming gay blade, seduces the young and pious wife of a stupid old husband. Byron would have learned from Dunlop's *History of Fiction* the "genealogy" of this fabliau at least from the *novelle* of Franco Sacchetti, *ca.* 1400 (who imitated the *Decameron*), to Casti's *Novelle Amorose* (1804). Dunlop selects as a typical example to relate the French version entitled *La Culotte des Cordeliers:* [4]

"It is there told, that a merchant's wife in Orleans had a clerk for a gallant. The husband came home one night unexpectedly. The clerk had time to escape, but left an essential article of dress behind him, which, on the following morning the husband put on by mistake. Before evening he remarked the change in his clothes, and on his return home reproached his wife with infidelity."

The wife gets out of her dilemma by providing that the clothing shall appear to have been a present from the Franciscans for the greater fertility of her husband. Dunlop says, "Of all these tales the origin may, perhaps, be a story in Apuleius, where a gallant is detected by the husband from having left his sandals." [5]

The *novella* of Casti mentioned by Dunlop in this series is *La Brache di San Griffone*, but Casti gives another version also in *I Calzoni Ricamati*. In this story, Giuditta, the wife of Master Piero of Amsterdam, yields to the love-making of Lord Boxton, who is touring Europe to discover whether there is any difference among the women of various countries. Her husband returns one night unexpectedly from a business trip and surprises them; Giuditta just has time to hide the milord under the sofa in the totally darkened room. She pretends to have the colic and sends Piero after some *acqua cattolica* at the chemist's. Piero dresses in the dark and hurries off full of concern for his wife's illness, but when he comes to pay for the medicine, he finds to his amazement that his money has turned into an English guinea, and that he has on a strange pair of richly embroidered breeches, with a watch and jeweled chain in the pocket. Advised by the chemist, he suppresses the obvious but dishonorable conclusion, and shames his wife into good behavior by his forbearance. "I have gained these rich spoils," he tells her, "and I shall take them from the closet every eight days in your honor."

Incidentally, still another of Casti's *novelle*, the fourth, entitled *La Diavolessa*, has been cited by many critics, E. H. Coleridge, Helene Richter, and R. D. Waller among them, as an analogue of *Don Juan*, Cantos I and II. Don Ignazio, a Spanish hidalgo, friend of Don Juan Tenorio and brought up with him in the same kind of education, pursues a brilliant career of scandalous amours in Seville, and at last runs away with his mistress Ermengilda. They are captured by pirates, their ship is wrecked, and Don Ignazio alone survives, cast up naked on the sandy beach. He gathers wreckage — "casks" and "biscuits" — to support himself; he finds a cave to live in, and then a hut; he becomes a penitent anchorite and is tempted by the Devil in many guises. Finally the Devil appears to him disguised as Ermengilda miraculously raised from the dead. Don Ignazio, forgetting his religious vows, marries with a common-law ceremony this Diavolessa. After a week, she whisks him off to Hell, where he rejoins his friend Don Juan.

The compressed simplicity and bareness of Casti's stories, however, convey none of the illusion of real life to be found in Byron's. Byron has borrowed, too, from richer versions of the Apuleian fabliau. He may have known it in romantic guise in C. P. Duclos's *Histoire de Madame de Luz*, in which he would also have read the history of his reputed French ancestor the Marechal de Biron. He undoubtedly knew it with all its trimmings of hypocrisy in Machiavelli's *Mandragola*. The heroine of that comedy, Lucrezia, is like Donna Julia in character — pious, easily led, capable of self-deception, femininely whimsical. Her mother, Sostrata, though a simpler character than Donna Inez, shares her complete hypocrisy and her function as half-conscious go-between. Regnard's play, *The Divorce*, is similar, especially in the tirades of the young wife feigning injured innocence to her irritating lord and master. The whole tradition of the fabliau from Boccaccio to Casti was in Byron's mind as he wrote, and the scene of climax that November night in Donna Julia's bedroom is improved by all that Byron had learned from English, French, and Italian comedy.

2

It seems unlikely that Casti's *La Diavolessa* played any important part in Byron's account of Don Juan's voyage and shipwreck. Aside from the fact that disaster at sea and the rescue of the hero by a simple maiden whom he proceeds to seduce were conventional features of the Don Juan legend, Byron's other models would have suggested their inclusion. Tempest and shipwreck have been conventional subjects of the epic since the *Odyssey*. Greek romance made the most of this convention, and picaresque romance in its turn did not neglect its advantages. The supreme example of shipwreck in *Robinson Crusoe* only gave a new impetus of realism and actuality to this favorite episode. The *Monthly Magazine*, as E. H. Coleridge notes in his edition of *Don Juan*, very soon brought out a complete analysis of Byron's indebtedness to Sir G. Dalzell's *Shipwrecks and Disasters at Sea*, 1812, a very remarkable col-

lection of firsthand accounts of wrecks. Coleridge adds to the documentation of Canto II the hints that Byron used from "his grand-dad's
narrative," from Bligh's *Mutiny on the Bounty*, from Hartford's *Remarkable Shipwrecks*, 1813, and from the *Memoirs of Cardinal de Retz*.

Byron told Trelawney, when they were fitting out the *Bolivar*, that
Trelawney would "find him nothing but a land-lubber. I hardly know the
stem from the stern, and don't know the name or use of a single rope or
sail. . . . All the sea-terms I use are from authority, and they cost me
toil and trouble to look them out." [6] The realism resulting from this
painful research was too strong for the British stomach. Byron's public
objected to the juxtaposition of the terrible and the ridiculous in such
unveiled terms. Even Shelley, in the midst of his enthusiastic comments
on the first two cantos, felt a little repelled:

"What a strange and terrible storm is that at sea," he wrote to Byron, "and
the two fathers, how true, yet how strong a contrast! Dante hardly exceeds
it. . . . The love letter, and the account of its being written, is altogether a
masterpiece of portraiture. . . . I cannot say I equally approve of the service
to which this letter was appropriated; or that I altogether think the bitter
mockery of our common nature, of which this is one of the expressions, quite
worthy of your genius." [7]

To us, who have been dulled by all too frequent repetitions in our daily
newspapers of this story of wreck and disaster at sea, the objections of
the public seem incomprehensible. They were prompted by that sentimentality which demanded prettiness and sublimity in poetry and refused ugliness and the grotesque, no matter how true to life. Such things
belonged in prose, in the picaresque novel for instance, like *Roderick
Random*, where we find in brief a wreck, decorated with rum and religion,
somewhat similar to that of the "Trinidada."

The prose documentation of Byron's shipwreck, like the Parolini episode, was merely an extension and corroboration of Byron's own experience, for one of the events in his first visit to Greece which made a deep
impression on him was the near-disaster at sea that he and Hobhouse
underwent in trying to sail from Prevesa to Patras in a Turkish ship of
war. Hobhouse gives his account of this experience in his *Journey
Through Albania*,[8] and Byron wrote a characteristically amusing description of it to his mother:

"Two days ago I was nearly lost in a Turkish ship of war, owing to the
ignorance of the captain and crew, though the storm was not violent. Fletcher
yelled after his wife, the Greeks called on all the saints, the Mussulmans on
Alla; the captain burst into tears and ran below decks telling us to call on
God; the sails were split, the main-yard shivered, the wind blowing fresh,
the night setting in, and all our chance was to make Corfu . . . or (as
Fletcher pathetically termed it) 'a watery grave.' I did what I could to console

Fletcher, but finding him incorrigible, wrapped myself up in my Albanian capote (an immense cloak), and lay down on deck to wait the worst. I have learnt to philosophise in my travels; and if I had not, complaint was useless. Luckily the wind abated, and only drove us on the coast of Suli. . . ." [9]

As Moore put it, Byron remembered the emotions he had felt on this occasion, though the circumstances and details of his poetic narrative might be imaginary or borrowed from other sources than his own experience.

But he had good poetic authority, as well as prose documentation, for his shipwreck. Probably William Falconer's *The Shipwreck*, 1762, predominated in Byron's mind as he wrote. This poem, one of the first publications of the Murray press, had been long a favorite with Byron. An 1804 edition of it by Clarke appears in the 1816 Sale Catalogue, and Byron mentions it in his notes to *Childe Harold*, Canto II, as one of the reasons why Cape Colonna is especially interesting to the English traveler, for it is the site of that famous wreck.[10] Two years after he wrote *Don Juan*, Canto II, he referred to it again at some length in his argument with Bowles over the "invariable principles of poetry." [11]

Superficially, Falconer's story of the storm and the shipwreck bears little resemblance to the *Don Juan* story. There is an exiled lover, Palemon, who gains the shore only to die after committing his sad tale of an unrelenting parent and an orphaned sweetheart to the charge of the Byronic hero, Arion. The scene is the Grecian archipelago, and there is much congenial talk of the ancient glories of Greece and its modern enslavement to the Turks. But the reasons for this poem's hold on Byron's imagination are shown in his comments on it in the Bowles controversy, revealing how it satisfied his predilections for human nature and action, for realism and authenticity:

"Is the sea itself [he wrote] a more attractive, a more moral, a more poetical subject, with or without a vessel, breaking its vast but fatiguing monotony? Is a storm more poetical without a ship? or, in the poem of *The Shipwreck*, is it the storm or the ship which most interests? both *much* undoubtedly; but without the vessel, what should we care for the tempest? It would sink into mere descriptive poetry. . . .

"In what does the infinite superiority of Falconer's *Shipwreck* over all other shipwrecks consist? In his admirable application of the terms of his art; in a poet-sailor's description of the sailor's fate. These *very terms,* by his application, make the strength and reality of his poem."

An authentic narrative of a great and losing struggle between man and inanimate nature, delivered in a high-pitched emotional key, was exactly the sort of thing to appeal to Byron's mind. Biased as he was in supposing that a piling up of facts was the same thing as the truth, he fell

into the same error of taste — though not to such an abysmal extent —
as Falconer, by using painstaking realism in the technical details. Falconer's *Shipwreck* was applauded, in spite of its boring factualness, but
Byron's was not, and the reason for its failure with the public was its
hard-boiled manner. A sustained high emotional tone was not the pitch
for *Don Juan,* but a humorous middle tone, varied by abrupt changes to
the sublime.

Ariosto's shipwreck, a famous passage in the *Orlando Furioso,* described entirely in his high heroic strain, must also have been in Byron's
mind, for his shipwreck matches Ariosto's in many details and fully
equals it when he chooses to raise the tone. Byron had some thoughts at
this time of translating Ariosto, but left the task to his friend W. S.
Rose, who was already engaged upon it. Perhaps Rose's translation was
to some extent influenced by Byron's poem — I am not expert enough
in Ariosto or Italian to decide; but it is interesting to compare their
markedly similar descriptions of the wreck.

Rogero and his seven kings set sail from Marseilles for North Africa,
but

> "Upon the darkening of the day, the wind
> Displays its fickle and perfidious kind."

Through the stormy night, the pilot, the sailors, and all on board struggle at various nautical tasks to steady the ungovernable vessel. Nothing
avails; fallen on her beam ends, split and leaking at every seam, the ship
is about to founder. "Meanwhile, his soul to Heaven each recommends."

> "A fierce assault and cruel coil doth keep
> Upon all sides that wintry tempest fell.
> Now to their sight so high the billows leap,
> It seems that these to heaven above would swell;
> Now, plunging with the wave, they sink so deep,
> That they appear to spy the gulf of hell.
> Small hope there is or none: with faltering breath
> They gaze upon inevitable death.
>
> "On a dispiteous sea, that livelong night,
> They drifted, as the wind in fury blew.
> The furious wind that with the dawning light
> Should have abated, gathered force anew."

The ship breaks up piecemeal, rudder, sails, and mast are carried away,
and they drive on helplessly toward a bare rock:

> "All to their private aims alone attend,
> And only to preserve their life have care.
> Who quickest can, into the skiff descend,
> But in a thought so overcrowded are,

Through those so many who invade the boat,
That, gunwale-deep, she scarce remains afloat.

"Rogero, on beholding master, mate,
    And men abandoning the ship with speed,
In doublet, as he is, sans mail and plate,
    Hopes in the skiff, a refuge in that need:
But finds her overcharged with such a weight,
    And afterwards so many more succeed,
That the o'erwhelming waves the pinnace drown,
And she with all her wretched freight goes down;

"Goes down, and, foundering, drags with her whoe'er
    Leaving the larger bark, on her relies.
Then doleful shrieks are heard, 'mid sob and tear,
    Calling for succour on unpitying skies:
But for short space that shrilling cry they rear;
    For, swoln with rage and scorn, the waters rise,
And in a moment wholly stop the vent
Whence issues that sad clamour and lament." [12]

Byron's story of shipwreck, also located in the Gulf of Lyons, carries
on for many stanzas in conversational humorous style, full of circum-
stantial details, but as the climax of the actual wreck approaches, the
tone rises and grows solemn:

" 'T was twilight, and the sunless day went down
    Over the waste of waters; like a veil,
Which, if withdrawn, would but disclose the frown
    Of one whose hate is masked but to assail.
Thus to their hopeless eyes the night was shown,
    And grimly darkled o'er the faces pale,
And the dim desolate deep: twelve days had Fear
Been their familiar, and now Death was here. . . .

"Then rose from sea to sky the wild farewell —
    Then shrieked the timid, and stood still the brave, —
Then some leaped overboard with dreadful yell,
    As eager to anticipate their grave;
And the sea yawned around her like a hell,
    And down she sucked with her the whirling wave,
Like one who grapples with his enemy,
And strives to strangle him before he die.

"And first one universal shriek there rushed,
    Louder than the loud Ocean, like a crash
Of echoing thunder; and then all was hushed,
    Save the wild wind, and the remorseless dash

> Of billows; but at intervals there gushed,
>   Accompanied by a convulsive splash,
> A solitary shriek, the bubbling cry
> Of some strong swimmer in his agony."

But even in the midst of these often quoted stanzas, Byron has inserted two in his customary voice, describing the last half-hysterical efforts of the ship's company to save themselves. The ship, having been lightened of every object that would float, at last

> "gave a heel, and then a lurch to port,
> And, going down head foremost — sunk, in short."

These lines epitomize the prosaic, tough realism with which he elected to relate a scene hallowed by romance.

Rogero, with the superhuman strength of a chivalric hero, swims with growing vigor and unwearied mind, buoyed up by noble resolves to reform his whole way of living, and so arrives on the rocky island shore not in the least exhausted and far from drowned. But Juan endures days and nights of torment, watching his comrades die lingering and cruel deaths, and reaches shore

> "With just enough of life to feel its pain,
> And deem that it was saved, perhaps, in vain."

There is symbolism in both these pictures of survival. Ariosto's is that of a good Catholic Christian, for Rogero finds on the rock the hermit who converts and baptizes him, in token of his salvation from death. Byron's symbolism, however, I venture to suggest derives from Lucretius, who strongly affected his views on man and the universe. One of the most famous images in the *De Rerum Natura*, which he read in the summer of 1813 with Lady Oxford, struck his imagination so forcefully that, as we have seen earlier, he used it as the basis of three separate scenes. The lines occur in a passage where Lucretius has gathered proofs of the imperfection of the universe and the undeniable existence of evil:

"Then further the child, like a sailor cast forth by the cruel waves, lies naked upon the ground, speechless, in need of every kind of vital support, as soon as nature has spilt him forth with throes from his mother's womb into the regions of light, and he fills all around with doleful wailings; as is but just, seeing that so much trouble awaits him in life to pass through." [13]

Faced with inexplicable and fated evil in his own life, Byron felt the pathos, the doubt, and the despair of Lucretius. The cosmic view of the hapless individual stranded in a vast, threatening, and even malignant universe is the backdrop for the Byronic melancholy, rebellion, and pessimism. Man, Byron wrote, "has always been, and always will be, an unlucky rascal." He encountered the Lucretian passage again in Burton's chapter on Discontents, Cares, and Miseries, where Burton calls to mind Lucretius' naked mariner "cast on shore by shipwreck, cold and comfortless in an unknown land. No estate, age, sex, can secure himself from this common misery." [14]

3

Peter Quennell has observed that Greece and youth were equated in Byron's mind. Byron thought in 1816 that he had said all he had to say on Greece; its scenes were fading and confusing in his memory, and he dreaded committing the error deplored by Voltaire of over writing his material. But nothing in his former pictures of Greece surpasses *Don Juan*, Cantos II–IV, in beauty and reality. It would be useless to conjecture about the autobiographical reminiscences contained in them; they are manifest and abundant. But the literary associations of the Haidée episode, as of the seraglio one to follow, are less obvious and should be noted. Here we enter the maze of connections linking oriental romance and European literature, which I do not propose to thread but only to sketch. For I am convinced that the nexus of oriental fiction, ancient and modern, was present in Byron's mind as a source of inspiration.

The formula of shipwreck, innocent, passionate love, and piracy in the Mediterranean is as old as the Greek romances, with which Byron's Venetian library was amply stocked. Dunlop's *History of Fiction* told him in its first chapter all about the Greek romances; in the second, about Apuleius and Petronius; copies of all these he bought in Venice. He would also have learned Dunlop's conjectures on the perpetuation of these romantic fictions, together with all classical mythology and superstitions, in the medieval romances, such as *Amadis de Gaul* [15] and *Huon of Bordeaux*. At the other end of time, in his own experience, he knew these aspects of oriental adventure at first hand, and had heard, collected, and translated some of the Greek ballads (dating, many of them, from the late middle ages) representing popular traditions on similar materials. His response to the whole body of oriental fiction resembles that of Scott and the other romanticists and Gothic novelists to the traditions of western medieval romance and balladry. Byron took the time-worn stuff of Greek and medieval oriental romance and breathed life and truth and passion into it. Dressed in the actual style and setting of the Orient, the Haidée episode is as fresh and real as an eye-witness account.

Byron says at the conclusion of Haidée's story:

> "But many a Greek maid in a loving song
> Sighs o'er her name; and many an islander
> With her Sire's story makes the night less long. . . ."

In a note to the *Bride of Abydos*, Byron mentions his acquaintance with the recent exploits of the contemporary historical Lambro; but his acquaintance with the Haidée story, and possible ballads recording it, is more shadowy. The name Haidée, we know from Byron's own translation of the ballad "Belovèd and Fair Haidée," occurred within his knowledge in popular Greek songs. Its meaning, "a caress," or "the caressed one," is appropriate to *Don Juan*, Cantos II–IV. Samuel Baud-Bovy, in his *La Chanson Populaire Grecque du Dodécanèse*, records many variants of ballads on "La fille injustement tuée" by cruel brothers or parents for her love to a stranger.[16] Any one of these may have been Byron's original. The testimony of historical reality furnished by the appearance of the story in ballad form would perhaps satisfy his fact loving nature, even if he had no more substantial proof of its occurrence in real life. As for the famous interpolated song, "The isles of Greece," its affinity to the Greek patriotic ballads, like "Arise, sons of the Hellenes," is obvious.

Daphnis and Chloe, however, and Theagenes and Characlea, are the literary ancestors of Juan and Haidée. Byron also knew their modern counterparts in Paul and Virginie; indeed, the eighteenth century tradition of the island romance is the "source" of Haidée's character and of her love for Juan. As in the Greek romances, the love-idyll of Juan and Haidée is interrupted by the pirate, blood and thunder, wounds and separation. The recognition scene between Lambro, apparently raised from the dead, and Haidée torn between filial devotion and fear for her endangered lover, is rendered in the best style of melodramatic romance. But unlike the Greek romances, or their medieval equivalents, no room is left for a happy reunion. Haidée dies a lingering death, her mind eclipsed by sorrow, and her unborn child dies with her. In three elegiac stanzas Byron records her tomb and her father's, the desolate isle, and the ballads of the Greeks upon her love and her father's exploits.

M. Anton Blanck, in an article entitled *"Floires et Blanceflor" et l'épisode de Haidée dans le "Don Juan" de Byron*,[17] has called attention to some interesting parallels between that twelfth century romance and Byron's story. Both stories begin in Spain and proceed to the Orient. In both, a pair of seventeen-year-old lovers, one Christian and the other Muslim (for Haidée, though said to be acquainted by name with Hell and Purgatory, is half-Moorish in blood and wholly pagan in ideas), experience a perfect love idyll, interrupted by the cruel guardian of the girl. In *Floires and Blanceflor*, the religious differences are reversed, for Floires is the Muslim, and Blanceflor the Christian. She is sold to the emir of Babylon, whither Floires patiently pursues her. He finds his way into the fantastic, highly decorated tower where she is kept, and there they enjoy their love in scenes of oriental luxury. At last the emir becomes suspicious and upon coming to the tower himself to find Blanceflor, discovers her fast asleep in Floires' arms. They wake to see his naked sword suspended over them, which he withholds until he can learn the young man's name. This romance has a happy ending, for the emir's heart is melted by Floires' constancy, and the young lovers are united in marriage. But the conception of innocent natural love, and the contrast between tender hellenic grace and oriental cruelty are the same in both *Floires and Blanceflor* and *Don Juan*.

It seems very improbable, however, that Byron knew either *Floires and Blanceflor* or its near relation *Aucassin and Nicolette*. M. Blanck grants the unlikelihood, but points out that Byron could have been acquainted with the story in Boccaccio's *Il Filocolo*, which Hunt had just drawn to the attention of Keats. Why should not Hunt have mentioned it to Byron also? This may have happened, but I feel sure that Byron would not have found the intensely prosaic *Filocolo* congenial, in spite of its "Questions of Love." He never mentions it, and whenever he speaks of Boccaccio, "the bard of prose," it is to speak of the *Decameron*, which he was reading in Venice as early as 1817.

Aside from the fact that *Floires and Blanceflor* is a medieval descendant of the Greek romances, the resemblance of the Haidée episode to it is more probably due to Wieland's *Oberon*. For *Oberon* is founded on the romance of *Huon of Bordeaux*, which in turn is closely allied to *Floires et Blanceflor*,[18] and Byron knew Wieland's modern version of *Huon* through Sotheby's translation. In Dunlop's *History of Fiction*, Byron would have found the entire story of *Huon of Bordeaux* with its analogues,[19] both from the Arabian Nights and from German prose fiction, all preceded by a short paragraph ascribing praise to Wieland's use of the material in *Oberon*, and to Sotheby's "beautiful translation" which has rendered the story "universally known." Dunlop concludes his discussion:

"Huon is a more interesting character than most of the knights of Charlemagne. Even his weakness and disobedience of Oberon arise from excess of love or the ardour of military enterprise; and our prepossession in his favour is much enhanced by a mildness of nature and tenderness of heart, superior to that of other heroes of chivalry." [20]

Alaric Watts, in the already mentioned articles on Byron's plagiarisms, was quick to pounce upon the similarity of *Don Juan* to *Oberon*. He had already been accusing Byron of borrowing without acknowledgment from Sotheby in the *Corsair*. The scene between Gulnare and the Corsair in prison, he found to resemble too closely the prison scene between Almansaris and Huon in *Oberon*, Canto XII. Now he points out the similarities between the island love affair of Juan and Haidée and that of Huon and Amanda. Unfortunately for the immediate effect of his arguments, Watts confused Amanda and Almansaris in his comparisons. Byron was able to toss this off: "Much is coincidence." But if he had not been borrowing from Sotheby's translation of *Oberon* in *Don Juan*, Cantos II–IV, he certainly had been in Canto V, written five months before he read Watts's articles, but not published until some months after. Watts reproaches Byron, and indeed he seems to deserve it, for his unkind criticisms of the good Botherby in *Beppo* and for his lines in *Don Juan*, Canto I:

> "Thou shalt not covet Mr. Sotheby's Muse,
> His Pegasus, nor anything that's his. . . ."

These remarks, Watts says, are particularly ungrateful from Byron, since "besides innumerable imitations of his style and diction, he has resorted to his pages . . . for ideas, language to clothe them in, and sometimes for principal portions of the machinery he employs in his poems." It is too bad for Watts that he could not have written this after *Don Juan*, Canto V, was published.

Byron wrote in his Journal at Ravenna, a few weeks after he had completed this canto, that he had read "much less of Goethe, and Schiller, and Wieland, than I could wish. I only know them through the medium of English, French, and Italian translations." [21] It is not possible to trace from published records when he first became acquainted with Sotheby's translation of *Oberon*, but by 1814 he must have known something of the original at least, not only from Dunlop, but from Mme. de Staël's enthusiastic account in *De L'Allemagne*:

"Wieland," she wrote, "a imité Voltaire dans ses romans; souvent Lucien, qui, sous le rapport philosophique, est le Voltaire de l'antiquité; quelquefois l'Arioste, et, malheureusement aussi, Crébillon." [22]

This was exactly calculated to arouse Byron's curiosity, mentioning as it does so many of his favorite authors as Wieland's models; it is not surprising to find him reading *Agathon*, to see a copy of *Aristippus* in the 1827 Sale Catalogue, and to suspect his acquaintance with *Don Sylvio de Rosalva*. Mme. de Staël went on to recite part of the story of *Oberon*, up to the island episode, but she left it unfinished. Byron must have resorted to Sotheby's translation, if he did not know it already, for it is the last three cantos of the poem on which he has relied for "materials" in the scene between Gulbeyaz and Juan in Canto V.

Juan has just been forcibly torn from his Haidée by her pirate father, and has been sent away to Constantinople to be sold as a slave. Huon likewise was separated from Amanda on the island, when she was brutally abducted by pirates to be sold into slavery in Tunis. After much suffering, Huon is wafted by enchantment straight to Tunis to the cottage of

Ibrahim, the head gardener of the royal palace. Huon assumes the disguise of a slave and works in the seraglio gardens, in the fond expectation of reunion with Amanda ; she, he hears, was miraculously preserved when the pirate ship was struck by lightning upon entering Tunis harbor, and is now the honored guest of the Sultan. Meanwhile Almansaris, the Sultana, neglected like Gulbeyaz, encounters Huon in the gardens and falls in love with him. As Gulbeyaz contrives with Juan, so Almansaris smuggles Huon into the seraglio for a private interview. Huon expects and hopes to see his Amanda again at any minute, and is firmly true to her through all temptations. But Juan has no hope of ever seeing Haidée again, and his mourning for her and faithfulness to her are more within the bounds of probability.

Gulbeyaz and Almansaris exactly resemble each other in circumstances, character, and even outward appearance. "Never," wrote Sotheby of Almansaris,

> "will Nature in her loveliest mould
> So fine a model for a Venus frame," [23]

and so on, for three stanzas of statuesque description. Byron described Gulbeyaz as

> "rising up with such an air
> As Venus rose with from the wave. . . .
> Her presence was as lofty as her state;
> Her beauty of that overpowering kind . . ."

and much more, to suggest, without describing, immortal perfection of beauty.

In *Oberon*, Huon is led through "a suit of endless chambers," beginning in dim shadows and leading out into a "blaze" of "highest lustre." A rich brocaded curtain parts and discloses the queen sitting on her golden throne, surrounded by twelve nymphs,

> "love's sisters, young and full of charms, . . .
> Each scarcely shaded by a roseate veil."

They are in the midst of a gorgeously decorated apartment —

> "There gold and lazuli the walls o'er laid;
> There Siam and Golconda's rifled mines
> Seem'd to have center'd their exhausted store,
> By wanton luxury lavished o'er and o'er." [24]

Huon "starts back like one bewilder'd and appal'd," for he had expected to see Amanda, not this "voluptuous visionary sight":

> "Ah what to him? — a dream without delight —
> 'T is not Amanda — ."

In *Don Juan*, the dwarfs open the great gilded bronze doors, and Baba and Juan, who have traveled "room by room, through glittering galleries, and o'er marble floors," enter a room "still nobler than the last," "a dazzling mass of gems, and gold, and glitter." Here follows a brief digression on tastelessness in décor, very good from Byron who was said to have had no taste in such matters. Gulbeyaz reclines under a canopy. Her attendants were

> "a choir of girls, ten or a dozen,
> And were all clad alike; like Juan, too,
> Who wore their uniform, . . .
> A very nymph-like looking crew,
> Which might have called Diana's chorus 'cousin.' "

Juan stands "admiring, at some distance." It is noteworthy that, though Byron cannot help some innuendoes on "Diana's chorus," he completely omits the ridiculous possibilities of Juan's feminine disguise in the dramatic scene that follows, reserving them for later when the dramatic tension has slackened.

Both ladies send away their attendants after some preliminaries, but the action between Almansaris and Huon, while similar on the whole, differs in details from that between Gulbeyaz and Juan. Both queens are imperious and straightforward in their love-making, expecting an instant response. Both Huon and Juan have their minds fixed on their absent mistresses. But Huon looks pale and sulks, and Juan bursts into tears. Both men are tempted by the voluptuous beauty of the Sultana, but each resists, Huon more staunchly, and Juan less so, who feels his virtue ebb

> "As through his palms Bob Acres' valor oozed."

Huon endures by consciously recalling Amanda, and at last openly confessing that he loves her only. Juan untangles himself from Gulbeyaz' embrace (Almansaris wants to embrace Huon but does not dare), and says he *has* loved, but that love is only for the free. Almansaris and Gulbeyaz respond equally to this check with passionate though silent rage, and with tears and humiliation. Throughout this scene, Byron is much more full and minute than Wieland in his psychological dissection of the feelings, assisted perhaps by Wieland's further promptings in the story of Danae and Agathon.

There are differences also in the sequels. In *Oberon*, Almansaris' ideas of vengeance hatch the scheme of compromising Huon in the garden myrtle-bower; there she tempts him, he resists again, and they are interrupted by the Sultan. Almansaris thereupon accuses Huon of trying to ravish her, and he is condemned to death by fire. Later she tries to rescue him from this fate, but he refuses to be rescued at the price of being untrue to Amanda, and Almansaris abandons him to his sentence, outraged at his scorn and consumed with jealousy of Amanda.

Gulbeyaz and Juan are interrupted by the arrival of the Sultan, and on the next day, when Gulbeyaz' suspicions and jealousy have been aroused by the thought of what may have passed in the harem with Dudù, she gives the order to Baba to have Juan liquidated. The double temptation of the hero, and the proof of chastity, were not in Byron's scheme.[25] His plot is looser, less dramatic, and more lifelike. Wieland goes on to a Tasso-like close in an incident paralleling the constancy of Olindo and Sophronia. Byron had no use for Oberon and all the fairy lore.

Once again Byron has taken a famous literary plot and retold it in terms of real life.[26] For the story of the Muslim lady and the Christian slave appears repeatedly in Italian, Spanish, and French literature, and probably in all the countries bordering the Mediterranean. Doubtless the adventure occurred repeatedly in real life, even up to Byron's day, in that pirate-infested sea and the neighboring Muslim and Christian civilizations. Piracy, capture, and holding for ransom persisted in the Mediterranean until 1830.

Byron knew several of the literary versions of this story. Dunlop gave him a clue to it, as follows:

"The first tale of Firenzuola, is one that has become very common in modern novels and romance. A young man being shipwrecked on the coast of Barbary, is picked up by some fishermen, and sold to the Bashaw of Tunis. He there becomes a great favourite of his master, and still more of his mistress, whom he persuades not only to assist in his escape, but to accompany him in his flight." [27]

Byron acquired the works of Firenzuola in Italy. The first *novella* [28] has some points in common with the first cantos of *Don Juan*, and is a fairly typical representative, as Dunlop says, of this plot.

Two devoted friends, wealthy nobles of Tuscany named Niccolo and Coppo, are separated by the necessity of Niccolo's going to Valencia to receive an inheritance. Setting sail from Genoa, Niccolo suffers shipwreck in a great storm, which with its effects on the ship's crew and passengers is described at length in the manner of *Don Juan*, Canto II, though without all the nautical accuracy. The ship breaks in two when it loses its mainmast, and Niccolo saves himself by clinging to a table, on which he floats to the coast of Barbary. The fishermen who rescue him sell him as a Christian slave to Amet of Tunis, a rich old Mussulman, who makes a pet of him and finally presents him to his young and beautiful wife. The wife falls in love with him, and after persuading herself in a long soliloquy that it is right for her to love Niccolo, who as a slave would naturally be more concerned about freedom than about love, makes a declaration to him "almost inarticulate between tears and blushes." When he realizes the truth of her offer, he is overcome by her beauty, superior sense, and refinement. He converts her to Christianity, marries her secretly, and they live together meditating escape.

Meanwhile Coppo has traced Niccolo to Tunis and arrives to rescue him. The two friends arrange to sail away with the lady, ostensibly on a pleasure cruise for the day, and so they escape to Messina. There, through the interposition of the ambassador of Tunis, the King of Sicily returns Niccolo and the lady, in spite of their protests, to the Dey of Tunis and the revenge of Amet. Good fortune, however, blows up another storm which carries their vessel toward Leghorn, where they fall a prey to some Pisan corsairs. Ransoming themselves from these pirates, they finally reach Pisa with some of their remaining treasure. When the lady has recovered from a dangerous fever, resulting from her trials and hardships, they proceed to Florence where their friends welcome them and feast them, and they are remarried with all due ceremony. Coppo marries Niccolo's sister, and the two couples live together in exemplary harmony and nobility of life.

It will be recalled that Byron's first plan for Juan and Gulbeyaz, as he outlined the story to Medwin, was that they should escape together, and then, if Juan tired of the lady, she could easily be made to die of the plague.

As this story progressed from Italy to Spain and then to France, it took on many additional features and new emphases. The questions of religious and political conflicts were made crucial in the plot. A new character, a renegado, or a servant of the Muslim lady (like Baba), who helps the lovers to escape, was added. Finally, its principal theme became the conflict between love and honor, or love and loyalty, as the friends developed into rivals for the lady's affections.

Cervantes has two versions; the simple one, in "The Captive's Story" in *Don Quixote*, and the complex version in *The Liberal Lover*, one of his *Exemplary Novels*. The latter, like Wieland's *Oberon*, makes the triangle into a quartette, by introducing a second lady, another Christian captive. The incident of a permitted conference between the Christian lovers in the harem was thereby added to the plot. Scudéri's *Ibrahim* presents still another version.[29] The novelette in Le Sage's *Le Diable Boiteux* called "The Force of Friendship" is a complete and a highly successful example of the tale. Canto I of Casti's *Tartar Poem* is another analogue, with the additional feature of threatened emasculation of the hero.

Byron probably knew all these versions, but if he was relating in *Don*

Juan, Canto V, merely his own account of a famous fictional plot, what becomes of his claim that every adventure of Don Juan is drawn from real life? He may, indeed, have heard of some such incident from an acquaintance, or he may have felt that Cervantes' autobiographical "Captive's Tale" was sufficient proof of its occurrence. But luckily he knew the version of the story set down by Jean-François Regnard as autobiography in his novelette *La Provençale.* Byron knew about Regnard's works from Grimm's *Correspondence,* and apparently before composing Canto V, he had just acquired a set of Regnard in the Paris edition of 1810, republished in 1820.[30] *La Provençale,* "a true story," appears in Volume I; it combines the features of Firenzuola's story and Cervantes' *Liberal Lover,* and is closely parallel to Wieland's *Oberon,* Cantos X–XII. Though it lacks the finesse and dramatic quality of Wieland's version, which are reflected in Byron's, it must have encouraged Byron to use Wieland, by furnishing evidence of Wieland's truth to reality in the purported actual adventures of Regnard.

Regnard's story, however, was more congenial to Byron in tone than Wieland's. Such passages as the following, would have struck sympathetic chords in Byron's mind:

"Love, among the Turks, is not armed with spikes but covered with flowers. . . . The ladies make all the advances: the law of nature is supreme, which they follow preferably to that of Mohammed, because they are women before they are Turks.

"[The hero's] restlessness did not permit him long to remain in the same place; and, like those people who have suffered from prolonged insomnia, he sought his repose in agitation. . . . It mattered little to him where he went, provided that he put himself at a distance. He flattered himself, even with pleasure, that the cold of the north might a little assuage his ardor. . . . Drawn along always by his restlessness, he traveled in Turkey, in Hungary, in Germany. But what good did it do him to flee afar, if he could not flee from himself, and if he was inseparable from his own grief? He found many other places, but he encountered nowhere indifference." [31]

Juan also, though not voluntarily, journeys away from love, Haidée, and the seraglio toward the north, and in the snows of Russia is overcome by melancholy and restless ennui.

4

Before leaving the seraglio scenes, we should consider the *Blackwood's Magazine* accusation that Byron had merely adapted Louvet's *Chevalier de Faublas* in *Don Juan,* Canto VI.[32] This little volume pretends to be the authentic memoirs of the sixteen-year-old De Faublas, covering his love adventures in Paris in 1783–84. It contains practically all the

hackneyed plots of secret amours; the central plot is a triangle situation among De Faublas, the Marquis and the Marquise de B., similar
to the plot of *Der Rosenkavalier*. De Faublas's mistress, the Marquise
de B., first receives him when, by a series of misunderstandings, his masquerade as a young lady is not penetrated, at least ostensibly, until he
is safely abed with her. The description of his unrobing from his masquerade costume is like *Don Juan*, VI, 61–62:

"I found myself in great embarrassment when it became necessary for me to
disengage myself from these garments whose usage was so little familiar to
me. I broke strings, I tore out pins, I pricked myself on this side and tore
myself on the other; the more I hurried, the less speed I made." [33]

The story is conducted with a high degree of verisimilitude and wit,
some scenes being actually dramatized like a comedy. I think it highly
possible that Byron had read this novel and many another like it, but as
for Canto VI being based upon it, that is nonsense. The gentle, almost
meditative beauty of that Canto has nothing in common with the lush,
brutal sentimentality of De Faublas's amours. On the contrary, I think
that Byron had in mind a satiric repudiation of that kind of "amatory
writing," and for that reason he fails to give any satisfaction to a las-
civiously imaginative reader. He skates on thin ice, with the utmost
grace, but he never breaks through. The chaste and touching description of Dudù is probably a portrait from life, perhaps of one of the
Macri girls at Athens, or the "Dudù" whom he knew there in 1810–11.[34]
Cervantes may also have assisted his comprehension of the innocence and
boredom of the harem life in his Exemplary Novel called *The Jealous
Husband*; Byron may have picked up his title for the duenna, "The
Mother of the Maids," from James Mabbe's translation of this novel.

5

The next tender episode of *Don Juan*, the rescue and adoption of Leila
in the midst of the sack of Ismail, was suggested by a footnote in Byron's acknowledged source, Castelnau's *Essai sur l'Histoire ancienne et
moderne de la Nouvelle Russie*.[35] The footnote is derived from the young
Duc de Richelieu's "mémoires," one of Castelnau's sources, in which
Richelieu describes his rescue of a young girl ten years old, innocent and
lovely in striking contrast to the rage in her surroundings. She was trying to hide from a pair of menacing Kossacks among the slain bodies of
four women, one of them her mother. Richelieu chased the Kossacks off
with blows, and was glad to find that the little girl had no injury other
than "a slight cut on the face from the same sword which had pierced her
mother."

Byron versified this incident, using almost the same words and faithfully detailing the facts. But his imagination, dwelling upon the future relations of Leila and Juan, seems to have reverted to one of Marmontel's *Moral Tales*, "Friendship Put to the Test," in which a similar incident is described. This love story, again with orientalism and "noble savage" traits to recommend it, is enhanced by the themes of conflict between love and honor, of humanitarianism in war, and of universal religion as opposed to sectarianism. These qualities would all have made it appeal to Byron.

Blanford, the hero, is seeking his fortune in India and happens to be present when Coralie's native village is being sacked by the British soldiers. Her father is dealt a mortal blow on the threshold of his dwelling:

"At that instant Blanford arrives. He comes to repress the fury of the soldiery. . . . 'Barbarians,' said he to the soldiers, 'be gone! Is it feebleness and innocence, old age and childhood, that you ought to attack?' "

Coralie, who is not yet fifteen years old, "witness to the piety, the sensibility of this stranger, thought she saw a god descended from Heaven to succour and comfort her father." The old Brahmin, though he perceives his end approaching, devotes his dying moments to a prolonged discussion of virtue, war, and religion with Blanford. He confides Coralie to Blanford's charge, and Blanford swears "that her chastity, innocence, and liberty, shall be a deposit guarded by honour, and for ever inviolable," and that she shall be brought up in "that modesty and virtue which are every where the glory of a woman":

"Blanford, whom his duty recalled from Asia to Europe, carried thither with him his pupil; and though she was beautiful and easy to seduce; though he was young and strongly taken, he respected her innocence. During the voyage, he employed himself in teaching her a little English; in giving her an idea of the manners of Europe, and in disengaging her docile mind from the prejudices of her country. . . . The sentiments which he had conceived for his pupil seemed to have given him rather the disposition of a father than of a lover."

The details of Marmontel's plot run far beyond the conceptions of Byron, insofar as they appear in his incompleted poem. But he has taken Marmontel's situation, authenticated by Richelieu's incident, and has reinterpreted it, with more delicacy and truth to life than Marmontel could muster. He rejects the improbable love at first sight of the young man for the child found in such frightful circumstances, and he refines on the strange mixed feelings each must feel for the other after the dramatic commencement of their affection. Moreover, he transfers to Leila some of the natural freshness of viewpoint to make satiric use of the observations of these travelers on European civilization.

A curious fact from Byron's life should be appended to this incident in *Don Juan*. Almost two years after the completion of Cantos VIII–XII, in which Leila figures, Byron secured the release of a group of Turkish civilian captives from the Greeks and sent them to their homes at his own expense, all but one little girl, Hato, or Hatagee. Hato, Byron wrote to Augusta,[36]

"has expressed a strong wish to remain with me, or under my care, and I have nearly determined to adopt her. If I thought that Lady B. would let her come to England as a Companion to Ada — (they are about the same age), and we could easily provide for her; if not, I can send her to Italy for education. She is very lively and quick, and with great black oriental eyes, and Asiatic features. All her brothers were killed in the Revolution. . . . Her extreme youth and sex have hitherto saved her life, but there is no saying what might occur in the course of the *war* (and of *such* a war), and I shall probably commit her to the charge of some English lady in the islands for the present. The Child herself has the same wish, and seems to have a decided character for her age. . . ."

Not content to leave the historical accuracy of this bit of *Don Juan* to the adventures of the Duc de Richelieu, Byron appears to be living out in his own life one of the adventures of his fictional hero. This is the exact reverse, in point of time-sequence, of the relation between the adventures of author and hero usually ascribed to Byron's storytelling. It is a measure of how deeply he could identify himself with his fictional creations.

6

The companionship of Leila on Juan's travels to seek his fortune in Russia and England may remind the reader of a similar situation toward the close of Thomas Hope's *Anastasius*. This novel, published anonymously by Murray in 1819, has been cited by Anton Pfeiffer [37] as the source of many incidents in *Don Juan*, Cantos III–X, and indeed deserves attention for its Byronism, which was immediately detected by the critics. Croker wrote to Murray:

"I have read just twenty pages of 'Anastasius,' and thank you for the information you gave me as to the author. Of course you know best, and what you volunteered to tell must be the truth, but then also I must believe in the 'Metempsychosis,' and that Tom Hope's late body is now the tabernacle of Lord Byron's soul." [38]

The *Edinburgh Review*, after the secret of the authorship of *Anastasius* was out, wrote enthusiastically:

"Mr. Hope will excuse us, — but we could not help exclaiming, in reading it, is this Mr. Thomas Hope? — Is this the man of chairs and tables — the gentleman of sphinxes — the Oedipus of coal-boxes — he who meditated upon muffineers and planned pokers? — Where has he hidden all this eloquence and poetry up to this hour? — How is it that he has, all of a sudden, burst out into descriptions which would not disgrace the pen of Tacitus — and displayed a depth of feeling, and a vigour of imagination, which Lord Byron could not excel?" [39]

The novel is a most extraordinary work and is less well known today than it deserves to be, having been overshadowed perhaps by Morier's *Hadji Baba*.

Murray must have sent a copy of *Anastasius* to Byron in the spring of 1820, after he had settled down at Ravenna, but Byron does not mention it until July 22, 1820. Murray was curious to know what Byron thought of this new rival in orientalism, and Byron finally wrote that it was "good, but no more written by a Greek than by a Hebrew." Murray was not satisfied with this lack of enthusiasm, and probably teased Byron further by letting him in on the secret of the authorship. In a later letter, Byron votes the book, rather petulantly, "excellent." It is hard to avoid the impression that he was genuinely envious of Hope's production. Here was the man whom Byron had ridiculed in *English Bards* as a dilettante, turning out exactly the type of novel Byron could have wanted to do himself, and receiving praise for it in the *Edinburgh* with invidious comparison to his own powers. By 1823, Byron had sublimated these envious feelings in a joke. He told Countess Blessington, after expressing high commendation of Hope's *Anastasius*, that

"he wept bitterly over many pages of it, and for two reasons: — first, that *he* had not written it, and, secondly, that *Hope* had; for that it was necessary to like a man excessively to pardon his writing such a book — a book, as he said, excelling all recent productions, as much in wit and talent, as in true pathos. He added, that he would have given his two most approved poems, to have been the author of 'Anastasius.' " [40]

It seems unlikely that Byron had read this novel before he composed Cantos III–IV in Venice, September–October 1819. Consequently, it is hard to accept part of Pfeiffer's observations on Byron's alleged indebtedness to Hope. But there are some hints that Byron may have followed for the later development of his poem. Anastasius, for example, dallies, for a page or so, with a project for a good adventure — to light out from Constantinople for St. Petersburg and become the next favorite of the Empress Catherine. Circumstances, however, direct him to the Arnaut-Turkish wars in the Balkans, then to Smyrna, the Arabian Desert, Egypt once more, and finally to Italy. In his second sojourn in Egypt, Anastasius falls in with Cirico, the wandering poet-revolutionist, whom he had already met after his disastrous love affair with Euphrosyne in Smyrna. Cirico always serves as a spur to his worthier ambitions, and urges him to try his fortunes in France in the French Revolution, where he might represent the cause of freedom for the Greeks. This hint may have reminded Byron of Anacharsis Cloots, for it was not until February 1821, some months after Byron had read *Anastasius*, that he first mentioned the plan of a French Revolutionary ending for *Don Juan*.

Anastasius is full of irony like *Don Juan*, but a dramatic irony expressed through the self-knowledge and self-characterization of the hero, who writes in the first person. He was born worldly-wise, with his impulses to mischief and wickedness infinitely stronger than his impulses to good feelings and good deeds. He says at one point that he feels impelled by destiny to "perform the things set down for him — be they good, or be they evil." But in the context this confession of fatalism is ironic, and reminds us of that sudden frankness of Byron's:

> "But Destiny and Passion spread the net
> (Fate is a good excuse for our own will). . . ."

Anastasius is master of his own soul, no matter how the wheel of fortune tosses him up and down. Periods of conversion and reformation occur from time to time, but not until his will, as well as his intellect, has been subdued by suffering does it finally turn toward good. This is the reverse of Don Juan's character, at least as far as we can see how it is to be projected. Both heroes, however, after living an extraordinarily active and congested life, were to die young in the odor of sanctity.

Many a thought of Anastasius in his roving career around the eastern Mediterranean parallels Byron's reflections in *Don Juan:* on the problems of free will, predestination, good and evil; on mutability in fortune; on avarice, the vice of the middle-aged; on female friendship and coquetry; on modern Greek patriotism and pride; on ennui — that it is a greater evil than loss or sorrow. Anastasius' reflections on his mother and her bad upbringing of him, when he came home to find her dead and only the dog to welcome him, must have struck Byron forcibly, and the conclusion, leaving Anastasius dying friendless and a solitary exile at the age of thirty-five, must have made an indelible impression on Byron's foreboding mind.

Coincidences also may be noted between the careers of Anastasius and Don Juan. Like Juan, Anastasius enters a new country, Arabia Deserta, famed for its liberty, and in the midst of uttering a rhapsody on freedom is held up by a fierce Bedouee, as the footpads hold up Juan with the words of praise to freedom-loving England scarcely out of his mouth. Like Juan, Anastasius leaves unwillingly the warm and familiar East for the chill and strangeness of the West, accompanied only by his child Alexis, the one being in the world whom he loves unselfishly:

"The people of Europe seemed heartless, the virtues of the Franks frigid, the very crimes of the West dull and prosaic; and I was like a plant which, reared in all the warmth of a hothouse, is going to be launched into . . . chilling blasts and nipping frosts. . . . Perhaps on the further borders of the chilly Neva, it may be my fate to cherish the last remembrance of Ionia and of Chios!" [41]

Anastasius' introduction into the society of Naples offers many parallels to Juan's experiences in England: intrigue in the *haut monde*, wits at the dinner table, the frenzies of romantic poets and blues, even a ghost which turns out to be substantial. M. de Silva, in a long diatribe against the corruptions of Rome, utters many of the thoughts Byron expresses in his castigation of England. Hope, like Byron, was using the observations of the traveler from another civilization to satirize his own.

While we are considering comparatively obscure works which have been nominated as sources of Byron's *Don Juan*, we should take a look at the Abate Casti's *Tartar Poem*,[42] credited with having suggested the St. Petersburg episode. There is no direct evidence that Byron knew this *ottava rima* epic in twelve cantos; but it seems probable, in view of his enthusiasm for Casti's other poems and the general similarity between the adventures of Casti's hero and *Don Juan*, that Byron had read it. Ugo Foscolo's much admired article in the *Quarterly Review*, April 1819,[43] on the *Narrative and Romantic Poems of the Italians*, would have told him something about it. Foscolo wrote of Casti:

"After amusing himself with kings in comedy and heroes in tragedy, he renewed his satires upon royalty in the person of Catherine the Second; with whom he made free in a very long poem entitled *Tartaro*. Casti succeeded the Abbate Metastasio as *Poeta Cesareo,* and lived at Vienna in high favour with Joseph the Second, who used to set him on against the monks and friars. When the 'Poema Tartaro' appeared the Emperor Joseph was on very ill terms with the Empress Catherine; but when each had got a slice of the kingdom of Poland, they made up their differences. The Czarina insisted that the Poeta Cesareo should be turned away; and Casti was banished from Vienna: but the emperor directed that the poet's pension should continue payable during the remainder of his life. Casti, with a spirit which would have honoured a better man, refused the gift, and when Joseph remitted the money to him, he would not touch it. The pecuniary losses consequent upon the publication of the Tartaro were not made up in fame. Foreigners did not relish it, and the Italians did not understand it; for they knew nothing of the court of St. Petersburgh beyond what they read in the newspapers. Neither did it add much to Italian literature. The style is unimpassioned, and the diction without grace or purity. But the poem abounds with point, and it succeeded amongst certain readers, in the same way that *small wits* take in society. They amuse for a moment because they flatter the bad passions of the human heart, and they end by becoming tedious." [44]

The *Poema Tartaro* is supposed to be another chivalric epic of the middle ages. The imaginary hero, Tommaso Scardassale, a handsome blond young Irishman, sells all his goods and sets out on a Crusade with other cavaliers from all over Europe. They go to Constantinople to support Baldwin II, and thence to Palestine, where Tommaso is captured in a battle against the Sultan of Egypt. The Sultan sends him, among a dozen of the handsomest and youngest of the Christian captives, as a present to the Caliph of Bagdad. At Bagdad, he works as a gardener slave in the pleasure grounds of the seraglio, and thus sees and falls in love with Zelmira, a lady of the harem. The Caliph, however, finds Tommaso so agreeable, or so dangerous, that he decides to promote him to the office of chief eunuch in the seraglio; Tommaso is saved from the dreadful fate only by escaping with Zelmira and his faithful valet. They journey to Circassia, and there fall in with Battù Khan, a marshal of Tartary.

Thus far the first canto has been sprightly comic-epic, but from this point the tone of the poem changes. Tartary stands for Russia, where Casti spent some years as an ambassador at Catherine II's court, and all the great and near-great of St. Petersburg and the warlike events of the first years of her reign are described and satirized in the remaining cantos. The love interest of Zelmira is shelved, for she is given by Battù to his little companion Prince Mengo, and she does not turn up again until the end of Canto XII, when chance makes her and Mengo the new rulers of Russia. The intervening cantos are all concerned with the actual eighteenth century Russia, a combination of travelogue and political and religious satire.

Tommaso goes with Battù to Caracora (St. Petersburg); there he is introduced at court and shown the sights of the city by a young Greek, Siveno, a well-instructed blasé cynic, who enters the poem merely to be Tommaso's guide, and then leaves it for good. As Siveno has predicted, Tommaso is preferred by Battù to Potemkin, who looks him over (in the bath) as a candidate for the next "Gentleman of the week" for Catherine. Potemkin is delighted with him, and writes a note to Catherine, sending Tommaso off to deliver it to her. Catherine reads the note, which causes her to smile and laugh to herself, approaches Tommaso to inspect him better, and promptly turns him over to Turfana, her lady in charge of all such candidates, or "L'Eprouveuse," as Byron calls her. The interview between Turfana and Tommaso is reported in full, and Tommaso is installed forthwith in Catherine's favor. Not until after all these preliminaries and the first weeks of Tommaso's servitude have passed, does the poet come to the great birthday ball, at which the public and the court first get a glimpse of the new favorite and whisper and speculate about him. Byron has telescoped all this dry, naked storytelling of Casti's to make one graceful, brilliant scene.

Tommaso is made of tougher material than Don Juan. Their predecessor Lanskoi, it is true, as Casti notes:

> "Divenuto era smunto, e quasi tisico,
> E i dover della carica annuale
>   Posto quasi l'avean di vita in risico,
> Onde per lo consiglio universale,
>   D'ogni esperto Dottor, Medico fisico,
> Andò a viaggiar negli stranieri stati,
> E il numero aumentò de riformati."

The same fate awaited Juan, but Tommaso, having no more sensibility, though a much more delicate looking frame, than any of Catherine's other aides-de-camp, flourished and outlived the wars and rebellions, and was finally disgraced only by the slander of Potemkin. From that point, Casti's poem leaves history and reverts to epic fancy.

Casti may have taught Byron, if he needed any instruction, to despise Catherine and all her works. He may have suggested to him the possibilities of double meanings and puns, even international ones, which are the only forms of humor in Casti's work, once it settles down to serious satire and description. Certain phrases and stanzas in Casti are echoed in Byron; for example:

> "Candida verità, figlia del Cielo,
>   Oh! se vederti occhio mortal potesse
> Senza ornamento alcun, senza alcun velo!
>   Oh! se scriver la storia ognun volesse
> Al par di quei che scrissero il Vangelo,
>   Nè tanto il ben col mal si confondesse,
> Oh! quanti, che di grandi il titol ebbero,
> Piccoli agli occhi nostri apparirebbero!"

The reflections of Tommaso on his curious adventures, after he has become the Empress's favorite, would be congenial to Byron and his hero:

> " . . . guari non fu,
> Che di Soria nel sanguinoso piano
>   Caddi de' Saraceni in schiavitù;
> E venni poi per vari casi in mano
>   Di Melech, del Califfo, e di Battù;
> Anzi, che Dio ne scampi insino un bruco,
> Poco mancò che divenissi eunuco.
>
> "E giunto poscia in sì lontan paesi
>   Tosto la sorte mia cangiò di scena,

Ed a cotanta altezza a un tratto ascesi
  Che agli occhi miei creder lo posso appena;
Per quai sentier non preveduti, o intesi
  Il lor chieco destin gli uomini mena!
Commedia è il mondo, e l'uom dal caso pende
Chi sa qual fine la mia sorte attende!"

But the general intention and scope of Casti's poem are quite outside those of Byron's and fail to be realized with the success that attended Byron's efforts.

CHAPTER EIGHT

The Literary Background of Don Juan: Ideas

1

Byron was indebted to literature not only for suggestions which enriched the situations, the sentiments, and the characterizations of *Don Juan*, but for the cultivation of many of his ideas. Ideas came to him, he freely acknowledged, as much from his reading as from his own observation of life, and these developed into convictions when he had tested them by experience and introspection.

The literary filiation of his ideas about war in *Don Juan* clearly demonstrates this alliance between literature and life. Omitting Shakespeare, though it should be noted that *Henry IV* and *Hamlet* were among Byron's favorite sources of quotation, we can begin with Burton, whose introduction to the *Anatomy of Melancholy* gives faithful expression in almost all its pages to Byron's inmost beliefs.

The stuff of the English Democritus' ideas is, however, as old as Lucian's *Menippus* and Juvenal's *Tenth Satire*, which were also direct sources of inspiration to Byron. Menippus descends to Hades to ask blind Teiresias what is the best way of life. He learns, like Hamlet, that the dead are indistinguishable from one another:

"So, with many skeletons lying together, all alike staring horridly and vacuously and baring their teeth, I questioned myself how I could distinguish Thersites from handsome Niraus, or the mendicant Irus from the king of the Phaeacians, or the cook Pyrrhias from Agamemnon."

Teiresias answers Menippus' question:

"The life of the common sort is best, and you will act more wisely if you stop speculating about heavenly bodies and discussing final causes and first causes, spit your scorn at those clever syllogisms, and counting all that sort of thing nonsense, make it always your sole object to put the present to good use and to hasten on your way, laughing a great deal and taking nothing seriously." [1]

Byron concludes the stanzas on Death at the beginning of *Don Juan*, Canto IX, bridging the transition from Camp to Court:

139

"And thus Death laughs, — it is sad merriment,
    But still it *is* so; and with such example
Why should not Life be equally content
    With his Superior, in a smile to trample
Upon the nothings which are daily spent
    Like bubbles on an Ocean much less ample
Than the Eternal Deluge, which devours
Suns as rays — worlds like atoms — years like hours?"

His thoughts wander on through the natural associations of this Lucianic (and Lucretian) passage, to Shakespeare's Hamlet, Alexander's
fame, Burton's object in life (good health and a sound digestion), the
problem of being, Montaigne's skepticism, and Newton's intellectual
modesty.

"It is a pleasant voyage perhaps to float,
    Like Pyrrho, on a sea of speculation;
But . . .
        . . . a calm and shallow station
Well nigh the shore, where one stoops down and gathers
Some pretty shell, is best for moderate bathers."

But skepticism for Byron, as for Burton, was only the cause for all the
greater moral indignation at the crimes and follies of human beings.
"*Lykanthropy*," Byron goes on, he comprehends, but he cannot for the
life of him imagine why men accuse him of misanthropy, when all he
writes is to show men the truth about mankind.[2]

Burton's thought on this Lucianic basis includes in the wonderful pro-
liferations of "Democritus to his reader" a long diatribe against wars
of conquest, chief among the vain follies of humanity:

"What would [Democritus] have said to see, hear, and read so many bloody
battles, so many thousands slain at once, such streams of blood able to turn
mills, *unius ob noxam furiasque* (through the mad guilt of one person), or to
make sport for princes, without any just cause, 'for vain titles' (saith Austin),
'precedency, some wench, or such-like toy, or out of desire of domineering,
vainglory, malice, revenge, folly, madness,' goodly causes all, *ob quas uni-
versus orbis bellis et caedibus misceatur* (for plunging the whole world into
an orgy of war and slaughter), whilst statesmen themselves in the meantime
are secure at home, pampered with all delights and pleasures, take their ease,
and follow their lusts, not considering what intolerable misery poor soldiers
endure, their often wounds, hunger, thirst, etc., the lamentable cares, tor-
ments, calamities, and oppressions that accompany such proceedings, they
feel not, take no notice of it. 'So wars are begun, by the persuasion of a few
deboshed, hair-brain, poor, dissolute, hungry captains, parasitical fawners,
unquiet Hotspurs, restless innovators, green heads, to satisfy one man's
private spleen, lust, ambition, avarice, etc.'; *tales rapiunt scelerata in proelia
causae* (such causes bring on war with all its crimes). *Flos hominum* (the

flower of mankind), proper men, well proportioned, carefully brought up, able both in body and mind, sound, led like so many beasts to the slaughter in the flower of their years, pride, and full strength, without all remorse and pity, sacrificed to Pluto, killed up as so many sheep, for devils' food, 40,000 at once." [3]

Burton continues, enumerating famous sieges and slaughters, the "engines, fireworks, and whatsoever the devil could invent to do mischief with 2,500,000 iron bullets shot of 40 pound weight, three or four millions of gold consumed." How may Nature, God, and all good men expostulate at this perversion of "an harmless, quiet, a divine creature! . . . yet . . . these are the brave spirits, the gallants of the world, these admired alone, triumph alone, have statues, crowns, pyramids, obelisks to their eternal fame. . . ." Burton dilates in a crescendo of rage on the slaughters, treachery, waste, rapine, maiming, murder, and rape of war: "So abominable a thing is war . . . the scourge of God, cause, effect, fruit, and punishment of sin, and not . . . the mere pruning of the human race, as Tertullian calls it, but *ruina*. . . ." Civil wars are particularly "feral" — "ten thousand families rooted out. . . . 'Why do the Gentiles so furiously rage?' saith the Prophet David. . . . But we may ask, why do the Christians so furiously rage? . . . Would this, think you, have enforced our Democritus to laughter, or rather made him turn his tune . . . and weep with Heraclitus. . . ."

But this is not all, nor even the worst, says Burton. For though "valor is much to be commended in a wise man," the world mistakes for the most part:

"They term theft, murder, and rapine, virtue. . . . 'They commonly call the most hair-brain bloodsuckers, strongest thieves, the most desperate villains, treacherous rogues, inhuman murderers . . . valiant and renowned soldiers, possessed with a brute persuasion of false honour,' as Pontus Heuter in his Burgundian History complains. By means of which it comes to pass that daily so many voluntaries offer themselves, leaving their sweet wives, children, friends, for sixpence (if they can get it) a day . . . to get a name of valour, honour and applause, which lasts not neither, for it is but a mere flash this fame, and like a rose . . . 't is gone in an instant. Of fifteen thousand proletaries slain in a battle, scarce fifteen are recorded in history, or one alone, the general perhaps, and after a while his and their names are likewise blotted out, the whole battle itself is forgotten. . . . Which is yet more to be lamented, [the orators] persuade them this hellish course of life is holy, they promise heaven to such as venture their lives . . . in a sacred war."

"Such brutish stories" that "put a note of divinity upon the most cruel and pernicious plague of humankind," should be suppressed. Meanwhile,

". . . a poor sheep-stealer is hanged for stealing of victuals, . . . but a great man in office may securely rob whole provinces, undo thousands, pill and poll,

. . . enrich himself by spoils of the commons, be uncontrollable in his actions, and after all, be recompensed with turgent titles, honoured for his good service, and no man dare find fault, or mutter at it."

The reader will recognize in this outburst the source of many and many a passage in English poetry and prose which borrowed freely not only the ideas but even the words of Burton's most eloquent oration, as Burton had freely gathered and brought up to date the Juvenalian eloquence of centuries on this subject. A set piece on the madness of conquerors and the outrage of war became a classic necessity in eighteenth century verse. Combined with reflections on the careers of Louis XIV, Charles XII, and Frederick the Great, these set pieces in sermons, periodicals, and poems began to be associated with the problem of Greatness and Goodness, as well as with the mockery of fame.[4] Byron's *Don Juan*, Cantos VII–VIII, was heir to all of these, but let us single out those passages that we know Byron had most in mind in 1821, as he was meditating the future of his suspended poem.

Pope, always fresh in his recollection, was particularly so in the early weeks of 1821, while he was writing his pamphlets in the Bowles controversy. He had been rereading Pope in Campbell's *Specimens*, and no doubt continuing his reflections on the worth of "the little Queen Anne's man" as opposed to contemporary poets. In March 1821 he wrote Murray a letter in which he comments in detail on Pope's superior imagery and imagination in satire. It is not surprising to find how deeply Pope's lines in *The Essay on Man*, Epistle IV, had been absorbed by Byron:

> "Look next on Greatness: say where Greatness lies.
> 'Where but among the heroes and the wise?'
> Heroes are much the same, the point's agreed,
> From Macedonia's madman to the Swede;
> The whole strange purpose of their lives to find,
> Or make, an enemy of all mankind!
> Not one looks backward, onward still he goes,
> Yet ne'er looks further forward than his nose. . . .
> What's fame? a fancied life in others' breath;
> A thing beyond us, ev'n before our death. . . .
> All that we feel of it begins and ends
> In the small circle of our foes or friends;
> To all beside as much an empty shade,
> An Eugene living as a Caesar dead; . . .
> One self-approving hour whole years out-weighs
> Of stupid starers and of loud huzzas."[5]

At the same time, Byron was studying carefully Johnson's *Vanity of Human Wishes*, as he records in his Journal, January 9, 1821:

"Read Johnson's *Vanity of Human Wishes*, — all the examples and mode of giving them sublime, as well as the latter part, with the exception of an occasional couplet. . . . 'Tis a grand poem — and *so true!* — true as the 10th of Juvenal himself. The lapse of ages *changes* all things — time — language — the earth — the bounds of the sea — the stars of the sky, and every thing 'about, around, and underneath' man, *except man himself,* who has always been, and always will be, an unlucky rascal. The infinite variety of lives conduct but to death, and the infinity of wishes lead but to disappointment. All the discoveries which have yet been made have multiplied little but existence. An extirpated disease is succeeded by some new pestilence; and a discovered world has brought little to the old one. . . ." [6]

Byron is reading with application of Johnson's lines to modern life.

The introduction of the *Vanity of Human Wishes* leads at once to war, the prime example of folly in human ambitions. We are told to observe

> "How nations sink, by darling schemes oppress'd,
> When vengeance listens to the fool's request. . . .
> Impeachment stops the speaker's pow'rful breath,
> And restless fire precipitates on death.
>   But scarce observ'd, the knowing and the bold
> Fall in the gen'ral massacre of gold;
> Wide-wasting pest! that rages unconfin'd,
> And crouds with crimes the records of mankind. . . .
> Once more, Democritus, arise on earth,
> With cheerful wisdom and instructive mirth,
> See motley life in modern trappings dress'd,
> And feed with various fools th' eternal jest. . . ."

Byron had recently commented to Murray, when he heard of the death of his dentist Waite, on his abomination of Wellington and all such " 'bloody, blustering boobies' who gain a name by breaking heads and knocking out grinders." Johnson's pictures of Charles XII, Xerxes, and "the bold Bavarian, in a luckless hour" furnished his thoughts with ammunition for the Siege of Ismail.

With the invocation to Democritus to rise once more, Johnson's poem would further have reminded Byron of Burton, for though it is a free imitation of Juvenal's Tenth Satire, it draws upon the *Anatomy of Melancholy* even for subject matter, notably in the passage on the woes of scholars.[7] Byron sent off to Murray for a copy of that well-remembered book, and had the luck to get back several months later his own former copy, rescued from the sale.

Meanwhile Byron had been writing *Sardanapalus*, "which he had for some time meditated," basing it on Diodorus Siculus and Mitford's *Greece,* though he had known the story since his school-days. While he worked in that tragedy on the problems of luxury and courage, tyranny and revolution, he had to deal in real life with the plans for an Italian revolution against the Austrians. On the day he commenced *Sardana-palus*, he notes in his Journal that news has come:

"the *Powers* mean to war with the peoples. The intelligence seems positive — let it be so — they will be beaten in the end. The king-times are fast finishing. There will be blood shed like water, and tears like mist; but the peoples will conquer in the end. I shall not live to see it, but I foresee it." [8]

From the luxury-loving warrior-prince, and the causes of freedom and justice, he turned to *Cain;* in that, he enlarged the perspective on the problems of good and evil, murder and revolution, from the historical to the cosmic, under the influence of his interest in metaphysics, popular geology, and astronomy. Compare the passages in *Don Juan*, especially Canto IX, 37–40, where war is viewed in a geological and archaeological vista. Meanwhile, also, he had been reading Shelley's *Revolt of Islam*, an effort, unsuccessful Byron felt, inspired by the French Revolution, to condemn tyrants and war and to praise freedom and brotherhood.

In the autumn of 1821, Byron was rereading Fielding. Judging from the references in his letters on the way to Pisa, he ran through not only *Joseph Andrews*, but the *Miscellanies*, and he noted his reflections in his *Detached Thoughts*, early in November:

"They talk of Radicalism, Jacobinism, etc., in England (I am told), but they should turn over the pages of 'Jonathan Wild the Great.' The inequality of conditions, and the littleness of the great, were never set forth in stronger terms; and his contempt for Conquerors and the like is such, that, had he lived *now,* he would have been denounced in 'the Courier' as the grand Mouth-piece and Factionary of the revolutionists. And yet I never recollect to have heard this turn of Fielding's mind noticed, though it is obvious in every page." [9]

The influence of Lucian, Juvenal, Burton, and Pope on Fielding's mind is also obvious in the various pieces comprised in the *Miscellanies*. The thread of meditation on war and conquest, greatness and fame runs through many of them. The *Essay of True Greatness* contains a typical set piece on war. It is almost a miniature, a text, of Byron's Siege of Ismail. Men, Fielding says, refuse honor to the lean wolf for his conquests over the flocks, though famine is his motive,

> "While Man, not drove by Hunger from his Den,
> To Honour climbs o'er Heaps of murder'd Men.
> Shall ravag'd Fields, and burning Towns proclaim
> The Hero's Glory, not the Robber's Shame?
> Shall Thousands fall, and Millions be undone
> To glut the hungry Cruelty of one?

"Behold the Plain with human Gore grow red,
The swelling River heave along the Dead.
See, through the Breach the hostile Deluge flow,
Along it bears the unresisting Foe:
Hear, in each Street the wretched Virgin's Cries,
Her Lover sees her ravish'd as he dies.
The Infant wonders at its Mother's Tears,
And smiling feels its Fate before its Fears.
Age, while in vain for the first Blow it calls,
Views all its Branches lopp'd before it falls.
Beauty betrays the Mistress it should guard,
And, faithless, proves the Ravisher's Reward:
Death, their sole Friend, relieves them from their Ills,
The kindest Victor he, who soonest kills.
    "Could such Exploits as these thy Pride create?
Could these, O Philip's Son, proclaim thee great? . . .
Not on such Wings, to Fame did *Churchill* soar,
For *Europe* while defensive Arms he bore.
Whose Conquests, cheap at all the Blood they cost,
Sav'd Millions by each noble Life they lost. . . .
Thee, from the lowest Depth of Time, on high
Blazing, shall late Posterity descry;
And own the Purchase of thy glorious Pains,
While Liberty, or while her Name remains."

Fielding's imitations of Lucian's *Dialogues* contains a noteworthy
one between Alexander and Diogenes. Alexander has been preening himself on his conquests and slaughters, and Diogenes retorts that Alexander is no better than any deadly pestilence, whom men fear equally as a
source of death:

"Alexander: Thou seemest, to my Apprehension, to be ignorant, that in pro-
fessing this Disregard for the Glory I have so painfully achieved, thou art
undermining the Foundation of all that Honour, which is the Encouragement
to, and Reward of, every thing truly great and noble: For in what doth all
Honour, Glory, and Fame consist, but in the Breath of that Multitude, whose
Estimation with such ill-grounded Scorn thou dost affect to despise. . . .
What other Reward than this have all those Heroes proposed to themselves,
who rejecting the Enjoyments which Ease, Riches, Pleasure, and Power, have
held forth to them in their native Country, have deserted their Homes, and all
those Things which to vulgar Mortals appear lovely or desirable, and in
Defiance of Difficulty and Danger, invaded and spoiled the Cities and
Territories of others; when their Anger hath been provoked by no Injury,
nor their Hope inspired by the Prospect of any other Good than of this very
Glory and Honour, this Adoration of Slaves. . . ."

Diogenes retorts that Alexander does not know the meaning of true
Honour if indeed he finds it in the applause of Wretches, the Mob, who

are truly contemptible; Honour is actually self-approval for one's own
Wisdom and Virtue. Alexander asks him what his Wisdom and Virtue
consist in:

"Diogenes: Not in ravaging Countries, burning Cities, plundering and
massacring Mankind.
"Alexander: No, rather in biting and snarling at them."

Byron doubtless noted the Lucianic irony and surprise ending.

The classic passages in *Jonathan Wild* are so well-known as hardly
to require quotation. They occur *passim* in Jonathan's reflections on
Greatness and his career. He early decides that the Great Man is he who
hires the most hands to perform his will, whether Conquerors, absolute
Princes, Prime Ministers, or Prigs. Goodness, on the other hand, is only
the expression of pusillanimity and soft-wittedness. As for murder,
Jonathan soliloquizes:

"What is the Life of a single Man? Have not whole Armies and Nations been
sacrificed to the Humour of *One Great Man?* Nay, to omit that first Class of
Greatness, the Conquerors of Mankind, how often have Numbers fallen by a
fictitious Plot, only to satisfy the Spleen, or perhaps exercise the Ingenuity
of a Member of that second order of Greatness the Ministerial!"

In the grand climax, Fielding declares that Wild's career exceeds in
Greatness even those of some few Heroes, such as traitors, or Conquerors, "who have impoverished, pillaged, sacked, burnt, and destroyed
the Countries and Cities of their fellow Creatures, from no other Provocation than that of Glory."

The same motifs are repeated in *A Journey from this World to the
Next,* and in the *jeu d'esprit, An Essay on Nothing,* where to the nothingness of the ambition of conquerors and emperors is joined the nothingness of the ambition of the Miser, unless "he can shew us some substantial Good which this Fortune is to produce," — a sequence followed
likewise by Juvenal, Burton, and Byron.

Pope, Johnson, Fielding, and Burton occupied a prominent place in
Byron's thoughts during 1821, but they would draw in their train a host
of reminiscences of other writers. I could repeat many instances, as Burton would say — Smollett, for example, Swift, and Steele. But turning
to Voltaire, who shared with Pope the most important place in Byron's
models, we find the same condemnation of wars of conquest. Although
Voltaire cannot help admiring the fortitude and daring of Charles "the
Great," in his biography of the Swedish conqueror, he condemns severely
Charles's wars of conquest, which laid waste the overrun territories and
reduced the conqueror's own country in men and money to the point of
perishing. He concludes that Charles XII was not at all a great man,

especially in comparison with his lifelong enemy, Peter the Great; for though Peter was equally cruel and aggressive, he is exempt from the charge of *wanton* highway robbery by the fact that his wars always enriched his country in material wealth and culture. Byron's interest in this biography is marked by his drawing upon it for the setting and story of *Mazeppa*, the famous Polish-Cossack ally of Charles XII.

In his tales, Voltaire elevates his moralizing on war to a philosophical level, in his search for the answer to the problem of the existence of evil and misery. In *Babouc's Vision, the World as it is*, the first spectacle that Babouc sees upon entering Persia is a senseless war between the Persians and the Indians over a trifling cause — a war in which brutality and treachery abound, while the individual soldiers on both sides fight heroically with no notion of their cause. Babouc interviewed the commanders in either army, and

"learned of actions of generosity, greatness of soul, humanity, which astounded and delighted him.

" 'Inexplicable human beings!' cried he. 'How can you unite so much baseness and grandeur, so many virtues and crimes?'

"Meanwhile peace was declared. The leaders of the two armies, neither of whom had gained the victory but on the contrary had shed the blood of so many men for their own interests, went off to seek rewards in their own Courts. The peace was praised in the public prints which announced nothing less than the return of virtue and felicity to the earth."

Babouc observes the same duality, the same mixture of good and evil, in all the institutions and customs of Persepolis, and concludes that "if all is not well, all is tolerable."

In *Candide*, however, the first overwhelming misfortune of the hero is caused by the carnage and rapine of war, which is recounted in a spirit of utter revolt against its brutality. The fantasy, grotesque emphasis, and exaggeration of this counterblast against false optimism would not appeal to Byron's sense of proportion and of fact, but he thoroughly agreed with the conclusion: "that man was born to live in the convulsions of distress or in the lethargy of boredom," and that the only solution to render life even tolerable is to work without argument or curiosity about problems beyond man's solving — to "cultivate his garden."

All these views of the problem of war have been largely from the moral and philosophical standpoint, but on the economic side of the question, Byron certainly knew the calm commercialism of the Whig viewpoint on the extravagance of conquest.[10] He probably also sympathized with Italian antimilitaristic propaganda, such as that expressed in Goldoni's comedy *La Guerra*. He must certainly have been acquainted with the most famous antimilitaristic statement of his own day, Benjamin Constant's pamphlet entitled *de l'Esprit de Conquête et de l'Usurpation*.[11]

Even if he had never read Constant's political works, he would have known the general tenor of his ideas from Madame de Staël and her friends in London, and again at Coppet in 1816, where Constant was a frequent topic of conversation.

The phrasing of *de l'Esprit de Conquête* makes it seem uncannily appropriate for our contemporary world, and underlines the resemblance of our times to the Napoleonic. It does not dwell on the horrors of war, but reasons on the impossibility of accomplishing any good by a war of conquest in the modern commercial world. It looks forward to the united nations and to the outlawing of war. But, most important for Byron, it dwells upon the hypocrisy incidental to war. When a nation sets out on a war of conquest, Constant says, it throws itself backward to a state of barbarous tyranny complicated by a disgusting hypocrisy:

"Authority has then to accomplish, in the intellectual faculties of the mass of its subjects, the same effect as in the moral qualities of the military. It must exert itself to banish all logic from the mind of the one, while it tries to stifle all humanity in the heart of the other: all words lose their sense; that of moderation must presage violence; that of justice must announce inequity. The right of nations must become a code of expropriation and of barbarism: every civilized notion which the light of centuries has introduced into the relations of societies, as into those of individuals, must be suppressed anew. The human race must revert to those times of devastation which seem to us the opprobrium of history. Hypocrisy alone must accomplish this difference; and that hypocrisy must be more corrupting than anyone can imagine; for the lies of authority are evil not only when they lead astray and deceive the people: they are all the more so when they do not deceive them." [12]

With all these thoughts in mind, Byron set out deliberately to write an anti-*Iliad*, and cast about for an historical source, which he found in the Marquis Gabriel de Castelnau's *Essai sur l'Histoire Ancienne et Moderne de la Nouvelle Russie*, Paris, 3 vols., 1820. Castelnau gives a rapid, detailed story of the Siege of Ismail, with all the facts as Byron uses them and in almost the same words. E. H. Coleridge, in his edition of *Don Juan*, has collated the parallel passages, but Coleridge's quotations do not show the general drift of Castelnau's narrative, which reveals its ideal appropriateness as a vehicle for Byron's satire. In the first place, it is an eyewitness account, compounded from a report of the siege made by a Russian officer who fought at it, from the journal of the young Duc de Richelieu, and from letters of the generals and Potemkin, which Castelnau claims to have in his hands. These ensure its authenticity, and set it in opposition to all the poetic accounts of sieges, dear to epic, from Homer and Tasso to Voltaire's *Henriade*. In the second place, Castelnau pretends to be writing a new sort of history — a kind that Byron approved — that not only exhibits the manners of a nation but includes those details of which historians are often so blamably negligent. Commenting on the foolhardy courage of the Russians under Suvaroff in attempting the assault of Ismail when their numbers were inferior to the Turks, Castelnau writes:

"Without that disposition [to obtain glory and honor at any cost], without the success which surmounted dangers easy to conceive, we would certainly not have entered into details at such length; but this assault of Ismail is an event to be noted among the most gallant of its kind; it gives an exact idea of the nation which undertook it, of the general who commanded it, and it honors all the military who took part in it. That the historian should slide over facts with little notice, that he should content himself with indicating and not bearing down upon them, is so many lines the less which he often spares the ennui of those who read; but that he should render an exact account of an action allied to heroism is a duty which he ought to force himself to fulfill well." [13]

Castelnau relishes the heroism and the action, for to him war is glorious. He mentions the generals and the men of rank personally and recounts laconically the suffering of the soldiers as part of the tactics of the battle. But the memoirs which he quotes are not so indifferent to the horrors of carnage and pillage, and Castelnau does not attempt to reconcile the marked difference between their eyewitness viewpoint and his own academic attitude. Two paragraphs forming a brief word picture of the sack of Ismail end thus:

"Let us turn our regard from the frightful spectacle of which we have only given an idea; let us pass over in silence acts of ferocity worse than death; let us draw the curtain on the disgusting excesses and the crimes impossible to prevent when the fury of the soldiers could not be restrained."

He goes on, in apology for the carnage, to say that it had nothing to do with the kindly nature of the Russians; it was the inevitable expression of their rage at the losses and resistance sustained in taking the city. On the whole, says Castelnau, the Siege of Ismail is unique in showing the exploit of 23,000 men (of whom over 8,000 were killed) against 36,000 in a fortified place (over 38,000 Turks were killed, counting civilians), and offers "to Europe the most handsome military deed which its annals could celebrate." This was an invitation to irony which Byron could not resist.

The main purpose of *Don Juan*, Cantos VII–VIII, is therefore a satiric attack upon wars of conquest, the major crime of civilization. On the other hand, the Siege of Ismail is only an episode in the experiences of Don Juan. Byron shows in these cantos what he had learned from the novels of Scott in the conduct of historical fiction. Without losing sight of the fortunes and characterization of his fictional hero, he manages to blend them into the historical narrative — the epic sweep of the siege and the sack, the portrait of Suvaroff, and the sketches of the other historical characters. Like Scott, he heightens, expands, and realizes in detail all the data in the source narrative.

In these efforts of imagination, he was inspired not only by the novel but by the epic. We have already mentioned the episode of Leila's rescue with its echo of Marmontel's novel. Even more strikingly, the episode of the Tartar Khan and his five sons, who sold their lives so dearly, reflects epic inspiration. Castelnau relates the story briefly with no elaboration, but Byron's expanded version of it recalls, not only his own earlier attempt at the same scene in Minotti's fight, as he "so gallantly bore the brunt of the fray," [14] but the episode of Latinus and his five sons in Tasso's Siege of Jerusalem.[15] Ginguené in his account of the episodes and characters chosen by Tasso to illustrate the two camps, Moslem and Christian, singles out this one of Latinus and his sons to narrate in full.[16] Thus Byron had recently been reminded of that heroic story. Like Latinus, Byron's old Khan sees his sons perish one after the other and feels himself at last childless and alone; with a final desperate spring upon his enemies, he catches his death blow and

"In one wide wound poured forth his soul at once."

Tasso's passage ends in a simile likening the fall of Latinus to that of a sturdy tree, and Byron echoes this figure in Canto VIII, 116. The coincidence of such passages in Castelnau and Tasso (compare also Byron's chief Pasha, who surrendered at last with oriental phlegm, and Tasso's wily Soldan of Jerusalem) would draw a cloud of epic reminiscences and enhance the value of Byron's Siege of Ismail to his readers. For the mingling of the heroic deeds of individuals with the barbaric ferocity of the whole siege is part of the epic satire on unnatural civilization.

2

The last six cantos of *Don Juan*, the English section, were less directly influenced by literature than the first ten. Although the circumstances of plot and characters are thoroughly fictionalized, the thoughts, the feelings, and the situations were largely Byron's at firsthand. Nevertheless, there are some interesting correspondences to be traced in his reading, which help to locate *Don Juan* XI–XVI in its proper literary setting.

In the first place, memoirs contributed to the pattern and the spirit of these cantos. The fine lines that separate the novel from biography and biography from memoirs are perhaps hard to define. All three were favorite types of reading with Byron. But the principal virtue of memoirs is that they describe beneath an infinity of ephemeral details, not individuals, but a real society and the spirit and ideals that actuate it. De Grammont's memoirs, for instance, convey the gaiety, essential health, and rude vivacity of the English court of Charles II. Grimm's expose the intellectuality, the sentimentality, and the decay and new life fermenting together in pre-Revolutionary France. The anecdotes, the portraits, the events recorded combine to impart to the reader the essential atmosphere in a given society at a given time.

Byron was keenly aware of this function of memoir writing. He wrote to the Earl of Blessington:

"I return the Count D'Orsay's Journal, which is a very extraordinary production, and of a most melancholy truth in all that regards high life in England. . . . The most singular thing is, *how* he should have penetrated *not* the *fact,* but the *mystery* of the English *ennui* at two-and-twenty. I was about the same age when I made the same discovery, in almost precisely the same circles, — (for there is scarcely a person mentioned whom I did not see nightly or daily, and was acquainted more or less intimately with most of them,) — but I never could have described it so well. *Il faut être Français,* to effect this.

"But he ought also to have been in the country during the hunting season, with 'a select party of distinguished guests,' as the papers term it. He ought to have seen the gentlemen after dinner (on the hunting days), and the soiree ensuing thereupon, — and the women looking as if they had hunted, or rather been hunted; and I could have wished that he had been at a dinner in town, which I recollect at Lord Cowper's — small, but select, and composed of the most amusing people. The dessert was hardly on the table, when, out of twelve, I counted *five asleep.* . . .

"Altogether, your friend's Journal is a very formidable production. . . . I have read the whole with great attention and instruction. . . . I showed it . . . to a young Italian lady of rank, . . . and she was delighted with it, and says that she has derived a better notion of English society from it than from all Madame de Staël's metaphysical disputations on the same subject, in her work on the Revolution." [17]

The diversity of subjects and pictures in the latter cantos of *Don Juan,* informed as they are with satiric purpose, has in a broader sense an affinity with memoir writing. It is Byron's attempt to sum up a real society, at the same time that he is satirizing it and writing a novel based on its realities.

A brief little volume of *Essays and Sketches . . . by a Gentleman who has left his Lodgings,* the anonymous production of Moore's friend, Lord John Russell, may have contributed some specific suggestions. Byron told Lady Blessington that he had been reading and enjoying them; they were excellent in detail, he thought, but on too small a scale. These papers contain sprightly descriptions of the London social season. Two long paragraphs describing a London Ball — the crush, the

inability to meet one's friends, the hostess ready to sink with fatigue —
closely parallel the stanzas in *Don Juan*, XI, 67–72. There is an essay
on fortune-hunting mammas who entrap young heirs into marrying their
daughters, "making society a cattle fair," a practice which "produces
in the end deceit amongst girls, and suspicion in young men." Compare
Don Juan, XII, 58–61. Other chapters comment on the corrupt prac-
tices of political career men, and the arithmetical legerdemain of the
Chancellors of the Exchequer. But these were commonplaces of the contemporary novel and journalism.

The topics for discussion in periodicals, indeed, are a rich source for
many of the digressions and allusions in *Beppo* and *Don Juan*. A perusal of the Quarterly List of New Publications in the *Edinburgh Review*, for instance, the issue of January 1820, suggests that here are
the points of departure for many of Byron's ramblings on contemporary
subjects: medicine, political economy, subjects under debate in Parliament and in religious synods, Ireland, slavery, post roads, travels to
the North Pole in search of a northwest passage, descriptions of country
seats, indicating the revival of interest in Gothic architecture, and gay
reviews of recent books on French cookery and the science of the gour-
met. Journals of the *Edinburgh Review* type are, in fact, a kind of public memoirs. It is a measure of the sureness of Byron's taste, the integrity
of his mind, that the journalistic topics of his poem require as little foot-
noting as they do, and seem fresh and interesting after the lapse of more
than a hundred years.

The subject of the marriage market, important in English fiction since
the days of Fanny Burney and greatly to be expanded by Victorian
novelists, has, like the indictment of war, a Juvenalian background.
Fielding touched on its main themes in his epistle *To a Friend on the
Choice of a Wife*, reflecting to some extent the ideas of the sixth satire
of Juvenal, which he translated later in the same volume of the *Miscellanies*:

> "Some sterner Foes to Marriage bold aver,
> That in this Choice a Man must surely err:
> Nor can I to this Lottery advise,
> A thousand Blanks appearing to a Prize.
> Women by Nature form'd too prone to Ill,
> By Education are made proner still,
> To cheat, deceive, conceal each genuine Thought,
> By Mothers, and by Mistresses are taught.
> The Face and Shape are first the Mother's Care;
> The Dancing-Master next improves the Air.
> To these Perfections add a Voice most sweet;
> The skill'd Musician makes the Nymph compleat.

"Thus with a Person well equipp'd, her Mind
Left, as when first created, rude and blind,
She's sent to make her Conquests on Mankind.
But first inform'd the studied Glance to aim,
Where Riches shew the profitable Game:
How with unequal Smiles the Jest to take,
When Princes, Lords, or Squires, or Captains speak;
These Lovers careful shun, and those create;
And Merit only see in an Estate."

Fanny Burney, representative of a host of women novelists in her time, elaborated these themes, illustrating them from the actualities of daily practice, and clustering around them subordinate themes on all the other malpractices of fashionable life. The fashionable, or "silver fork," novels were well known to Byron; they must have constituted a large portion of those "four thousand novels" he claims to have read before 1807. In *Don Juan* XI–XVI, he drew heavily upon their types and themes: the knowing duenna, the marriageable bachelor, the "drapery-misses," the blues, the desperate dandies, the complacent husbands, the matchmaking relatives, the dissatisfied wives.

The Gothic novel, however, comes in for a greater share of burlesquing attention. The description of Norman Abbey, fond though it is, is nevertheless with its details of architecture, grounds, and furnishings, a hit at Gothic novel descriptions, even at the novels of Scott. Byron concludes it:

"Oh, reader! if that thou canst read, — and know
'T is not enough to spell, or even to read,
To constitute a reader — there must go
Virtues of which both you and I have need; —
Firstly, begin with the beginning — (though
That clause is hard); and secondly, proceed:
Thirdly, commence not with the end — or sinning
In this sort, end at last with the beginning.

"But, reader, thou hast patient been of late,
While I, without remorse of rhyme, or fear,
Have built and laid out ground at such a rate,
Dan Phoebus takes me for an auctioneer.
That Poets were so from their earliest date,
By Homer's 'Catalogue of ships' is clear;
But a mere modern must be moderate —
I spare you then the furniture and plate."

Incidentally, the four stanzas following the description of Newstead with its gently humorous close, form a delightful burlesque of "nature-poetry" like Keats's *Ode to Autumn*.

The principal resemblance between *Don Juan* and the Gothic novel is, of course, the ghost scenes in the sixteenth canto. To celebrate his twenty-first birthday, Byron gave a house party at Newstead for several of his college friends. One of the pranks that contributed to their merriment was a bit of ghostly faking that Hobhouse recalled years later in his journal:

"On Tuesday, I set off for Nottingham, and passed by Newstead. . . . When I was admitted I was shown up into the old gallery, then refitted, and scarcely to be recognised. It was there that Lord Byron placed the old stone coffin found in the cloisters; and I well recollected that, passing through the gloomy length of it late one night, I heard a groan proceeding from the spot. I went to the coffin, and a figure rose from it, dressed in a cloak and cowl, and blew out my candle. . . . It was my friend C. S. Matthews." [18]

From this incident, the local legends, the atmosphere of the dilapidated old Abbey, and Byron's bump of superstition, grew not only Don Juan's vision of the Black Friar, but the earlier ghostly vision in *Lara*. A comparison of these two episodes shows the essential differences between Byron's romantic and his realistic, satiric muses, both under the influence of Gothic novel fashions.

The scene and the circumstances in both poems are identical, but in *Lara*, the details emphasized in evoking a ghostly atmosphere are feverishly heightened and vaguely localized, while in *Don Juan*, they are sharply and matter-of-factly defined. Lara and Juan both turn from a contemplation of the moonlight, the lake, and the stream, to walk in the shadowy gallery, under the portraits of grim Knights and pictured Saints. Juan hears a sound like a mouse rustling in the corner, and is petrified to behold the hooded figure pass him three times, glancing on him a bright eye. Lara sees nothing except his vastly enlarged shadow on the walls, but some nameless horror causes him, or an unworldly visitant, to shriek and rouse the whole house; he falls down in a deathlike trance from which he is recovered with difficulty. Juan recovers his senses unaided, finds that his eyes still work all right, reads an old newspaper to compose his mind, and goes to bed and to sleep without causing any disturbance. A reluctance to speak of their experience, however, and an effort to hide any traces of perturbation mark the behavior of both heroes the morning after.

Thus far the *Don Juan* ghost story is merely the *Lara* one seen through an unclouded, unemotional pair of eyes. *Lara*, which is pure Gothic in the manner of the *Castle of Otranto*, has been translated into the idiom of real life. The specter, or the supernatural appearance, is given equal credit in both poems. It belongs to the vast army of ghosts whom Gothic novelists loved to employ as monitors of dire events to come. In *Lara*, the supernatural experience is dropped — it has served its purpose — and the bloody and catastrophic events ensue. In *Don Juan*, like Mrs. Radcliffe's novels, or more properly like Monk Lewis's, the natural explanation of the supernatural is suggested in her Grace of Fitz-Fulke's impersonation of the ghost. Byron's treatment of this ghost-story is typically Don Juanesque; it is antisentimental and self-mocking, but it shows under a mask of skepticism, humor, and disillusionment, an undeniable will to believe.

3

Claude Fuess has noted the possibility that Byron in his description of the assemblage at Norman Abbey "was influenced to some extent by Thomas Love Peacock." [19] Whether it is influence or coincidence, the affinity between Byron's and Peacock's satires of society is well worth examining.

Byron's acquaintance with Peacock was only at second hand through Shelley, who sent Byron a copy of *Melincourt* as soon as it appeared in 1817. In 1821, out of all the pamphlets and articles occasioned by the first few cantos of *Don Juan*, the one that elicited a favorable response from Byron was "John Bull's" *Letter to the Right Hon. Lord Byron*. He admired the author's clever writing, full of "fun and ferocity," and was no doubt pleased by the comparison of *Don Juan* to Scott's novels and the suggestion that Byron should continue the poem by writing about England in the reign of George IV. Byron wrote to Murray to learn who was the author; he suspected Hobhouse, Peacock, and D'Israeli, possibly Washington Irving. But a few weeks later he had settled on Peacock, who learned from Shelley's letter, when Shelley was visiting Byron at Ravenna: "Lord B. thinks you wrote a pamphlet signed *John Bull;* he says he knew it by the style resembling *Melincourt*, of which he is a great admirer." [20] Byron seems to have accorded Peacock the sincere flattery of imitation in his latter cantos of *Don Juan*, for his satire on England and English society shares many of the techniques and opinions of Peacock's.

Melincourt is perhaps not so successful a sample of the Peacockian recipe for the intellectual novel as his later *Crotchet Castle*, but it contains all the essential ingredients and is almost equally diverting. The most obvious mechanical resemblance between it and *Don Juan* is the use of the house party and the banquet as settings for the meeting of minds and of fools. Both Peacock and Byron use allegorical names, a trick borrowed from Greek and English satiric comedy. Peacock has his Rev. Mr. Grovelgrub, Mr. Hippy, Mr. Fax, Mr. Feathernest, and Mr. Mol(e)y Mystic (*i.e.* Coleridge) in his Cimmerian Lodge. Byron gives

us the young bard Rackrhyme, Sir John Pottledeep, the six Miss Raw-
bolds, and the Reverend Rodomont Precisian. All the types of politicians,
intellectuals, social climbers, fools and eccentrics, many of them thin
disguises for real people, make up the parties at Norman Abbey, Miss
Anthelia Melincourt's castle, and Mr. Forester's country house. Byron
complains, however, that

> "The days of Comedy are gone, alas!
>   When Congreve's fool could vie with Molière's *bête:*
> Society is smoothed to that excess,
>   That manners hardly differ more than dress."

He is unwilling to go to such lengths of fantasy as Peacock in his social
satire.

The interpolated songs in *Melincourt*, usually sung by Miss Anthelia
to the harp, recall Lady Adeline's ballad of the Norman Abbey friar.
The electioneering of Sir Oran-haut-ton and Mr. Sarcastic at the bor-
ough of Onevote, aided by the citizens of Novote, suggests Lord Henry's
electioneering, for it is based on the same principles of maintaining Place
and Patronage. The chess-dance, following Mr. Forester's Anti-
Saccharine banquet, recalls Byron's metaphor:

> "Good company's a chess-board — there are kings,
>   Queens, bishops, knights, rooks, pawns; the World's a game;
> Save that the puppets pull at their own strings,
>   Methinks gay Punch hath something of the same."

Dr. Killquick and his medicines, from whose fatal ministrations Mr.
Hippy is always just being saved by some lucky accident, are echoed in
Byron's gibes at the medical profession. Other butts of Peacock's incidental satire are the same that Byron loved to shoot at: Southey (Mr.
Feathernest), Wordsworth (Mr. Paperstamp), Coleridge, the Legitimate Review (*i.e.* the *Quarterly*), and Lord Castlereagh, with his strange
jargon, especially the phrase "venerable feature."

The "plot" of Peacock's novel, like Byron's, is matchmaking. Anthelia,
the heiress, brought up like Aurora Raby in a truly unworldly fashion,
is looking around for a husband, and she becomes involved in Mrs. Pinmoney's matchmaking efforts on behalf of her nephew Sir Telegraph
and her daughter Miss Danaretta Contantina. *Melincourt*, like *Don
Juan*, contains strong satire on the marriage market, marriage *à la
mode*, the importance of money in making a good match, and the feeble
and pernicious education of fashionable women. Mrs. Pinmoney, incidentally, enumerates among other fads of the day, "a taste for enjoying the country in November, and wintering in London till the end of
the dog-days."

But the story of Anthelia and her suitors is only a narrative line on which to hang the main matters of *Melincourt*, contained in the discussions and diversions. Mr. Fax and Mr. Forester hold informal debates on political and social economy. Mr. Fax represents the theories of Malthus and Bentham, while Mr. Forester, the Rousseauistic philosopher and hero, holds less pedantic and more traditional views, relying on reason and the natural goodness of man. It is obvious where Peacock's sympathies lie. A whole chapter is concerned with the Principle of Population, and the intellectual climax of the book occurs in Chapter XL, "The Hopes of the World," in which the two gentlemen, just about to conclude successfully their rescue of the kidnapped Anthelia, sit down gravely to discuss with deep philosophy the future of England. Byron avoided this burlesque of reality by merely suspending his story while, as author, he digresses into philosophy, instead of trying to dramatize it in dialogue.

The thesis of Peacock's novel, demonstrated in these discussions and in the story of poor Desmond and his experiences with Mr. Vamp, the editor of the Legitimate Review, is that a politically corrupt society is being duped into hypocritical complacency by prating about morals. In the council of war held by the Legitimate Reviewers at Mainchance Villa, for example, the slogan "The church is in danger" is raised whenever reason threatens to take hold of the proceedings and defeat the sophistries of those defending the *status quo*. At Mr. Forester's banquet, Mr. Sarcastic delivers an oration against the power of Custom to entrench error and wickedness. Later comments in a more elegiac strain bewail the feebleness of natural feelings laid asleep by Custom.

"Vices of unfrequent occurrence stand sufficiently self-exposed in the insulation of their own deformity. The vices that call for the scourge of satire, are those which pervade the whole frame of society, and which, under some specious pretence of private duty, or the sanction of custom and precedent, are almost permitted to assume the semblance of virtue, or at least to pass unstigmatized in the crowd of congenial transgressions." [21]

This saying of Mr. Forester's represents the primary thesis of Byron's satire on society, and sums up the difference between the satire in Pope's poetry and that in Peacock's novels and Byron's *Don Juan*. "Manners now make men," says Byron; "Be not what you seem, but what you see." Byron will be content to live in exile with beautiful Truth, as long as error and hypocrisy rule in England. The same classicist admiration of reason, common sense, and moderation, tinged by Shaftsburian and Rousseauistic conceptions of the natural goodness of man and the pernicious influence of society, pervades both Peacock's and Byron's thought.

CHAPTER NINE

Conclusion

The confluence in *Don Juan* of literary motifs from every age and clime of European literature gives the poem the richness of its texture and the universality of its appeal. Here is the evidence that the mind of Byron, brooding on his own strange fortunes and explaining himself in the story of Don Juan, is the mind of a true poet. Imprisoned like every human being in the mystery of life on this planet, and that imprisonment made doubly bitter for him by the peculiarities of his physical nature and by his errors which he interpreted fatalistically, he could nevertheless give voice for common human nature to the mystery and the bitterness. That Byron the poet rose with such urbanity and such triumph over the limitations of Byron the man is the final act in the drama, the act which makes the drama a tragedy in the true sense.

What sustaining power literature brought to Byron's life, I have tried to indicate. In spite of his stormy and disrupted career, books were Byron's constant companions. They instructed him, steadied him, comforted him, fed his imagination, and enlarged his intellectual horizon. The role of books in his life is extremely important, though secondary to his intense personal experience.

To be a little fanciful, we might say that he behaved toward books as he did toward his friends and enemies, though more cavalierly, without the polish and restraint of manners. He trusted books rather naïvely, but he was rough with them. As Leigh Hunt recollected, the fiercely creased, double and triple dog-ears in books which Byron had read were symbolic of Byron's attitude toward them. Books were tools to be used, servants to supply the overwhelming needs of that amalgam of thought and feeling that was Byron's mind. The same arrogance, ruthlessness, and absorbing egotism are demonstrated here as in Byron's other relationships. But on the other hand, we find likewise the same awe, genuine admiration of excellence, envy and emulation of a recognized superior, the same tenderness, passionate opinionated loyalty, and hard commonsense.

Useful, informational reading appealed to Byron, but, as with most of us, to a less degree than the reading of poetry and fiction. Byron's commonsense told him how to acquire information by means of short

cuts. He relied on historical and biographical dictionaries and on "epit-
omes of information" like Burton's *Anatomy* and Aulus Gellius' *Attic
Nights*, and on rich historical surveys like Gibbon and Mitford. But the
power generated by such reading and rereading was certainly not secondary to what a lesser mind might have accomplished by more painful
study. The drudgery of study Byron usually avoided, though he undertook it from time to time, when his mind "needed something craggy to
break itself on," or when he had a definite purpose of composition in
view.

In poetry and fiction, the range, the catholicity, one might almost say
the tastelessness, of his choice of favorites reflect faithfully the division
of direction in his own poetic productions. Lucian, Juvenal, Lucretius,
Ariosto and Tasso, Pope and Scott, Rousseau and Voltaire — the mind
which could embrace all these at once was bound to be a divided mind
and to produce a mixed poetry. Byron's mind was autocratic and in-
capable of receiving a single decisive influence. Even Shelley, who had
the most far-reaching effect on him, could teach him only temporarily
and by indirection. Byron's intellectual integrity was stubborn; he
learned from opposition, from the pressure of circumstances, and from
the long percolation of ideas derived from books, colleagues, and personal experience. But his catholicity of taste was only an extreme case
of romantic eclecticism. Byron's library and his poetic principles and
practice demonstrate the clash of systems and tastes in all the world of
thought and of creative art at the meeting of the eighteenth and nineteenth centuries. Some poets and some thinkers were removed farther to
the right or to the left of the clash. Byron was squarely at its center.
He stayed there through his career, feeding on conflict, achieving poise
in the midst of opposing forces.

Byron read with intense vitality and awareness. He defined the chief
value of living as the feeling of being alive, and this full liveliness appears in the contemporaneity of his viewpoint toward books. He had a
strong sense of the past, enlarging as his studies went on to include
archaeology and geology. But he judged all the past, even the most remote, in the light of the present. To him, everything was vivid, near, and
personally applicable even in the most ancient books. What came out of
the presses from modern authors might be disappointingly inferior, but
it was immediately compared with all the literature of the past. For
Byron there is no division between poets, the great dead and the mere
living. The race of poets goes on uninterrupted; there is a tradition to
preserve, a right and wrong to uphold or to combat, a future to poetry.

The sense of competition increased Byron's urgency to know everything new. His avid interest in contemporary literature contains a de-

gree of amusing furtiveness and shame, which, however, a less candid nature than Byron's would never have revealed. In his mind, the hierarchy of the great, the near great, the passable average, and the unworthy is constantly ranged to join the similar hierarchy of past poets. He thought he knew where he belonged in that grouping — on a fairly low level, though he was ambitious to rise. One of his methods of rising was to exhibit himself publicly and associate himself privately with what he considered the best, the aristocracy of poets. But he did not deny himself the pleasure of absorbing what he thought the second- and third-rate too. What he could do with the second- and third-rate, when he adapted it for his own poetry, my analysis of *Don Juan* has indicated. In this, his practice was like Shakespeare's and many another English poet's.

Byron once confessed that his mind was a fragment, and that it was no wonder he produced fragments of poetry. Lord Ernle has called *Don Juan* "the least incomplete portrait of Byron himself," and perhaps its gigantic fragmentariness is the most characteristic feature of the portrait.

Why did Byron not complete this poem? Had he lost interest in it, or said all that he had to say? Had he lost interest in writing anything in the face of the call to action in Greece? My conviction is that he had carried Juan's story as far as he could on the basis of his present positive knowledge and belief. The introduction of the supernatural was a brake on his creative momentum, for it brought him up sharply against his inhibiting skepticism.

For sixteen cantos, skepticism had been held in suspense in the ruminative digressions, while the story marched on in positive conviction. But at the end of Canto XVI, Byron was confronted with a choice that he still did not feel ready to make: he had either to show Juan drifting toward disaster, as he had drifted in similar circumstances, or he had to show him maturing in character to make a heroic stand against circumstances, so that he might survive for his destined role as a hero of liberty. Juan's maturity could be based only on a conviction of the value of moral action, and that could spring either from "principles" or from experience. Juan had no principles, and very little experience of moral action; sudden maturity would be a rather too surprising development in his character. Byron's "principles," on the other hand, were unsettled by the chaotic state of his philosophic and religious thinking, and he had had less experience than he craved in positive moral action. I picture him as coming to the point in Juan's story over which his forecasting mind had been painfully hesitating for years, and having to postpone the completion of the poem until he had acquired more experience and a greater degree of certainty. He might have carried on the *satire* of *Don Juan* indefinitely, but the direction of the *story* required positive rather than antagonistic or oppugnant views.

Over and above this intellectual dilemma lay the terrifying emotional tangle. To go back in memory and merely to recount the conflicts and the bitter passions and remorse would have been a self-punishment not to be endured. But to attempt to extract their essence, to resolve the tangle, perhaps to blame himself by implication, to confess and repent publicly — Byron could not objectify that story, not in poetry.

Don Juan, for all its negations, is fundamentally an affirmative poem. In the analysis of the themes, I have dwelt on the moral earnestness, at the expense of the whimsicality, mockery, humor, and the sometimes rather low forms of verbal wit, to justify Byron's claim that he was writing "a most moral poem." His earliest aim, a poem "to giggle and make giggle" (a phrase he borrowed from Ginguené's description of Pulci), persisted, but it was the comedian's method of conveying grave truths.

Like his master Pope, Byron felt a primary and almost exclusive concern with human nature and human society. Though he dabbled unceasingly in metaphysical speculation, he postponed defining and elaborating abstractions, from a hard-headed conviction that he could know only what came to him through his senses. He cared supremely for reality, and in one sense, the outward show of things is the only reality for him; but he knew that in a truer sense, there must be abstract reality behind the outward show. This was what he was searching for and what he partially found. For there are abstract conceptions at the back of his individualizing. While the behavior of human beings is the important object of his observation, abstract morality is the center of his universe. His cynicism, if at bottom he has any, springs from his ideal of perfection in human nature which he sees everywhere betrayed by frailty and ignorance. He has the preternaturally clear sight and just sense of proportion that belong to the satirist and the humorist, and also to the perfectionist.

Paradoxically for a poet, and especially for one who affirmed the power of the word, Byron distrusted verbiage. Verbal explanations and systematizations may satisfy some minds, but action is what counts. Life, for him, is made up of the action of feelings and the action of deeds, and manifests itself in a pageant of tangible effects. Time and change subdue all these appearances ("all things are a show"), but the mind of man, the source of feeling and action, is eternal and unchangeable. The mind with its innate feelings is for Byron the manifestation of a central, unshakable Godhead, the reason that, for all his skepticism, he could and did frequently affirm his belief in God, in truth, in right, and in immortality. God is a moral being, and man is his image.

With this scale of value Byron measured mankind and the world with a just proportion. The denials of value or of constancy in the temporary show of things passed in review through *Don Juan* are the repeated answers of the perfectionist forced to comment on an imperfect world. They should be read in the light of Byron's subsequent behavior in the imperfect world of Greek revolution and political skullduggery as much as in his surrender to imperfection of life in Venice and London. For, as Lord Ernle has pointed out, Byron had one solitary conviction on the value of moral action, that bridged the hiatus between his abstract beliefs and his practice: through courageous moral action, the world will achieve the ideal of liberty.

The history of Byron's intellectual skepticism is the drama of the opposing tendencies in his nature toward participation and toward isolation. He is a skeptic who would like to persuade himself that he is perfectly poised in his skepticism, but who is really so uncomfortable in it that he is constantly launching out on a new, though hopeless, struggle toward belief. He longs to believe and shrinks from believing because he thinks himself incurably solitary and independent at the center of opposing systems. During most of his life he is unwilling to commit himself, either in poetry or in action. Nature and fate have made him solitary and an outsider. He cannot give himself wholly to anything, to an individual, a social group, a party, or a system of belief. He is the Pilgrim of Eternity. Yet he longed to submit and to be absorbed. The glory of Byron's life is that at last he did commit himself in the cause of Greek liberty. It does not do to explain away this last decided commitment by references to his ambition, to his boredom, and to all the other motives for the Greek expedition which were most undoubtedly and compellingly present. The fact of heroic self-sacrifice remains. Byron was right when he said that we should not dig for motives and causes and thereby destroy the value of a good deed and a good effect:

> " 'T is sad to hack into the root of things,
>   They are so much intertwisted with the earth;
> So that the branch a goodly verdure flings,
>   I reck not if an acorn gave it birth."

He begged Colonel Stanhope to judge him by his actions and not by his words. This final commitment was what Byron was working out for himself in *Don Juan*, explaining his origin and his history, not in any crassly objective autobiography, but in the deepest sense, in the mirror of poetry. Don Juan was to have died for human freedom. Byron left the word and took up the deed: he completed *Don Juan* in action.

Notes

CHAPTER ONE

1. David V. Erdman has gathered very convincing evidence that Byron guarded himself with every precaution against the possibility of failure. He was so afraid of failure to secure the public applause for which he longed that he hedged each venture around with nonchalance, anonymity, "published at request of friends," "not for representation on the stage," etc. See Erdman's article, "Byron's Stage Fright: the History of his Ambition and Fear of Writing for the Stage," *JELH*, September 1939, 219–243.

2. Moore, *Life of Byron,* 151.

3. March 10, 1814.

4. March 20.

5. February 18.

6. March 4, 1822.

7. *Childe Harold,* IV, 122.

8. Hobhouse, *Recollections,* II, 80.

9. Smiles, I, 362.

10. *Ibid.,* 371.

11. Its relations to Schiller's *Armenian* and to Maturin's *Melmoth* are noteworthy. In France, it was understood to be Byron's work entirely, and had a great influence, especially in the work of Charles Nodier.

12. Moore, *Life of Byron,* 322.

13. Hobhouse, *Recollections,* II, 88. A copy of Florian's *Mémoires* appears in the 1827 Sale Catalogue of Byron's library. Florian told the story of his education, adventures in society, and amatory intrigues, substituting Spanish names and customs for French, *e.g.* Lope de Vega for Voltaire, the Infante Don Juan instead of the Duc de Penthièvre.

14. Moore, *Life of Byron,* 527.

15. *Ibid.,* 303.

16. *Byron in Italy,* 129.

17. *L. & J.,* IV, 217.

18. Smiles, I, 393.

19. Moore, *Life of Byron,* 386.

20. Although Byron's and Southey's relations have been frequently and well explained, it is worth noting here that Byron's reasons for his attack on Southey were two-fold: First, Southey was spreading calumny about Byron and Shelley and their "league of incest" with Godwin's daughters; and second, Southey had reviewed Hunt's *Foliage* in the *Quarterly,* "attacking Shelley in an oblique and shabby manner," and including Byron by inference with Hunt's friends, who were "trying to revive the system of Epicurus." Byron wrote Murray: "Does he know what that review has done? I will tell you. It has *sold* an edition of the *Revolt of Islam,* which otherwise, nobody would have thought of reading, and few who read can understand — I for one." Moreover, he has classed together "men of the most opposite habits, tastes, and opinions in life and poetry (I believe), that ever had their names in the same volume — Moore, Byron, Shelley, Hazlitt, Haydon, Leigh Hunt, Lamb. . . ." This classification did not suit Byron's book, now that he was going to champion Pope single-handed, if need be. See *L. & J.,* IV, 272–273.

21. Hobhouse, *Recollections,* II, 107.

22. Moore, *Memoirs,* II, 266 & 329.

23. Hobhouse, *Recollections,* II, 109.

24. *L. & J.,* IV, 277–279.

25. October 31, 1819.

26. August 1819, V, 512–522.

27. *L. & J.,* IV, 366. As a matter of fact, the sale of *Don Juan,* I and II, was eventually very good. See Byron's letter to Kinnaird, September 13, 1821: "Murray, by system for some time, avoids letting me have any favourable news in *his* line. For instance, I learned from an Englishman, that notwithstanding the *row,* the popularity and sale of the *two first Juans* had been excessive. Of this he told me nothing." (Murray, *Lord Byron's Correspondence,* II, 198.)

28. *L. & J.,* IV, 346–347. Mr. Roberts, editor of the *British Review,* had taken *Don Juan,* Canto I, stanzas 209–210, quite literally and published a solemn declaration that Byron lied in claiming that he had bribed the editor.

29. *L. & J.,* IV, 341.

30. Smiles, I, 407.

31. *L. & J.,* IV, 402.

32. Moore, *Life of Byron,* 439.

33. Smiles, I, 413–416.

34. *Ibid.,* I, 413.

35. Murray, *Lord B.'s Correspondence,* II, 179.

36. *L. & J.,* V, 375.

CHAPTER TWO

1. Moore mentions these broadsides as notorious, in his edition of Byron's works, 1833, XV, 101, quoted by E. H. Coleridge, Byron's *Works,* VI, 3.

2. Byron had been reading S. T. Coleridge's *Biographia Literaria.* See his letter to Murray of Oct. 12, 1817.

CHAPTER THREE

1. Chew, *Byron in England,* 47–48.

2. Countess Guiccioli, *My Recollections of Lord Byron,* 39, quoted by Chew, *op. cit.* Earlier, on page 31, she mentioned "the last four cantos, written in Greece." This discrepancy in the number of destroyed cantos casts further doubt on her story, but it seems possible to me that she may have made an innocent mistake. When Byron recovered from her his promise not to continue *Don Juan,* he must have had to satisfy her with a forecast of his plans for the poem. Could he not then have told her in greater detail and at greater length than he told anyone else what he planned to write? And may not his letters to her from Greece — over three hundred of his letters to her are lost — have contained remarks on his plans for Cantos XVII–XXII? She may never have understood that these plans had not yet been reduced to verse.

However, another remark included in the appendix to Stanhope's *Greece,* "Reminiscences of Lord Byron" (page 505), bears on this question. "A Friend" who accompanied Byron on his voyage from Genoa to Cephalonia and lived with him while they were anchored there, asked Byron "whether he had ever thought of writing an epic poem. His answer was, that he would never attempt any thing which approached it nearer than Don Juan. All great subjects, he added, are exhausted; and, in our days, even the most celebrated epics are never read. He said that he would continue Don Juan to one hundred and fifty cantos, if the public would have patience; and, as far as I understood him, twenty-two cantos were ready for the press." Stanhope himself says that he knew Hobhouse destroyed "a beautiful poem of Lord Byron's, and perhaps, the last he ever composed. The same reason that induced Mr. H. to tear this fine manuscript will, of course, prevent him or me from ever divulging its contents." (page 534).

3. In a letter to Murray, December 25, 1822, when he had finished the twelfth canto.

4. In Wieland's *Agathon,* II, however, Byron read a chapter condemning romantic

invention and ideal heroics in fiction, and supporting historical accuracy and truth to nature. "Romantic heroes . . . are no more to be found in the circle of nature, than winged dragons or mermaids. . . . The hero of this history [Agathon] . . . is less a hero than a man; and is therefore fitter to warn us by his own experience, and better able to profit by his own errors." Moore discovered Byron reading this book in Venice in October 1819, and supposed that he was imbibing information on epicureanism from it. But it is more likely that Fieldingesque passages such as this, scattered through *Agathon,* and its clever psychological delineation of love, were the sources of attraction.

5. In the conversation with Medwin about Don Juan, already quoted from, which Medwin solemnly says he "committed to paper half an hour after it occurred," Byron defended *Don Juan* as an epic. "People are always advising me," said he, "to write an epic. You tell me that I shall leave no great poem behind me; — that is, I suppose you mean by great, a heavy poem, or a weighty poem. . . . As to epics, — have you not got enough of Southey's? There's 'Joan of Arc,' 'The Curse of Kehama,' and God knows how many more curses, down to 'The Last of the Goths.' If you must have an epic, there's 'Don Juan' for you. I call that an epic: it is an epic as much in the spirit of our day as the Iliad was in Homer's. Love, religion, and politics form the argument, and are as much the cause of quarrels now as they were then." Byron proceeded to point out parallels between *Don Juan* and the *Iliad,* outlining the future conduct of his story. "It shall have twenty-four books too, the legitimate number; and my spirits, good or bad, must serve for the machinery. If that be not an epic, if it be not strictly according to Aristotle, I don't know what an epic poem means." (Medwin, *Journal,* London, 1824, 111–114.)

Peter Quennell has well defined *Don Juan* as a modern epic poem "purposely stripped of all heroic trimmings," emerging from a troubled intellectual background that perplexed all his contemporaries as well as Byron himself. (*Byron in Italy.*)

6. *E.g.* those mentioned by Chew, *op. cit.,* 42, Thornton's *Don Juan,* and others on pages 51–53.

7. *Blackwood's Magazine,* May 1821, IX, 227–233, an editorial signed "Y" entitled "Lord Byron and Pope." "Y" quotes this sentence from Byron's first letter in the Bowles-Pope controversy, published March 1821.

8. A copy of Goldoni's *Memoirs* was sold in the 1816 auction of Byron's library, and Byron traded with Moore in 1819 another copy of it for an edition of Ariosto.

9. E. H. Coleridge, preface to *Don Juan,* in Byron's *Works,* 1905, VI. Richter, *Lord Byron: Persönlichkeit und Werk,* Max Niemeyer Verlag, Halle, 1929, 448–466.

10. Coleridge, *Biographia Literaria,* Chap. XXIII, "Critique on Bertram." (2nd ed., London, Pickering, 1847, II, 262–273.) Coleridge quotes from Acts IV and V of the *Libertine,* but he calls the subject of his discussion "the old Spanish play, entitled *Atheista Fulminata,* formerly, and perhaps still, acted in the churches and monasteries of Spain, and which under various names (*Don Juan, the Libertine,* &c.), has had its day of favor in every country throughout Europe." This *"auto sacramental,"* El Ateista fulminado, of an earlier date than Tirso de Molina's *Burlador,* must certainly have existed, but no manuscripts of it survive. Coleridge heard of it through the preface to *The Libertine,* in which Shadwell says he has heard that it used to be acted in the churches of Italy under the name *Atheista fulminato.* Shadwell's own sources for his play, however, were Rosimond and Molière at second-hand. (See Victor Said Armesto, *La Leyenda de Don Juan,* Madrid, Sucesores de Hernando, 1908, pp. 64–65, and August Steiger, *Thomas Shadwell's "Libertine,"* Berne, A. Francke, 1904, p. 4.)

11. Richter, *op. cit.,* 453.

12. Ronald Bottrall, "Byron and the Colloquial Tradition in English Poetry," a paper read before the Cambridge University English Club, November 1937, and published in *The Criterion,* January 1939, XVIII, 204–224.

13. Richter, *op. cit.,* 452–453. (My own translation.)

14. Selma Stern, *Anacharsis Cloots, der Redner des Menschengeschlechts, Historische Studien,* CXIX, Berlin, 1914.

15. See Byron's appendix to *Childe Harold,* Canto II (*Works,* II, 199), in which he recounts his "commission by a Greek of Athens named Marmarotouri to make arrangements, if possible, for printing in London a translation of Barthelemi's *Anacharsis* in Romaic. . . ."

16. Medwin, *op. cit.,* 113. Juan apparently was to have become enamored in earnest of Gulbeyaz and to have escaped with her. Byron forsook this project in the six months that elapsed between his statement to Medwin and the composition of Canto VI.

CHAPTER FOUR

1. Byron's *jeux d'esprit* and minor poems are full of "Hudibrastics," *e.g.* "Lines written on board the Lisbon packet," and "Adieu, ye Joys of La Valette." As a comic rhymer, he was rivaled among contemporaries only by Moore, and when Trelawney complimented him on the felicity of his rhymes in *Don Juan,* Byron referred him to Swift — "he beats us all hollow, his rhymes are wonderful." (Trelawney, *Recollections,* 21.)

2. Medwin, *Journal,* 167. The passage previously quoted in footnote 5, Chap. III, p. 165, is also typical.

3. Guiccioli, *My Recollections,* 548.

4. *Ibid.,* 474.

5. *Ibid.,* 549.

6. Byron's stanzas were composed in December 1819, Keats's in May 1819. Byron's were sent to Murray in January 1820, but were not published until August 1821. Meanwhile, Keats's Odes were published in mid-summer 1820 and reached Byron from Murray early in October 1820. Byron, however, protested that he would not and could not correct any of Cantos III and IV, and there is no record, as with Cantos I and II, that any additional stanzas were sent at a later date. Therefore the resemblance in phrasing and ideas between *Don Juan,* IV, 8–28, and Keats's *Odes* must be merely one of those coincidences that Byron said accounted for so many of the charges of plagiarism brought against him. It may be due to their common inspiration from things Greek and natural, and their common romantic melancholy. But it must have infuriated Byron to read those Odes and recognize where the Cockney poet had been before him. No wonder he burst out in a frenzy in his letters to Murray against Johnny Keats, the opponent of Pope and Boileau. In his heart, Byron could recognize that, for all his resolutions to the contrary, he was still tarred with the same brush. He never failed to depreciate Cantos III and IV of *Don Juan.*

7. See his remarks on the relative difficulty of the Spenserian stanza, the couplet, and blank verse, Medwin, *Journal,* 169.

8. Dated December 12, 1814.

9. *Don Juan,* II, 108–110, composed December 1818.

10. *The Island,* 1823, especially Canto I, stanza IX, "the abandoned skiff."

11. Hobhouse, *Italy,* London, John Murray, 1859, I, 43–49.

12. Fuess, *Lord Byron as a Satirist,* 161.

13. R. D. Waller, introduction to his edition of Frere's *Monks and Giants,* 27. Waller's introduction provides the best compact survey of *ottava rima* and Pulcian imitations in English, and I have relied heavily upon it in the following pages.

14. See Fischer, *Leigh Hunt und die Italienische Literatur,* Freiburg, 1936, 6 ff.

15. *L. & J.,* III, 242.

16. *Ibid.,* 418–419. See also Miller, *Leigh Hunt's Relations with Byron, Shelley, and Keats,* Columbia University Press, 1910.

17. In a letter to Ugo Foscolo, May 7, 1818, quoted by Waller, *op. cit.,* 34. Foscolo came to England and entered the Murray circle only in late 1816, and hence the belatedness of Frere's confession to him.

18. XXI, 486–556.

19. 508–509.

20. Waller, *op. cit.,* 22.

21. Rose, *The Court and Parliament of Beasts,* London, John Murray, 1816, and 1818.

22. Rose says that the acid test is women's disagreement over what is a gore and what a gusset. Their imprecision on this point in their own natural province proves them to be not fit for rule.

23. Published by Murray, 1816, and 1818.

24. Waller notes this echo of Casti in his edition of Frere's poem, page 136.

25. See the excellent criticism of *Don Juan* in Waller, *op. cit.,* 47–57.

CHAPTER FIVE

1. *Correspondence of Baron de Grimm and Diderot with the Duke of Saxe-Gotha,* London, 1814, I, 263. See Byron's stanzas in *Don Juan,* IX, 55–56.

2. *Don Juan,* XIII, 40.

3. Cf. Lucian, *Dialogues of the Dead,* "Menippus and Teiresias." Menippus refers to Euripides' *Medea,* one of Byron's favorite plays, for an expression of pity toward the female sex in childbirth.

4. I am indebted to Professor H. M. Jones for pointing out the full extent of the sinister sub-plot of Canto I.

5. Byron could not forego this dig at Campbell's *Gertrude of Wyoming,* though he was indebted to Moore for first noticing the ridiculous phrase.

6. *Don Juan,* X, 53–57.

7. Lord Henry is probably a caricature of William Lamb, but he has also certain characteristics of Lord Holland and Wedderburn Webster.

8. *L. & J.,* I, 195.

9. See, however, Brown, "Byron and English Interest in the Near East," *Studies in Philology,* January 1937, XXXIV, 55–64. "Close parallels between descriptions and incidents in Byron's poetry and those in contemporary travel books are legion, and have been pointed out by editors and biographers of the poet from Galt and Tom Moore to E. H. Coleridge. Such parallels show that Byron, consciously or not, was actually conforming closely in his poetry to the materials and points of view emphasized in the travel books." (Page 61.)

10. Hobhouse's *A Journey Through Albania* confirms Byron's addenda to *Childe Harold,* II, that the two young liberals were seriously affected by the plight of the Greeks and the cause of Greek freedom in 1809–10. I think it is safe to assume that their political ideas were more in accord at that time than later; with that proviso, what Hobhouse has to say in volume II, pages 49–53, on Greek patriotism and ardor for freedom, during which he mentions Lambro, may throw some light on Byron's viewpoint in *Don Juan,* III–IX. Hobhouse tells how the Greeks, betrayed by the Russians, had made the French under Napoleon their next chief hope. Then, disappointed in Napoleon, they turned to England, only to have their hopes of assistance frustrated by checks and reverses they felt they did not deserve. The Greek patriots, Hobhouse says, felt that the privileged classes including the clergy, even among their own nation, and more especially the tyrannical rulers of Europe, were set against their ever regaining even partial freedom and autonomy.

11. *Works,* Poetry, II, 193, in the second of the supplementary papers referred to in Byron's note 33 to *Childe Harold,* Canto II. Cf. also Baggally, *The Klephtic Ballads,* 34, 58, & 97.

12. Cf. Byron's note to the *Bride of Abydos, Works,* III, 194: "Lambro Canzani, a Greek, famous for his efforts, in 1789–90, for the independence of his country. Abandoned by the Russians, he became a pirate, and the Archipelago was the scene of his enterprises. He is said to be still alive at Petersburgh. He and Riga are the two most celebrated of the Greek revolutionists." Hobhouse also mentions Lambro Canziani [*sic*] twice in his *Journey.* The pirate's real name was Lambros Katsones. I wonder whether Byron may have confused him with another famous klepht, the Suliote Lambro Tsavelas, the ballad about whose exploits is given by John Baggally, page 59.

Tsavelas was a leader in the Suliote wars against Ali Pasha in 1790–92. The ballad contains these interesting lines, in Baggally's translation:

"To know the sword of Lambro, the musket of Botsaris,
The arms of the Suliot women, of renowned Haido' — "

But this is only a shadowy suggestion of a link between the names Lambro and Haidée. Byron was obviously perfectly clear on the historical background of his Lambro, and could not have confused Suli and the Cyclades.

I am indebted to Mr. Alan Willard Brown for the suggestion that Cantos II–IV of *Don Juan* bear some relation to the Greek ballads which Byron collected during 1809–11.

13. Baggally, *op. cit., passim.*

14. *The Works of Byron,* Macmillan ed., 1286, footnote.

15. *Works,* Poetry, VII, 28, footnote; also Raymond's *The Political Career of Lord Byron,* 72.

16. *Childe Harold,* III, 35. Note the use of the phrase "united nations."

17. See Byron's *Detached Thoughts.* Coolidge wrote up his impressions of this visit in an article in the *New Monthly Magazine and Literary Journal,* October 1835, XLV, 193–203.

18. Whether Coolidge ever sent him the books about Daniel Boone which he promised, Byron owned two books on the American wilderness — Birkbeck's *Notes on a Journey in America,* and Cobbett's *Year's Residence in America* — which told him something about Boone and about Rapp and the Harmonists. The *Quarterly Review* from 1819 to 1823 contains a series of articles on the travel books of this sort describing the prospects for English emigrants to the United States of America. The *Quarterly's* hostility to republicanism produced this regular campaign against the wave of emigrations which they considered practically treasonable. To desert England the land of liberty for America, a repulsively hypocritical, atheistical, and hi-jacking community, was still worse, for the emigrants took all their solid English gold with them.

19. *Don Juan,* X, 46–48.

20. Blessington, *Conversations,* 134–135.

CHAPTER SIX

1. Nichol, *Byron,* E. M. L. series, 21.

2. 1807 Memorandum of his reading.

3. Moore, *Memoirs,* V, 190, July 1827.

4. *L. & J.,* II, 251 & V, 42.

5. Moore, *Life,* 30.

6. *L. & J.,* I, 23.

7. Moore, *Life,* 39.

8. *L. & J.,* IV, 411, & V, 168.

9. Moore, *Life,* 46–49.

10. *L. & J.,* I, 172.

11. Galt, *Life,* 65–66, 73.

12. Murray, *Correspondence,* I, 30. See the third paper appended to Note 33, *Childe Harold,* Canto II (*Works,* II, 196 ff., especially 201), in which Byron had the pleasure of catching the Edinburgh Reviewer in this number on several errors of fact and vocabulary.

13. Moore, *Life,* 116. Bland was Byron's sixth form master in Greek at Harrow.

14. *A Catalogue of books, the property of a nobleman about to leave England on a tour to the Morea. To which are added a silver sepulchral urn, containing relics brought from Athens, in 1811; and a silver cup, the property of the same noble person; which will be sold by auction by R. H. Evans, at his house, No. 26, Pall Mall, on Thursday, July 8th, and the following day. . . . Printed by W. Bulmer, and Co.,* Cleveland-Row, St. James's, 1813.

In Byron's correspondence with Murray about preparing the books for sale, he refers to "Aphrodites," which should be burnt, "a small vol. of abominable poems by the Earl of Haddington which must not be in yᵉ Catalogue on Sale — also a volume of French Epigrams in the same predicament," and "an inscription" on the title-page of Meletius' *Geography*, "which must be *erased* and made illegible."

15. Moore, *Life*, 238.
16. *L. & J.*, II, 401.
17. *Ibid.*, 407–408.
18. *Ibid.*, III, 70.
19. *Ibid.*, II, 86–87.
20. *Ibid.*, II, 375–376.
21. *Ibid.*, II, 183. Byron found in it a poem in manuscript by Fulke Greville, Lord Brooke, which he sent to Murray for identification.
22. Murray, *Correspondence*, I, 189.
23. See Murray's description of the bleak appearance of Newstead when he visited it in the autumn of 1814. Smiles, I, 256.
24. *L. & J.*, III, 164 & 177.
25. Murray, *Correspondence*, I, 293.
26. Smiles, I, 360.
27. *L. & J.*, V, 442.
28. Moore, *Life*, 289, and Smiles, I, 352.
29. Moore, *Life*, 289.
30. Smiles, I, 363.
31. *L. & J.*, III, 271.
32. *A Catalogue of a Collection of Books, late the Property of a Nobleman about to leave England on a tour, including the Large Plates to Boydell's Shakespeare . . . Birch's General Dictionary . . . Moreri, Dictionnaire Historique . . . Lavater's Physiognomy . . . Sophocles Brunckii . . . Malcolm's History of Persia . . . Dryden's Works . . . Beauties of England . . . Cobbett's Parliamentary Debates . . . State Trials. . . . And some Romaic books of which no other Copies are in this Country . . . . which will be sold by auction, by Mr. Evans, at his house, No. 26, Pall-Mall, on Friday, April 5, and following day.*
33. Smiles, I, 363.
34. *L. & J.*, III, 280.
35. *Ibid.*, V, 391, footnote.
36. Gordon, *Personal Memoirs*, II, 328.
37. Moore, *Life*, 300.
38. Hobhouse, *Italy*, I, 37 & Chap. III.
39. Hobhouse, *Recollections*, II, 48.
40. *L. & J.*, III, 444–445.
41. Hobhouse, *Recollections*, II, 56, and *Italy*, I, Chap. III.
42. *L. & J.*, III, 376 & 382.
43. Hobhouse, *Recollections*, II, 51.
44. Murray, *Correspondence*, II, 23–24.
45. Smiles, I, 366.
46. *L. & J.*, IV, 108.
47. *Ibid.*, 271.
48. Murray, *Correspondence*, II, 90.
49. Smiles, I, 370.
50. *L. & J.*, IV, 222–224; Smiles, I, 393; Hobhouse, *Recollections*, II, 85.
51. *L. & J.*, V, 177.
52. Murray, *Correspondence*, II, 62.
53. *L. & J.*, IV, 198.
54. *Ibid.*, 367.
55. He sent to Murray for a copy of "Zeluco" Moore's *View of Italy*, which contained a remembered passage on the history of the Doge, but only to condemn and refute it in his introduction to *Marino Faliero*. Moore, *Memoirs*, II, 173, Journal of

1818, records a curious and to me inexplicable library connection of Byron's: "Caroline Strutt has written a letter from Venice, in which she says, Lord Byron lives quite retired, never going out but to the American Ambassador's library. . . ." This was in September when Byron was commencing *Don Juan* and writing at top speed. But I cannot identify an American ambassador at Venice then or ever after.

56. Murray, *Correspondence*, II, 43–46.
57. *L. & J.*, IV, 399 & 428, and V, 13.
58. *Ibid.*, V, 55, 98, & 234.
59. *Ibid.*, 64, 72, 93–96, & 109.
60. *L. & J.*, V, 373 ff. Cf. Moore, *Life*, 533.
61. *L. & J.*, V, 390–391.
62. Hunt, *Lord Byron and Some of his Contemporaries*, 45–46, & 61.
63. *L. & J.*, VI, 211.
64. Murray, *Correspondence*, II, 240.
65. *Ibid.*, 264, and Moore, *Life*, 591.
66. See Stanhope's *Greece*, 511, from extracts of letters (written in Greece May and June 1824) from Mr. George Finlay to Colonel Stanhope: "At Metaxata, . . . in the month of October, 1823 . . . I found the greater part of Walter Scott's novels, Mitford's History of Greece, Sismondi's Italian Republics, and an English translation of Pausanias," in Byron's rooms. These were strewn over a table and chair and "ranged in order on the floor."
67. Moore, *Memoirs*, V, 193.
68. *Catalogue of the Library of the Late Lord Byron.* . . . July 6, 1827, reprinted with an introductory essay by Gilbert H. Doane.
69. "Smith's Philosophical Essays" in the 1827 Catalogue is probably: E. Smith, M.D., *Illustrations of the Moral Government of God*, London, n.p., n. d. This book is mentioned by Countess Guiccioli in *My Recollections*, 154, in dealing with Byron's encounters with Dr. Kennedy. "Byron said that the author of the book proved that hell was not a place of eternal punishment."
70. Blessington, *Conversations*, 70.
71. See *L. & J.*, VI, 428, Charles Hancock's description of Byron's last day on Cephalonia before he left for Missolonghi: "The day before he left the island I happened to receive a copy of *Quentin Durward*, which I put into his hands, knowing that he had not seen it and that he wished to obtain the perusal of it. He immediately shut himself in his room, and in his eagerness to indulge in it, refused to dine with the Officers of the 8th Regt. at their Mess or even to join us at table, but merely came out once or twice to say how much he was entertained, returning to his chamber with a plate of figs in his hand."
72. See Byron's letter to Rogers, *L. & J.*, IV, 209, begging Rogers to secure from Beckford "a copy in MS. of the remaining *Tales*." "I think I deserve them, as a strenuous and public admirer of the first one."
73. *L. & J.*, IV, 92–93.
74. Cf. Murray, *Correspondence*, I, 178.
75. Goode, *Byron as Critic*, Chap. 6.
76. Trelawney, *Recollections*, 134.
77. Edgeworth, *The Modern Griselda*, 1804.
78. "Car, au moyen des femmes, disait-elle, on fait tous qu'on veut des hommes; et puis ils sont les uns trop dissipés, les autres trop préoccupés de leurs intérêts personnels, pour ne pas négliger les vôtres; au lieu que les femmes y pensent, ne fût-ce que par oisiveté. Parlez ce soir à votre amie de quelque affaire qui vous touche; demain à son rouet, à sa tapisserie, vous la trouverez y rêvant, cherchant dans sa tête le moyen de vous y servir. Mais de celle que vous croirez pouvoir vous être utile, gardez-vous bien d'être autre chose que l'ami, car, entre amants, dès qu'il survient des nuages, des brouilleries, des ruptures, tout est perdu. Soyez donc auprès d'elle assidu, complaisant, galant même si vous voulez, mais rien de plus, entendez-vous." (J. F. Marmontel, *Oeuvres Complètes de Marmontel*, Paris, Verdière, 1818, I, 246.) Cf. *Don Juan*, XIV, 93:

"No friend like to a woman Earth discovers,
So that you have not been nor will be lovers."

79. Blessington, *Conversations*, 96.

80. Moore, *Life*, 600.

81. *Childe Harold*, IV, 75–77, and *Don Juan*, I, 52–53. See also Moore, *Life*, 65.

82. Moore, *Life*, 117–120.

83. *L. & J.*, VI, 59.

84. Blessington, *Conversations*, 95.

85. *L. & J.*, V, 151–156.

86. An interesting series of Byron's critical marginalia in Ruffhead's *Life of Pope*, inscribed in autograph "Byron — Cambridge A.D. 1808," is recorded in the Rev. James Hodgson's *Memoir of the Rev. Francis Hodgson*, London, Macmillan, 1878, I, 97. For example, Byron wrote: "Of Pope's pithy conciseness of style Swift — no diffuse writer himself — has so emphatically said —
'For Pope can in one couplet fix
More sense than I can do in six.' "
"Imitators of Horace and Juvenal were Boileau and Pope — of one as well as of the other of whom it may be said — 'Même en imitant toujours original.' " In another note, Byron summarizes Pope's indebtedness in the *Rape of the Lock* to Villars, Shakespeare, Homer, Virgil, and Ariosto, quoting a line to prove the last mentioned.

87. See D'Israeli's Prefaces to the editions of 1818 and 1828. Also Byron's letter to Murray, *L. & J.*, V, 390.

88. Blessington, *Conversations*, 60.

89. The first published attack was a series of articles by Alaric A. Watts, in the *Literary Gazette*, a Tory journal, February–March 1821, on Byron's Plagiarisms. Watts's son, in a biography of his father, explains how Watts, who had been acquainted with Byron in 1814 and was one of Byron's most ardent admirers and defenders, became disillusioned, like the general public, after the publication of *Don Juan* I–II, and under the influence of William Jerdan and the Longmans, swung completely to the other party. See Alaric Alfred Watts, *Alaric Watts, A Narrative of His Life*, by his son, 2 vols., London, Richard Bentley and Son, 1884, I, 48–49, 99, & 107–118.

90. Miss Hazel Edwards, in her essay on *Byron's Early Reading and Its Influence on his Early Works* (Univ. of Texas Library, unpublished), counts 1549 references made by Byron to books he had read before 1807.

91. Blessington, *Conversations*, 62. Cf. also 96 & 104, where she records Byron's exhibitions of memory in repeating passages from Hallam's *Middle Ages*, Scott's *Peveril of the Peak*, and a letter from Madame du Deffand to Voltaire. If Byron was trying to impress her, he made his point almost too well, and found one of his favorite prejudices impaled upon it. One day, after she has recorded a prolonged conversation with him on the relative merits of Shakespeare and Pope, Byron defending the latter as usual against all comers, she says: "Could there be a less equivocal proof of his admiration of our immortal bard than the tenacity with which his memory retained the finest passages of all his works? When I made this observation to him he smiled, and affected to boast that his memory was so retentive that it equally retained all that he read; but as I had seen many proofs of the contrary, I persevered, . . . that . . . Byron was in his heart a warm admirer of Shakespeare." *Ibid.*, 159.

92. Gibbon's *Decline and Fall*, I, 347. Cf. *Don Juan*, XVI, 1.

93. See Medwin, *Journal*, 140. Byron, who has been pointing out Scott's borrowings, is twitted by Medwin for being too severe, and retorts, "Set a thief to catch a thief."

94. See Nichol, *Byron*, 212.

95. Blessington, *Conversations*, 161.

96. George Finlay remarked: "The memory of Lord B. was very extraordinary; it was not the mere mechanical memory which can repeat the advertisements of a newspaper and such nonsense; but of all the innumerable novels which he had read, he seemed to recollect perfectly the story and every scene of merit." Stanhope's *Greece*, 525.

97. Byron satisfied Galt that this was only coincidence, but Galt could not refrain,

in recording the incident, from including with malicious amusement a few more instances of his lordship's "pilfering the thoughts and fancies of others."

98. Cf. Goethe's critique of *Manfred* in *Kunst und Alterthum*. Moore translated it in the *Life*, 448–449: ". . . This singular intellectual poet has taken my Faustus to himself, and extracted from it the strongest nourishment for his hypochondriac humour. He has made use of the impelling principles in his own way, for his own purposes, so that no one of them remains the same; and it is particularly on this account that I cannot enough admire his genius. The whole is in this way so completely forged anew, that it would be an interesting task for the critic to point out not only the alterations he has made, but their degree of resemblance with, or dissimilarity to, the original. . . ."

99. *L. & J.*, IV, 174.

100. *L. & J.*, V, 346.

101. Moore, *Life*, 524. But he concludes the passage with an example of reminiscence in Byron's verse of Beaumont and Fletcher's *Two Noble Kinsmen*.

102. *L. & J.*, III, 254.

103. He discussed the matter, as he records July 3, 1821 (*Memoirs*, III, 248), with Lord Holland. "I said that Lord Byron could not describe anything which he had not actually under his eyes, and that he did it either on the spot or immediately after. This, Lord Holland remarked, was the sign of a true poet, to write only from *impressions;* but where then do all the imaginary scenes of Dante, Milton, &c. go, if it is necessary to *see* what we describe in order to be a true poet?"

104. Moore, *Life*, 420–421. In a footnote, Moore comments on the similarities between Byron and Wieland, in their experiences, temperaments, and methods of composition.

105. *Ibid.*, 51.

106. *Ibid.*, 217.

107. Blessington, *Conversations*, 60. See the *Autobiography of John Galt*, London, Cochrane and McCrone, 1833, II, 355–367, Appendix No. 3, consisting of an interesting comparison between Joshua Pickersgill's *The Three Brothers*, 4 vols., 1803, and *Manfred* and others of Byron's poems. The comparison was made at Galt's instance in a letter to the Editor of the *Monthly Magazine*, signed "A. P."

108. Cline, "Unpublished Notes on the Romantic Poets by Isaac D'Israeli," *Univ. of Texas English Studies*, 1941, 140.

109. See H. S. L. Wiener's *Literary Sources of Byron's "Turkish Tales"* in *Nineteenth Century Studies*, Cornell Univ. Press, 1940.

110. Goode notes the confusion in Byron's mind between truth and fact. Cf. *Don Juan*, VII, 81.

111. Galt, *Life*, 191. Galt objects, on no substantial critical grounds, I believe, that the parts of *Don Juan* admittedly derived from books are vague and "justify the opinion, that invention was not the most eminent faculty of Byron, either in scenes or in characters." *Ibid.*, 255.

112. *Don Juan*, I, 214–215.

CHAPTER SEVEN

1. Horace, *Satires, Epistles, and Ars Poetica*, with an English translation by H. Rushton Fairclough, Loeb Classical Library, London and New York, 1929.

2. Hobhouse, *Recollections*, II, 107.

3. Murray, *Correspondence*, II, 101.

4. Dunlop translates from Le Grand, I, 299.

5. Dunlop, *History of Fiction*, II, 75.

6. Trelawney, *Recollections*, 70.

7. Murray, *Correspondence*, II, 149–150.

8. I, 162–163.

9. *L. & J.*, I, 253–254.

10. *Works*, II, 169.

11. *L. & J.,* V, 544–545, & 551. Byron's arguments are negligible, for he constantly confuses his usage of the words "nature" and "art," the opposing terms in the argument, as indeed they are the opposing forces in *The Shipwreck* — the power of the storm at sea pitted against the art of the ship and the mariners.

12. Ariosto, *Orlando Furioso,* transl. by W. S. Rose, Canto XLI.

13. Lucretius, *De Rerum Natura,* Bk. V, ll. 222 ff., Loeb Classical Library translation. Other phrases, images, and ideas in Lucretius, too numerous to mention, which Byron made his own, include: *"Alma Venus . . . genetrix"* ("thou alone dost govern the nature of things, since without thee, nothing comes forth into the shining borders of light, nothing joyous and lovely is made. . . ."); Lucretius' description of the mind-soul, which Byron called "that very fiery particle"; and Byron's favorite tag: *"medio de fonte leporum surgit amari aliquid. . . ."* Burton also loved to quote this aphorism, *e.g.* I, 144, of the *Anatomy of Melancholy.* Byron believed with Lucretius in the changing universe, but he rejected Lucretius' explanation of the process of death in the dissolution of soul and body. Cf. *Don Juan,* V, 33–39.

14. *Anatomy of Melancholy,* I, 272.

15. The *Amadis of Greece,* a continuation of *Amadis de Gaul,* is especially oriental; it contains a Christian-Moorish love affair, conducted by aid of female disguise, in the harem, similar to *Florice and Blanchefleur* and to *Don Juan,* Cantos V and VI. See Dunlop, I, 312–313.

16. Geneva, 1936, 220–224.

17. In *Mélanges d'Histoire Littéraire . . . offerts à Fernand Baldensperger,* I, Paris, 1930.

18. See *Florice and Blanchefleur,* ed. A. B. Taylor, Oxford, 1927, 16.

19. Dunlop, I, 253–267.

20. *Ibid.,* 265.

21. *L. & J.,* V, 171.

22. De Staël, *De L'Allemagne,* 269.

23. *Oberon,* Canto XI, 8, and following stanzas.

24. *Ibid.,* XI, 47.

25. Besides, there was an interval of eighteen months between the composition of Canto V and Canto VI.

26. Leigh Hunt, reviewing *Don Juan,* III–V, in the *Examiner,* August 26, 1821, remarks that the love scene between Gulbeyaz and Juan is "an Oriental version of the scene between *Lady Booby* and her servant in *Joseph Andrews.*" Others have noticed its resemblance to the story of Potiphar's wife and Joseph.

27. Dunlop, II, 99.

28. As translated by Thomas Roscoe in *The Italian Novelists,* London, Simpkin and Marshall, 1836, II.

29. Reported in Dunlop, II, 292–293.

30. *Don Juan,* Canto V, was composed October 16 to November 20, 1820.

31. My translation.

32. July 1823, XIV, 88–92.

33. 30–31. My translation.

34. Cf. Murray, *Correspondence,* I, 16.

35. Paris, 1827, II, 216.

36. From Missolonghi, February 23, 1824, *L. & J.,* VI, 331.

37. *Thomas Hope's "Anastasius" und Lord Byrons "Don Juan,"* Munich, 1913.

38. Smiles, II, 76.

39. No. LXIX, 92–102.

40. Blessington, *Conversations,* 36.

41. *Anastasius,* II, 356.

42. Composed in 1778, and published at Paris, 1797.

43. *Quarterly Review,* XXI.

44. P. 491.

CHAPTER EIGHT

1. Lucian, Loeb Classical Library transl., IV, 97–99 & 107–109.

2. *Don Juan*, IX, 13–21.

3. *Anatomy of Melancholy*, Everyman edition, I, 55–56.

4. See Irwin, *The Making of Jonathan Wild*, New York, Columbia University Press, 1941.

5. ll. 217–258.

6. *L. & J.*, V, 161–163.

7. I am indebted to Professor Marjorie Nicolson for the reminder that Burton's passage on this subject is founded upon an equally famous and earlier one, that in Bacon's *Advancement of Learning*, which was also known and admired by Johnson.

8. *Ibid.*, 173.

9. *Ibid.*, 465.

10. Cf. Henry Martyn's letter to Steele (*Spectator*, No. 180).

11. Composed at Hamburg in 1813, and republished in Constant's *Cours de politique constitutionelle*, 4 vols., 1817–1820. See its recent republication as *Prophecy from the Past; on the Conquest and Usurpation*, ed. and transl. by Helen Lippmann, N. Y., Reynal and Hitchcock, 1941.

12. My translation.

13. Vol. II, 206–207. My translation.

14. *Siege of Corinth*, ll. 781 ff.

15. *Gerusalemme Liberata*, Canto IX, Fairfax's translation.

16. V, 447.

17. *L. & J.*, VI, 186–188.

18. Hobhouse, *Recollections*, III, 29.

19. Fuess, *Lord Byron as a Satirist*, 172, footnote.

20. *Letters of Shelley*, ed. by Roger Ingpen, London, Pitman, 1909, II, 897. Peacock discounted Byron's praise of *Melincourt*, laying it to Shelley's kindness.

21. *Melincourt*, 178.

Selected List of Works Consulted

ARMESTO, VICTOR SAID, *La Leyenda de Don Juan,* Madrid, Sucesores de Hernando, 1908.

BAGGALLY, JOHN W., *The Klephtic Ballads in Relation to Greek History (1715–1821),* Oxford, Basil Blackwall, 1936.

BAUD-BOVY, SAMUEL, *La Chanson Populaire Grecque du Dodécanèse,* Geneva, A. Kundig, 1936.

BEALES, A. C. F., *The History of Peace,* New York, MacVeagh, The Dial Press, 1931.

BEYER, WERNER, *The Prestige of Christophe Martin Wieland in England,* an unpublished essay, New York, Columbia University Library, 1936.

BEYLE, M. HENRI (DE STENDHAL), "Lord Byron en Italie," *Revue de Paris,* XII (1830), 186–204.

———, *Oeuvres Complètes de Stendhal,* edited by Edouard Champion, Paris, 1919, III; 1925, IX.

BLANCK, ANTON, " 'Floires et Blanceflor' et l'épisode de Haidée dans le 'Don Juan' de Byron," *Mélanges d'Histoire Littéraire . . . offerts à Fernand Baldensperger,* Paris, 1930. I, 54–62.

Blackwood's Magazine,
> May 1818, III, 216–218, [Review of *Childe Harold,* Canto IV].
> June 1818, III, 323, "Letter to the Author of Beppo."
> July 1818, III, 369–381, "On the Lake School of Poetry."
> August 1819, V, 512–522, "Remarks on Don Juan."
> May 1821, IX, 131–140, "Familiar Letter from the Adjutant to Christopher North" (Odoherty Papers).
> May 1821, IX, 227–233, "Lord Byron and Pope."
> August 1821, X, 107–115, [Review of *Don Juan,* Cantos III–V].
> July 1823, XIV, 88–92, [Review of *Don Juan,* Cantos VI–VIII].

BLESSINGTON, MARGUERITE POWER, COUNTESS OF, *Conversations of Lord Byron with the Countess of Blessington,* Philadelphia, Carey and Hart, 1836.

BLUNDEN, EDMUND, *Leigh Hunt,* London, Cobden-Sanderson, 1930.

———, *Leigh Hunt's "Examiner" Examined,* London, Cobden-Sanderson, 1928.

BOISSY, TERESA GAMBA GUICCIOLI, MARQUISE DE, *My Recollections of Lord Byron; and Those of Eye-Witnesses of His Life,* translated by Hubert E. H. Jerningham, London, Richard Bentley, and New York, Harper, 1869.

BOTTRALL, RONALD, "Byron and the Colloquial Tradition in English Poetry," *The Criterion,* XVIII (January 1939), 204–224.

BREDVOLD, LOUIS I., Introductory Essay, *Lord Byron, Don Juan and Other Satirical Poems, Doubleday Doran Series in Literature,* edited by Robert Shafer, Garden City, Doubleday, Doran, 1935.

British Critic, The,
> August 1819, XII, 195–205, [Review of *Don Juan,* Cantos I–II].
> September 1821, XVI, 251–256, [Review of *Don Juan,* Cantos III–V].

BROUGHTON, JOHN CAM HOBHOUSE, LORD, *Italy,* London, John Murray, 1859. 2 vols.

———, *A Journey Through Albania, and . . . Turkey in Europe and Asia . . . , 1809 and 1810,* (London, 1813), Philadelphia, M. Carey and Son, 1817. 2 vols.

———, *Recollections of a Long Life,* New York, Scribner's, 1909. 6 vols.

BROWN, WALLACE CABLE, "Byron and English Interest in the Near East," *Studies in Philology,* XXXIV (1937), 55–64.

———, "English Travel Books and Minor Poetry about the Near East, 1775–1825," *Philological Quarterly,* XVI (1937), 249–271.

———, "Popularity of English Travel Books about the Near East, 1775–1825," *Philological Quarterly,* XV (1936), 70–80.

DE BRUCHARD, HENRI, "Notes sur le Don Juanisme," *Mercur de France*, XXVI (April 1898), 58–73.

BYRON, GEORGE NOEL GORDON, LORD, *The Works of Lord Byron, Poetry*, edited by E. H. Coleridge, and *Letters and Journals*, edited by R. E. Prothero, London, John Murray, 1898–1905. 13 vols.

———, *The Complete Poetical Works of Lord Byron*, with an introductory memoir by Sir Leslie Stephen, New York, Macmillan, 1907.

CALVERT, WILLIAM J., *Byron: Romantic Paradox*, Chapel Hill, University of North Carolina Press, 1935.

Catalogue of a Collection of Books, late the Property of a Nobleman about to leave England . . . which will be sold by auction, by Mr. Evans, at his house, No. 26, Pall-Mall, on Friday, April 5 . . . [1816]. Photostatic copy of copy in British Museum Library.

CHEW, SAMUEL C., *Byron in England*, New York, Scribner's, 1924.

———, "The Centenary of Don Juan," *American Journal of Philology*, XL (1919), 117.

———, *The Dramas of Lord Byron*, Göttingen, Vandenhoeck und Ruprecht, 1915.

CLINE, C. L., "Unpublished Notes on the Romantic Poets by Isaac D'Israeli," *University of Texas Studies in English*, Austin, University of Texas Press, 1941. 138–146.

"Conversations of an American with Lord Byron," *New Monthly Magazine and Literary Journal*, XLV (October 1835), 193–203, 291–302.

DALLAS, R. C., and A. R. C. DALLAS, *Recollections of the Life of Lord Byron*, Philadelphia, Small, Carey and Lea, 1825.

DOANE, GILBERT H., editor, *Catalogue of the Library of the Late Lord Byron . . . July 6, 1827*, reprinted with an introductory essay by G. H. Doane, Lincoln, Nebraska, privately printed, 1929.

DÖRKEN, HILDEGARD, *Lord Byrons Subjektivismus in seinem Verhalten zur Geschichte untersucht an seinen Verserzählungen*, Leipzig, Tauchnitz, 1929.

Dublin University Magazine,
    May 1875, LXXXV, 630–637, "The Morality of 'Don Juan.'"
    December 1875, LXXXVI, 727–731, "A Monument to Byron."

DU BOS, CHARLES, *Byron et le Besoin de la Fatalité*, Paris, Au Sans Pareil, 1929.

DUNLOP, JOHN, *History of Fiction*, 2nd edition, Philadelphia, Carey and Hart, 1842. 2 vols.

Edinburgh Review,
    January 1808, XI, 285–289, [Lord Brougham's Review of *Hours of Idleness*].
    December 1816, XXVII, 277–310, [Francis Jeffrey's Review of *Childe Harold*, Canto III].
    February 1818, XXIX, 302–310, [Review of *Beppo*].
    March 1821, XXXV, 92–102, [Review of Hope's *Anastasius*].
    February 1822, XXXVI, 413–452, [Francis Jeffrey's Review of Byron's Dramas and Poetry].

EDWARDS, EDWARD, *Libraries and Founders of Libraries*, London, Trübner, 1865.

———, *Memoirs of Libraries*, London, Trübner, 1859. 2 vols.

EDWARDS, HAZEL, *Byron's Early Reading and Its Influence on His Early Works*, an unpublished essay, Austin, University of Texas Library.

EGGERT, GERHARD, *Lord Byron and Napoleon*, Leipzig, Mayer and Müller, 1933.

EICHLER, A., *John Hookham Frere . . . sein Einfluss auf Lord Byron, Wiener Beiträge zur Englischen Philologie*, XX, Vienna and Leipzig, W. Braunmüller, 1905.

ELLIS, GEORGE, *Specimens of Early English Metrical Romances*, 2nd edition, London, Longman's, 1811. 3 vols.

ELZE, KARL, *Lord Byron*, London, John Murray, 1872.

ERDMAN, DAVID V., "Byron's Stage Fright," *ELH, Journal of English Literary History*, VI (1939), 219–243.

ERNLE, R. E. PROTHERO, LORD, "The End of the Byron Mystery," *Nineteenth Century and After*, XC (1921), 207–218.

———, "The Poetry of Byron," *Quarterly Review*, CCXLI (April 1924), 229–253.

Examiner, The, (see Leigh Hunt).

FAURIEL, C., *Chants Populaires de la Grèce Moderne,* Paris, Firmin Didot, 1824. 2 vols.

First Edition Club, The, *Bibliographical Catalogue of First Editions . . . of Books by Lord Byron,* Plaistow, England, Curwen Press, 1925.

FISCHER, ERIKA, *Leigh Hunt und die Italienische Literatur,* Quakenbrück, Trute, 1936.

FOÀ, GIOVANNA, *Lord Byron, Poeta e Carbonaro,* Florence, "La Nuova Italia," 1935.

FOSCOLO, UGO, "Narrative and Romantic Poems of the Italians," *Quarterly Review,* XXI (April 1819), 486–556.

FUESS, CLAUDE M., *Lord Byron as a Satirist in Verse,* New York, Columbia University Press, 1912.

FUHRMANN, LUDWIG, *Die Belesenheit des jungen Byron,* Berlin, Kindler, 1903.

GALT, JOHN, *The Life of Lord Byron,* New York, J. & J. Harper, 1830.

GAMBA, PIETRO, *A Narrative of Lord Byron's Last Journey to Greece,* London, John Murray, 1825.

GINGUENÉ, P. L., *Histoire Littéraire d'Italie,* 2nd edition, Paris, Michaud, 1824.

GOODE, CLEMENT TYSON, *Byron as Critic,* Weimar, R. Wagner Sohn, 1923.

GORDON, PRYSE LOCKHART, *Personal Memoirs; or Reminiscences of Men and Manners at Home and Abroad, During the Last Half Century,* London, Colburn and Bentley, 1830. 2 vols.

GREEN, F. C., *Stendhal,* Cambridge, Cambridge University Press, 1939.

GRIERSON, SIR H. J. C., "Lord Byron: Arnold and Swinburne," *The Background of English Literature,* New York, Henry Holt, 1926.

HARRINGTON, LEICESTER F. C. STANHOPE, EARL OF, *Greece, in 1823 and 1824,* revised edition, London, Sherwood, Gilbert and Piper, 1825.

HARTMANN, HEINRICH, *Lord Byrons Stellung zu den Klassizisten seiner Zeit: Rogers, Campbell, Gifford, Crabbe und Moore,* Bottrop i. W., W. Postberg, 1932.

HEBER, RICHARD, [Review of Byron's Dramas], *Quarterly Review,* XXVII (July 1822), 477–524.

HENLEY, WILLIAM ERNEST, "Byron's World," *Essays, The Works of William Ernest Henley,* London, David Nutt, 1908. IV, 1–167.

——, "Byron," *Views and Reviews, The Works of William Ernest Henley,* London, David Nutt, 1908. V, 65–73.

HODGSON, REV. JAMES, *Memoir of the Rev. Francis Hodgson,* London, Macmillan, 1878. 2 vols.

HOFFMANN, KARL, *Ueber Lord Byrons "The Giaour,"* Halle, Karras, 1898.

HOPPNER, RICHARD BELGRAVE, "Byron at Venice," *The Athenaeum* (May 22, 1869), 702.

HOWARTH, R. G., editor, *Letters of George Gordon, 6th Lord Byron,* with an introduction by André Maurois, London, J. M. Dent, 1933.

HUNT, LEIGH, *The Examiner,*

  September 4, 1814, "Illustrations from Lord Byron's Work."
  October 31, 1819, [Review of *Don Juan,* Cantos I–II].
  August 26, 1821, [Review of *Don Juan,* Cantos III–V].
  July 29, 1822, "Sketches of the Living Poets."
  November 24, 1822, "A Defense of *Don Juan.*"
  July 5, 1823–November 29, 1823, [Review of *Don Juan,* Cantos VI–XIV].

——, *The Feast of the Poets,* London, James Cawthorn, 1814.

——, *Lord Byron and Some of His Contemporaries,* Philadelphia, Carey, 1828.

——, *Men, Women, and Books,* London, Smith and Elder, 1847.

INGPEN, ROGER, editor, *The Letters of Percy Bysshe Shelley,* London, Pitman, 1909. 2 vols.

IRWIN, WILLIAM ROBERT, *The Making of Jonathan Wild,* New York, Columbia University Press, 1941.

"John Murray, 1778–1843, 'The Anax of Publishers,'" London *Times Literary Supplement,* No. 2160 (June 26, 1943), 308.

JONES, HOWARD MUMFORD, "The Byron Centenary," *Yale Review,* XIII (July 1924), 730–745.

JONES, JOSEPH JAY, "Lord Byron on America," *University of Texas Studies in English,* Austin, University of Texas Press, 1941. 121–137.

KAHN, GUSTAVE, "Don Juan," *Revue Encyclopédique,* VIII (1898), 326–329.

KENNEDY, JAMES, *Conversations on Religion with Lord Byron* . . . , London, John Murray, 1830.

KIND, THEODOR, *Anthologie Neugriechischer Volkslieder*, Leipzig, Veit and Comp., 1861.

———, *Neugriechischer Volkslieder*, Leipzig, Hermann Fritzsche, 1849.

KRAEGER, HEINRICH, *Der Byronische Heldentypus*, Munich, C. Haushalter, 1898.

LEGRAND, EMILE, *Recueil de Chansons Populaires Grecques*, Paris, Maisonneuve et Cie., 1874.

LEONARD, W. E., *Byron and Byronism in America*, New York, Columbia University Press, 1905.

"Letters, etc. of Lord Byron," *Sharpe's London Magazine*, XXXVI, n.s. (July–August 1869), 14, 70.

LEVI, EZIO, "Un Episodio Sconosciuto nella Storia della Novella Spagnuola," *Bolitin de la Academia Española*, XXI (December 1934), 687–736.

Literary Gazette, The,
    July 17, 1819, [Review of *Don Juan*, Cantos I–II].
    July 24, 1819, [Review of *Don Juan*, Cantos I–II, cont'd].
    August 11, 1821, [Review of *Don Juan*, Cantos III–V].
    July 19, 1823, [Review of *Don Juan*, Cantos VI–VIII].
    December 6, 1823, [Review of *Don Juan*, Cantos IX–XI].
    April 3, 1824, [Review of *Don Juan*, Cantos XV–XVI].

MARJARUM, EDWARD WAYNE, *Byron as Skeptic and Believer*, Princeton, Princeton University Press, 1938.

MARSHALL, RODERICK, *Italy in English Literature, 1755–1815*, New York, Columbia University Press, 1934.

MASI, ERNESTO, "Il romanzo d'un' Imperatrice," *Nuova Antologia*, CXXXI (October 16, 1893), 593–613.

MAUROIS, ANDRÉ, *Byron*, translated by Hamish Miles, London, J. Cape, 1930.

MAYNE, ETHEL C., *Byron*, 2nd edition, New York, Scribner's, 1922.

———, *The Life and Letters of Lady Byron*, New York, Scribner's, 1929.

MAZZINI, GIUSEPPE, "Byron e Goethe," *Life and Writings*, London, Smith and Elder, 1891. VI, 61.

McKENZIE, KENNETH, "Italian Fables of the Eighteenth Century," *Italica*, XII (June 1935), 39–44.

MEDWIN, THOMAS, *Journal of the Conversations of Lord Byron*, New York, Wilder and Campbell, 1824.

MERIVALE, J. H., [Articles on Pulci's *Morgante Maggiore*], *The Monthly Magazine, or British Register*, XXI–XXIII (May 1, 1806–July 1, 1807).

MILLER, BARNETTE, *Leigh Hunt's Relations with Byron, Shelley, and Keats*, New York, Columbia University Press, 1910.

Monthly Magazine, or British Register, The,
    August 1, 1819, XLVIII, 56–57, [Review of *Don Juan*, Cantos I–II].

Monthly Review, The,
    March 1818, LXXXV, 285–290, [Review of *Beppo*].
    July 1819, LXXXIX, 309–321, [Review of *Don Juan*, Cantos I–II, and other poems].
    August 1821, XCV, 418–424, [Review of *Don Juan*, Cantos III–V].
    July 1823, CI, 316–321, [Review of *Don Juan*, Cantos VI–VIII].
    October 1823, CII, 217–221, [Review of *Don Juan*, Cantos IX–XI].
    February 1824, CIII, 212–215, [Review of *Don Juan*, Cantos XII–XIV].
    April 1824, CIII, 434–436, [Review of *Don Juan*, Cantos XV–XVI].

MOORE, THOMAS, *Life, Letters and Journals of Lord Byron*, London, John Murray, 1920.

———, *Memoirs, Journal, and Correspondence of Thomas Moore*, edited by Lord John Russell, London, Longman's, 1853. 7 vols.

MORLEY, JOHN, "Byron," *Critical Miscellanies*, London, Macmillan, 1886. I, 203.

MURRAY, JOHN, editor, *Lord Byron's Correspondence*, London, John Murray, 1922. 2 vols.

NATHAN, ISAAC, *Fugitive Pieces and Reminiscences of Lord Byron: containing . . . the Hebrew Melodies . . .* , London, Whittaker, Treacher and Co., 1829.

NEFF, E. E., *A Revolution in European Poetry, 1660–1900,* New York, Columbia University Press, 1940.

NICHOL, JOHN, *Byron,* London, Macmillan, 1880.

PASSOW, ARNOLD, *Popularia Carmina Graeciae Recentioris,* Leipzig, Teubner, 1860.

"PASTON, GEORGE," (EMILY MORSE SYMONDS), "New Lights on Byron's Loves," *Cornhill Magazine,* CXLIX–CL (April–September 1934), April, 385–400; May, 513–537; June, 641–655; July, 1–16; August, 129–144; September, 257–276.

"PASTON, GEORGE," and PETER QUENNELL, *"To Lord Byron,"* New York, Scribner's, 1939.

PFEIFFER, ANTON, *Thomas Hopes "Anastasius" und Lord Byrons "Don Juan,"* Munich, Schuh, 1913.

POLIDORI, J. W., *The Diary of Dr. John William Polidori, 1816, Relating to Byron, Shelley, etc.,* edited by William Michael Rossetti, London, Elkin Mathews, 1911.

PRAZ, MARIO, *La Fortuna di Byron in Inghilterra,* Florence, "La Voce," 1925.

PRICE, L. M., *The Reception of English Literature in Germany,* Berkeley, University of California Press, 1932.

PUDBRES, ANNA, "Lord Byron, the Admirer and Imitator of Alfieri," *Englische Studien,* XXXIII (1903), 40–83.

PUGHE, F. H., *Studien über Byron und Wordsworth,* Heidelberg, C. Winter, 1902.

QUENNELL, PETER, *Byron, the Years of Fame,* New York, Viking, 1935.

——, *Byron in Italy,* New York, Viking, 1941.

RAYMOND, MRS. DORA NEILL, *The Political Career of Lord Byron,* New York, Henry Holt, 1924.

REDFERN, JOAN, "Berni as Byron's Precursor," London *Times Literary Supplement,* No. 1799 (July 25, 1936), 476.

RICHTER, HELENE, *Lord Byron: Persönlichkeit und Werk,* Halle, Max Niemeyer, 1929.

ROBERTSON, J. G., editor, *Goethe and Byron, Publications of the English Goethe Society, New Series,* II, London, A. Moring, 1925.

DE ROBERTIS, ACHILLE, "Satira e censura in Toscana," *Giornale Storica della Letteratura Italiana,* CIII (1934), 281–301.

SCHMIDT, OTTO, *Rousseau und Byron,* Oppeln and Leipzig, Eugen Franck's Buchhandlung (Georg Mashe), 1890.

SCOTT, SIR WALTER, *The Letters of Sir Walter Scott,* edited by H. J. C. Grierson, London, Constable and Co., 1932–37. 12 vols.

SICKELS, E. M., *The Gloomy Egoist,* New York, Columbia University Press, 1932.

SMILES, SAMUEL, *A Publisher and His Friends: Memoirs and Correspondence of the Late John Murray,* London, John Murray, 1891. 2 vols.

STEIGER, AUGUST, *Thomas Shadwell's "Libertine,"* Berne, A. Francke, 1904.

STERN, SELMA, *Anacharsis Cloots, der Redner des Menschengeschlechts, Historische Studien,* CXIX, Berlin, Ebering, 1914.

STOKOE, F. W., *German Influence in the English Romantic Period,* Cambridge, Cambridge University Press, 1926.

SWINBURNE, A. C., "Wordsworth and Byron," *Critical Miscellanies, Complete Works,* London, William Heinemann, 1926. XIV, 155–244.

TEXTE, JOSEPH, *Jean-Jacques Rousseau and the Cosmopolitan Spirit in Literature,* translated by J. W. Matthews, New York, Macmillan, 1899.

TICKNOR, GEORGE, *History of Spanish Literature,* 3rd edition, Boston, 1864. 3 vols.

TRELAWNEY, EDWARD, *Recollections of the Last Days of Shelley and Byron,* with an introduction by Edward Dowden, London, Humphrey Milford, 1923.

TRIBOLATI, FELICE, "Lord Byron à Pisa," *Nuova Antologia,* XXVI (1874), 631–655.

VARÉ, DANIELE, "Byron and the Guiccioli," *Quarterly Review,* CCLXII (1934), 206–226.

VARNHAGEN, HERMANN, *Ueber Byrons dramatisches Bruchstück "der Umgestaltete Misgestaltete,"* Erlangen, 1905.

Vigo, Pietro, "L'Abate Casti e un' Edizione Clandestina del 'Poema Tartaro,'" *Rassegna Bibliografica*, XV (1907), 184–186.

Watts, Alaric A., "Lord Byron's Plagiarisms!," *Literary Gazette*, No. 214 (February 24, 1821), 121–124; No. 216 (March 10, 1821), 137–139; No. 217 (March 17, 1821), 150–152; No. 219 (March 31, 1821), 168–170.

Watts, Alaric Alfred, *Alaric Watts; a Narrative of His Life by His Son*, London, Richard Bentley, 1884.

Wiel, Taddeo, "Lord Byron e il suo soggiorno in Venezia," *L'Ateneo Veneto*, Anno 28 (1905), I.

Wiener, Harold S. L., "Literary Sources of Byron's 'Turkish Tales,'" *Nineteenth Century Studies*, Ithaca, Cornell University Press, 1940.

Wildstake, Karl, *Wielands Agathon und der Französische Reise- und Bildungsroman von Fenelons Telemach bis Barthelemys Anacharsis*, Murnau, 1933.

Wilmsen, Friedrich, *Ossians Einfluss auf Byrons Jugendgedichte*, Berlin, Felber, 1903.

Zabel, Ernst, *Byrons Kenntnis von Shakespeare und sein Urteil über ihn*, Halle, 1904.

Zacchetti, Carrado, *Lord Byron e l'Italia*, Palermo, R. Sandron, 1919.

Index